S0-AZD-878

Praise for *Walk in Love*
Illumination Book Award Winner for Theology

"*Walk In Love* is the perfect introduction to what it means to not only worship as an Episcopalian but also to live out the Christian life in this tradition. In informative, easily digestible portions, the authors walk through *The Book of Common Prayer*, the place of the Bible, the practices of faith, and the structure of the Episcopal Church, connecting them to everyday life. This book should be a staple for newcomers classes, adult forums, and anyone looking to learn more about living life the Episcopal way."

Derek Olsen
Biblical scholar
Author, Inwardly Digest: The Prayer Book
as Guide to a Spiritual Life

"Scott Gunn and Melody Wilson Shobe have written another winsome resource for Episcopal newcomers, veterans, and everybody in between. Read it if you want to learn the relationship between our prayer, our belief, and our daily life. Read it to get re-rooted in the unique Anglican approach to the Way of Jesus. Just read it."

Stephanie Spellers
Canon to the Presiding Bishop for Evangelism,
Reconciliation, and Creation
Author, The Episcopal Way

"The most comprehensive, and comprehensible, guide to Episcopal faith and practice available. A perfect book for newcomers, longtime members, and anyone in between."

Adam Trambley
Rector, St. John's Episcopal Church
Sharon, Pennsylvania

"Scott Gunn and Melody Wilson Shobe do a great job of putting together a rich, comprehensive, and accessible book on the beliefs and practices of the Episcopal Church. Clergy and lay Christian education professionals across the liturgical and theological spectrum will find this book useful in presenting the basics of our common life of faith to newcomers and sixth-generation Episcopalians alike."

Steven J. Pankey
Rector, Christ Episcopal Church
Bowling Green, Kentucky

"Whether you've lived with the prayers of *The Book of Common Prayer* for decades or are just encountering the richness that is the Episcopal faith, *Walk in Love* welcomes you to know the story of Christianity in the Episcopal Church and be inspired to share it."

Laurie Brock
Rector, St. Michael the Archangel
Lexington, Kentucky
Author, Horses Speak of God

"Our adult confirmation class, a mix of generations and faith traditions, has enjoyed *Walk In Love* very much. It has lots of helpful information with a personal touch, encourages the reader to develop a relationship with the Book of Common Prayer, and includes useful questions for reflection and discussion. We have used it for several years and will continue to do so. This is an excellent addition to our library of formation resources."

Penny Bridges
Dean, St. Paul's Cathedral
San Diego, California

Walk in Love

Episcopal Beliefs & Practices

Scripture quotations are from the New Revised Standard Version of the Bible, copyright © 1989 National Council of the Churches of Christ in the United States of America. Used by permission. All rights reserved.

Psalm passages are from the Psalter in *The Book of Common Prayer*, unless otherwise noted.

© 2018 Forward Movement
Sixth printing, 2023.

All rights reserved.

ISBN: 9780880284554

Printed in USA

Forward
Movement
inspire disciples. empower evangelists.

Walk in Love

Episcopal Beliefs & Practices

Scott Gunn
Melody Wilson Shobe

FORWARD MOVEMENT
Cincinnati, Ohio

Table of Contents

Introduction

Walk in love, as Christ loved us and gave himself for us, an offering and sacrifice to God.

—*The Book of Common Prayer*, p. 376

Every Sunday in Episcopal churches across the world, people gather for Holy Eucharist. We all pray using *The Book of Common Prayer* so we hear and use many of the same scriptures over and over. One of the verses that we often hear week after week is, "Walk in love, as Christ loved us and gave himself for us, an offering and sacrifice to God."

This verse is used in the offertory sentence, which comes just as the people's offerings are collected, and is a way of pointing people toward the sacrament of Holy Eucharist that we are about to receive. We are encouraged to make connections between our Sunday prayers and our daily lives. We are encouraged to be generous in our offerings as God has been generous to us.

While there are nine choices for offertory sentences, the most popular choice—by far—is the one in whose honor this book is named. The words come from the fifth chapter of Ephesians, Paul's lovely letter about how Christ's sacrificial life and love is meant to shape and form us all.

Why is this offertory sentence the most popular choice?

We can't say for sure, but maybe it's the first three words. Walk. In. Love. These words embody action, just as the Christian life is about action and movement. They emphasize love. The phrase paints a clear picture, a vision of how we ought to love and move. But maybe there's more. The rest of the sentence gets real. To love "as Christ loved us and gave himself for us" is to be all in. This kind of love goes way beyond nice. It is all-consuming. Christ-like love, like Jesus' very life, is "an offering and sacrifice to God."

Christ-like love is not about us; it is about God and our neighbors. It is impossibly generous. In fact, this type of love is only possible by God's grace. We'll never manage to love this way on our own. And this is where our liturgies come into play. To see bread and wine become the Body and Blood of Christ is to behold God's grace, to see radical transformation. Taking part in the sacraments helps us to see God's grace at work in the world around us. Seeing God's grace at work trains us to open our hearts and our eyes to God's action in the sacraments.

For Episcopalians—Anglican Christians—prayer, belief, and life itself are inextricably related. Right belief helps our prayer and our lives. Daily prayer shapes our belief and guides our lives. A sacrificial, loving life feeds our prayer time and transforms our faith from passive to active.

This book is about walking in love. For Christians, this journey begins at the baptismal font, is nourished by the

Suggested Offertory Sentences

Offer to God a sacrifice of thanksgiving, and make good your vows to the Most High. *Psalm 50:14*

Ascribe to the Lord the honor due his Name; bring offerings and come into his courts. *Psalm 96:8*

Walk in love, as Christ loved us and gave himself for us, an offering and sacrifice to God. *Ephesians 5:2*

I appeal to you, brethren, by the mercies of God, to present yourselves as a living sacrifice, holy and acceptable to God, which is your spiritual worship. *Romans 12:1*

If you are offering your gift at the altar, and there remember that your brother has something against you, leave your gift there before the altar and go; first be reconciled to your brother, and then come and offer your gift. *Matthew 5:23, 24*

Through Christ let us continually offer to God the sacrifice of praise, that is, the fruit of lips that acknowledge his Name. But do not neglect to do good and to share what you have, for such sacrifices are pleasing to God. *Hebrews 13:15, 16*

O Lord our God, you are worthy to receive glory and honor and power; because you have created all things, and by your will they were created and have their being. *Revelation 4:11*

Yours, O Lord, is the greatness, the power, the glory, the victory, and the majesty. For everything in heaven and on earth is yours. Yours, O Lord, is the kingdom, and you are exalted as head over all. *1 Chronicles 29:11*

Let us with gladness present the offerings and oblations of our life and labor to the Lord.

These can be found in The Book of Common Prayer, *page 376.*

riches of the church, and is lived out in the world beyond the walls of churches. You can see an artistic hint of this idea on the cover of the book. You see the inside of a church, but instead of a back wall, the church mystically opens up to a lovely path through a forest. Our churches invite us to follow

Jesus into the world. And of course, our faith invites us to bring our world into the church.

We hope you find in this book not only an overview of the beliefs and practices of the Episcopal Church but also a foundation for a life that is guided and nourished by the church and the Gospel of Jesus Christ.

The Christian Faith

Some readers of this book will be new to the Christian faith. Others will be veterans but may wonder about the authors and what they believe. If you want a more comprehensive view of the basics of the Christian faith, we also co-wrote *Faithful Questions: Exploring the Way with Jesus* (Forward Movement, 2015). But for now, we offer a very basic summary of the faith so that you can see our perspective—or maybe get the lay of the land if you are new to the faith.

Of course, we accept the teaching of the ancient creeds of the church (see Chapter 13). Since we are both priests, we have also gladly promised to teach the doctrine of the church as it is set out in *The Book of Common Prayer*. And we take scripture very seriously, agreeing in our ordination vows that the Bible contains all things necessary to salvation. Perhaps it is helpful for us to share our faith as a story—not our story but the story of scripture.

In the beginning, before there was anything else, there was God's love. God brought forth everything, including this planet where we live, creating light and dark, land and sea, animals and plants, and finally making people. God gave us our freedom—the ability to choose right or wrong and whether to even follow God—and we squandered our gift. We chose to walk away from God, preferring selfishness and fear.

God sent prophets to remind us of God's way. From time to time, we listened to the prophets, and we remembered who we are and how we are meant to live. Each time, we eventually rejected the prophets and their message, always returning to selfishness and fear.

Finally, God's own son was sent into the world. Jesus Christ was born like any other human, tiny and vulnerable, in the middle of nowhere in a backwater region of the Roman Empire. The most important birth in history might seem to some to be insignificant and ordinary. We learn a lot about the God we worship when we see that God chose to enter our world not in power and might, but in vulnerability.

Jesus Christ was Perfect Love enfleshed. Jesus showed us who God is and how we are to love. Jesus' love is expansive: He especially loved the unlovable and people at the margins of society. Jesus' love is honest: He always told the truth. Jesus' love is invitational: He wanted to draw people into his way of life and love.

Then as now, the powers of the world feared and hated Perfect Love. This kind of love is a threat to empires and all powerful people. The love of Christ cares about people, but it cares nothing for power, for might, or for prestige. The authorities in Jesus' day tried to extinguish Perfect Love by killing Jesus. They put him on a cross to die.

Jesus died. But on the third day, as God had promised, Jesus was raised to new life. Jesus wasn't kind-of dead, kind-of raised to a sort-of new life. No, we believe that Jesus was stone-cold dead, and God the Father raised him completely to new life. We celebrate this new life at Easter, but we celebrate more than the power of something that seems impossible. We celebrate that in the raising of Jesus to new life, we see God's love is stronger than death, stronger than fear, and stronger than anything that can happen to us in this earthly life.

Jesus soon returned to dwell with his Father in heaven, but before he left, he promised that he would send the Holy Spirit to abide with the church and lead people into all truth. Fifty days after that first Easter, when the disciples were gathered to celebrate their Feast of Pentecost, the Holy Spirit descended on the church in all its diversity, from many nations and peoples. In that act, God showed us all that the church is for everyone of every culture.

The New Testament presents several letters and documents from the time of the early church. In these letters, Saint Paul and others write to fledgling Christian communities that are trying to figure out what it means to follow Jesus. This is where we are in the story. Like those early Christians, we are trying to figure out how to follow Jesus in our own imperfect way. Fortunately, we have the Holy Spirit, God's abiding presence, who can lead us into all truth.

Being a Christian is not meant to be easy, and no one who reads the gospels could think otherwise. The way of Jesus can be a source of profoundly deep joy, as we are offered a way to live as God hopes: for love alone. Being a follower of Jesus means that we will "take up our cross" and follow him, that we will choose the difficult path at times, but it is not easy to overcome our intrinsic fears and selfishness. Being a follower of Jesus means we will proclaim Jesus Christ to all people, teaching them about his commandments.

Most of this book is an exploration of what it means to be an Episcopal or Anglican Christian. We believe there is not just one way to be a Christian, but we are head-over-heels in love with the Anglican way of following Jesus. You will read more in the chapters to come, but the shortest version is that Anglican Christianity is a way of following Jesus that is rooted in the Bible and the sacraments of the church, united by shared ways of praying. We will unpack that in the chapters to come.

In This Book

After sharing what we see as the Anglican or Episcopal understanding of prayer (Chapter 1), we move through the sacraments of the church (Chapters 2-8). We spend a bit more time on baptism and eucharist, since they are the primary sacraments. We turn next to how the church keeps time, including daily cycles (Chapter 9) and yearly cycles (Chapter 10). We look very closely at Holy Week, the most important week of the year for a Christian (Chapter 11). And we look at the end of our earthly pilgrimage, funerals, and burial (Chapter 12).

Because our faith is not just about liturgy but also about beliefs, we explore some basic teachings. We discuss the ancient creeds (Chapter 13) and how we read the Bible (Chapter 14). The idea of salvation or redemption only makes sense if we talk about sin and grace, so we do that in Chapter 15. This section wraps up with a chapter on prayer (Chapter 16).

The church itself is an important part of our faith, so we spend time exploring the community of people who follow Jesus. Chapter 17 is an overview of church, while Chapter 18 explores how we Episcopalians organize ourselves. Chapter 19 reminds us that the church is not just the living holy ones but also those who have gone before us, the holy ones who dwell with God as saints. And Chapter 20 considers how we are all called to follow Jesus in particular ways.

The next three chapters look at how we might care for God's creation (Chapter 21), at the implications of God having become human in Jesus Christ (Chapter 22), and at how we nurture the spiritual gifts that God has given us (Chapter 23). Finally, we end with encouragement to continue as followers of Jesus. We share spiritual practices, such as daily prayer or service of others (Chapter 24). Lastly, we hope you will learn how God's story is your story and how you might share that story with a world in need (Chapters 25 and 26).

How to Use This Book

We encourage you to have a copy of *The Book of Common Prayer* handy as you read *Walk in Love*. You'll want the 1979 version of the Episcopal Church's *Book of Common Prayer*; you can find a free PDF online or buy a copy at your favorite bookseller. Maybe your priest will loan or give you a copy. There are numerous citations from *The Book of Common Prayer*, including collects (or prayers) that start each chapter. We encourage you to look up the citations in *The Book of Common Prayer* to provide tangible connections between beliefs and practices. Whenever you see a number by itself, framed by parentheses, that is a page number in *The Book of Common Prayer*.

You can certainly read your way through *Walk in Love* on your own. Maybe your curiosity is stoked by something in one of the chapters, and so we have provided some suggestions for additional reading or exploration.

A book group could make productive use of *Walk in Love*, relying on the discussion questions here to get things going. Hopefully your group will have a rich conversation. This book's publisher, Forward Movement, also offers a free downloadable course about Episcopal beliefs and practices, *Practicing Our Faith*. Funded in part by a generous grant by the Constable Fund of the Episcopal Church, the curriculum is available for children, youth, and adults in English and Spanish. This course, *Practicing Our Faith*, is part of a three-year set of courses; the others are *Celebrating the Saints* and *Exploring the Bible*. You can learn about these offerings at www.forwardmovement.org.

About This Book

We developed much of what you read here as we worked together as parish priests in Rhode Island. As you can tell, we spent a lot of time and energy thinking about liturgy, the prayer book, and the Bible. We witnessed the fruits of that work as lives were transformed by Jesus Christ and people were drawn into deeper commitment to following Jesus in their daily lives.

When we tell stories here, we use "I." Sometimes that "I" is Melody writing, and sometimes it is Scott. Don't worry too much about that, and just enjoy the stories.

We hope you find this book helpful. More than that, we hope you fall in love with Jesus just a bit more through a deep and abiding life of prayer and enriched beliefs.

Scott Gunn   Melody Wilson Shobe
Cincinnati, Ohio   Dallas, Texas

Feast of the Epiphany of Our Lord Jesus Christ, 2018

The Anglican Way
of Christianity

Chapter 1

Not Only with Our Lips, but in Our Lives

Beliefs and Practices

As a priest, having a favorite prayer is perhaps similar to having a favorite child: How could you possibly pick one? There are things beloved and beautiful about so many different prayers; each has its strengths and its moments. When people ask me about my favorite prayers, I usually wax poetical about the wonderful diversity of *The Book of Common Prayer*, which contains thousands of options for prayers for nearly every circumstance and situation. I might rattle off a list of my favorites of the day, while encouraging people to explore the riches of the prayer book for themselves. I also remind people that we aren't limited to the forms of *The Book of Common Prayer*: Prayer is "responding to God, by thought and by deeds, with or without words" (856). We can pray using scripted prayers, by using our own words, or using no words at all. The options are, quite literally, limitless!

But let me tell you a secret. The truth is, I do have a favorite. If I could only pray one prayer for the rest of my life, it would be the General Thanksgiving from Morning Prayer, especially the traditional-language (Rite I) version.

Almighty God, Father of all mercies,
we thine unworthy servants
do give thee most humble and hearty thanks
for all thy goodness and loving-kindness
to us and to all men.
We bless thee for our creation, preservation,
and all the blessings of this life;
but above all for thine inestimable love
in the redemption of the world by our Lord Jesus Christ,
for the means of grace, and for the hope of glory.
And, we beseech thee,
give us that due sense of all thy mercies,
that our hearts may be unfeignedly thankful;
and that we show forth thy praise,
not only with our lips, but in our lives,
by giving up our selves to thy service,
and by walking before thee
in holiness and righteousness all our days;
through Jesus Christ our Lord,
to whom with thee and the Holy Ghost,
be all honor and glory, world without end. Amen.

—*The Book of Common Prayer,* pp. 58-59

This prayer is my favorite for a host of reasons. One is nostalgia. I grew up in a church that said Morning Prayer on a regular basis. Through sheer repetition, the General Thanksgiving was one of the first prayers I memorized as a child, right alongside the Lord's Prayer and the Apostles' Creed. I love this prayer with a child's devotion, the way I love Winnie the Pooh or macaroni and cheese. It resonates for me because it is a part of my story, a part of who I am.

It is also my favorite because I am a bibliophile, and I am in love with the poetry and language of this prayer. I remember coming home from church one day in about fourth grade and looking up the words inestimable and unfeignedly in the dictionary. I loved how they sounded on my tongue and was delighted to learn what they meant. As a child, saying such big, beautiful, mysterious words felt holy to me, a reminder that I love and follow a God who is big and beautiful and mysterious. Those beautiful, mysterious words, so different from our everyday speech, continue to connect me with God's holiness today.

Finally, and perhaps most importantly, this prayer of thanksgiving is my favorite because of the line "that we may show forth thy praise, not only with our lips, but in our lives." If the poetry isn't stunning enough, this sentiment will stop you in your tracks: not only with our lips, but in our lives. We are called to offer God praise, not simply in what we say, but also with what we do. God doesn't want lip service; God wants life service. An intimate, unbreakable connection exists between the words that we say in prayer and the things that we do in our daily lives.

Lex Orandi, Lex Credendi

This line from my favorite prayer articulates a foundational principle of the Episcopal Church: *Lex orandi, lex credendi.* This Latin phrase is loosely translated "the law of prayer is the law of belief." Or, said another way, "you are what you pray." In the Episcopal Church, prayer, belief, and action are intimately tied together.

The more we pray something, the more deeply it becomes a part of us. We are shaped by the prayers that we pray, as both the act of prayer and the content of those prayers inform how we think about ourselves and the world. Even more than shaping our beliefs, our prayers shape our actions, pushing us to live out in our daily lives the things we have said with our lips. Our prayers demand that we ask ourselves some difficult questions: How does what we say on Sunday inform how we think on Thursday? What do our prayers and beliefs call us to *do* on Monday and Tuesday and every other day? As we pray, we are shaped by our prayers, so that over time, with God's help, we become the very things for which we pray. In this way, *The Book of Common Prayer* is the source, not only of the prayers that the Episcopal Church uses regularly but also of the content of our beliefs and the guideline for how we practice our faith.

The Book of Common Prayer

The Episcopal Church is defined by how we worship, which is guided by *The Book of Common Prayer*. And the way we pray is what binds together the Anglican Communion—a worldwide communion that includes the Episcopal Church. Our pattern of prayer is both ancient and modern, drawing on the tradition of the church through the centuries and responding to the needs and concerns of faithful Christians in this day and age.

The Anglican Communion is the third largest Christian communion in the world, after the Roman Catholic Church and the Eastern Orthodox Church. It includes 85 million people in over 165 countries. Learn more about the Anglican Communion at www.anglicancommunion.org.

The Book of Common Prayer was first published in 1549 under the direction of Thomas Cranmer, Archbishop of Canterbury. The book was the result of an extraordinary idea: The prayers that we say in worship should be held in common, that is, they should be available to all people in their native language. Prior to the publication of *The Book of Common Prayer*, books of liturgy were mostly reserved for clergy (bishops, priests, and deacons) and monastics (monks and nuns). These books also were largely written in Latin, a language spoken by only the educated elite. In the wake of the Reformation, Cranmer and others believed that prayer, like scripture, should be available to all people, clergy and laity alike, and that people should be able to read and understand the prayers of the church in their own language.

From this deep conviction arose *The Book of Common Prayer*. Some of the prayers in *The Book of Common Prayer* were written by Cranmer himself. With the sensibility of a poet, he crafted words to give voice to the deep longings of human hearts and to put us in conversation with God. But for many other prayers, Cranmer relied on centuries of tradition, painstakingly translating into English prayers that had been passed down through the generations, reaching back to the earliest celebrations of the eucharist and creating a living connection with our ancestors. The first *Book of Common Prayer* was ancient and modern, holding on to patterns of prayer that were hundreds of years old yet speaking in the language of its time.

In writing that first *Book of Common Prayer*, Cranmer also sought to find a *via media*, a middle way, between Catholic and Protestant sensibilities. It was a time when the church was still being rocked by the waves of the Protestant Reformation. In response to the criticisms levied against the Roman Catholic Church, many were willing to throw the baby out with the bathwater, changing their practice of prayer radically so as to sever any connection with the practices of the Roman Catholic Church.

Cranmer and others sought a middle ground, a liturgy that retained some aspects of Catholic thought and practice while being informed by the best of Protestant theology. Finding that middle way was costly, angering extremists on both sides. It ultimately led to Cranmer's execution for heresy when Roman Catholic Queen Mary took the throne. But the legacy of *via media* lives on as a foundational principle

Ancient Prayers

The 1549 *Book of Common Prayer* included some wonderful collects composed for that first edition, and we still use some of these prayers today.

O Almighty God, who hast built thy Church upon the foundation of the apostles and prophets, Jesus Christ himself being the chief cornerstone: Grant us so to be joined together in unity of spirit by their doctrine, that we may be made an holy temple acceptable unto thee; through the same Jesus Christ our Lord, who liveth and reigneth with thee and the Holy Spirit, one God, for ever and ever. Amen. (p. 178)

Blessed Lord, who hast caused all holy Scriptures to be written for our learning: Grant that we may in such wise hear them, read, mark, learn, and inwardly digest them; that, by patience and comfort of thy holy Word, we may embrace and ever hold fast the blessed hope of everlasting life, which thou hast given us in our Savior Jesus Christ; who liveth and reigneth with thee and the Holy Spirit, one God, for ever and ever. Amen. (p. 184)

Thomas Cranmer and his team also made use of some ancient prayers that they translated for use in 1549.

Stir up thy power, O Lord, and with great might come among us; and, because we are sorely hindered by our sins, let thy bountiful grace and mercy speedily help and deliver us; through Jesus Christ our Lord, to whom, with thee and the Holy Ghost, be honor and glory, world without end. Amen. (p. 160) This prayer is based on a liturgical book from the eighth century called the *Gelasian Sacramentary*.

Almighty and everlasting God, who hatest nothing that thou hast made and dost forgive the sins of all those who are penitent: Create and make in us new and contrite hearts, that we, worthily lamenting our sins and acknowledging our wretchedness, may obtain of thee, the God of all mercy, perfect remission and forgiveness; through Jesus Christ our Lord, who liveth and reigneth with thee and the Holy Spirit, one God, for ever and ever. Amen. (p. 166, also from the *Gelasian Sacramentary*)

If you would like to learn more about the origin of different prayers in *The Book of Common Prayer*, refer to *Commentary on the American Prayer Book* by Marion J. Hatchett.

in our *Book of Common Prayer* and in Episcopal/Anglican belief and practice.

Over the years, *The Book of Common Prayer* has been edited and revised a number of times, with each iteration balancing the ancient with the modern, seeking a middle way between extremes. The Church of England still uses the 1662 *Book of Common Prayer*, which bears a great resemblance to the original 1549 edition. The Episcopal Church in the United States of America adopted its first *Book of Common Prayer* in 1789; that *Book of Common Prayer* was deeply informed by both the original *Book of Common Prayer* and the Scottish Episcopal Church's *Book of Common Prayer*. The *Book of Common Prayer* currently authorized for use in the Episcopal Church was last revised in 1979. All of the congregations across the Episcopal Church are expected to worship according to the 1979 *Book of Common Prayer*.

Praying as a Community

When we come together each week and pray according to *The Book of Common Prayer*, we are praying, in a deep sense, as a community. Our liturgy—the words and actions of worship—is not about "each man for himself," or about how "*I* like to pray" or even how the priest likes to pray. Instead, we are keeping a tradition of worship that stretches through time and is shaped by a tradition of prayer that has been passed down from generation to generation.

Our prayers connect us not only through time but also through space to all the other members of the Anglican Communion, a worldwide body bound by a shared history and shared worship. While Anglican congregations across the globe have varying beliefs and practices, Anglican Communion churches are all connected, in some way, to

Liturgy is a commonly misunderstood term, with people saying that it means work of the people, suggesting that participation by everyone in the gathering is the point. While it is surely important for each person in a eucharistic gathering to participate in her or his own way, this is not what liturgy is about. A better translation of the Greek word is public work. Back in ancient Greece, people offered a liturgy if they donated money for a civic building, for example. Liturgy was an offering for the good of all people, for the public. In this way, our liturgies are meant to be public works, that is, offerings for the good of the whole world.

the Church of England, and each has a prayer book that has been influenced and informed by *The Book of Common Prayer.* If you visit an Anglican church anywhere in the world, you will have a basic idea of what is going on. Even if you can't understand a word of the language being spoken, the order of service and the actions of worship will be very familiar.

All Episcopal priests take a vow at their ordination to the priesthood to be faithful to the doctrine, discipline, and worship of the Episcopal Church. At baptism and again at confirmation, every Episcopalian promises "to continue in the apostles' teaching and fellowship, in the breaking of bread, and in the prayers." Note that this promise doesn't say prayer but rather "in the prayers."

In baptism and confirmation, we commit to more than a general idea of prayer; we promise to pray *like this* and *in community*. The Book of Common Prayer contains the prayers that we promise to be faithful to—the prayers that mark us both as Christians and as Episcopalians.

Breadth and Opportunity

Now, a person might hear about these promises of prayer and think that *The Book of Common Prayer* is a straitjacket that limits and restricts how we interact with God. Nothing could

The Episcopal Church's *Book of Common Prayer* is not an eternal, stagnant document; it has been revised, sometimes significantly, multiple times since the first American version in 1789. But the prayer book is also not meant to be taken lightly or to be subject to whims and passing fads. Because we believe that we are shaped by what we pray, the form and content of these prayers matters deeply. For that reason, revision of *The Book of Common Prayer* is a lengthy process.

Any revision to *The Book of Common Prayer*, whether it is the matter of a few words or significant changes, requires approval by majority vote in both houses at two successive meetings of the General Convention, which meets every three years. This means that it takes a minimum of six years to revise the prayer book, and any revision requires the input and majority support of all the orders of ministry: bishops, priests, deacons, and lay people.

be further from the truth. One of the greatest gifts of *The Book of Common Prayer* is its breadth. *The Book of Common Prayer* offers tremendous opportunity for creativity and diversity.

❖ The prayer book includes an incredible variety of liturgies, including Holy Eucharist and Holy Baptism, marriage and burial, confirmation and ordination. But there are also forms—guides for worship—for daily prayer, including Daily Devotions and the Daily Office, an ordered routine of praying at different times throughout the day. In addition, the prayer book features prayers for those who are sick and for grace at meals, for victims of addiction, for schools and colleges, for rain and for travelers, and many more.

❖ Most liturgies offer forms of prayer for Rite I and Rite II—essentially two versions of the prayers that espouse the same principles. This can seem confusing, but it is actually a beautiful part of our Anglican heritage, another way that we hold on to the ancient while also responding to the world around us. Rite I is full of thees and thous, the more formal and traditional language that echoes the earliest prayer books. It is a language of beauty, poetry, and mystery. Rite II is more contemporary, changing the thees and thous to yous and translating some of the more complex words and concepts so they are easier to understand, while still holding on to the beauty and tradition. In this way our *Book of Common Prayer* is both ancient and modern, and our prayers benefit from a greater richness because we have many options.

❖ Even within the language of a certain rite, there is a great deal of variety. In Rite II Holy Eucharist, for example, there are four different options for eucharistic prayers: A, B, C, and D. Each eucharistic prayer uses different phrases and images to draw us into the mystery of Holy Eucharist. For instance, Eucharistic Prayer D is connected to some of the oldest eucharistic prayers, grounding us in ancient tradition. Eucharistic Prayer C talks about outer space, reminding us of our modern context. The different prayers emphasize different aspects of our understanding of God, in order to help us have a greater appreciation for what happens when we come together for Holy Communion.

❖ In addition to the different liturgies, *The Book of Common Prayer* is also attentive to the different seasons of the church year. The liturgies offer various options for opening greetings, prayers, and refrains that reflect the different times of the church year. From Advent to Lent to Epiphany to Easter, the seasonal options give our prayers context and nuance.

❖ While *The Book of Common Prayer* does have some requirements, much is left unwritten as well. This allows for a great variety of practice, from the vestments that people wear, the decorations on the altar, and the colors of the seasons to the hymns, anthems, and instrumental music of our worship.

❖ *The Book of Common Prayer* also includes more open-ended liturgies for Holy Eucharist (400), marriage (435), and burial (506). This approach leaves room for flexibility and adaptation while staying within the parameters and wisdom of our faith. These rites "require careful preparation by the Priest and other participants" (400) and include certain prayers to be said or guidelines to be followed. But the rites also allow congregations to respond to specific pastoral needs while remaining bound by common prayer.

❖ Actions such as when we cross ourselves, processions into and out of church, whether or not to use incense, and many other things, are decisions for individual communities.

Worship according to *The Book of Common Prayer* offers unity in the midst of diversity, allowing individual congregations to have both variety and constancy. Many aspects of prayer and worship are the same across all Episcopal churches, no matter where they are located, while other components differ from one community to the next.

Praying with Our Bodies

Prayer is a full-contact sport. Prayer is not just a matter of the mind or the mouth—it is a matter of the whole body. It is meant to involve every part of ourselves. We live out that reality in worship by the different actions we use when we pray. *The Book of Common Prayer* sometimes directs us to sit, sometimes to stand, sometimes to kneel. Sometimes we are told to speak, sometimes to remain silent, other times to sing. Some people even include actions: crossing themselves at certain moments, bowing their heads at the name of Jesus, and genuflecting (dropping to one knee in reverence) before the altar. The different actions can make it seem like we aren't engaged in prayer but rather Episcopal aerobics! The truth is that these different actions and postures of prayer help us to engage our *whole selves* in worship. They are ways of living out the truth that we praise God "not only with our lips, but in our lives."

By actively engaging our bodies in prayer, we acknowledge that prayer demands more than just our words. We proclaim in our actions that God wants all of us—and that we are offering all of ourselves to God.

Our actions and our motions are only part of our prayers; worship involves all of the senses. In worship, we see light and darkness as candles flicker, and we see the variety of colors in changing vestments, church hangings, and stained glass windows. We hear music sung or played and words spoken and chanted, and we experience silence that tells its own story. We smell the beeswax of burning candles, the holy perfume of incense, the beautiful scent of anointing oil. We taste the bread and wine. And we touch: the smooth surface of altar rails, the thin pages of prayer books and hymnals, the hands of our neighbors and strangers. Our worship engages all of our selves: our bodies and souls, our mouths and our movements. And it engages all of our senses: sight, hearing, taste, touch, and smell. Our prayer is embodied action.

This tenet extends beyond our worship. Praising God "not only with our lips, but in our lives" means that our prayers must shape the way we live, not only for an hour on Sunday but also for every hour of every day of every week for our entire lives. We don't just involve our bodies in worship on

Sunday by kneeling or standing, smelling and tasting. We involve our bodies in worship every day, by living in our lives what our lips profess in prayer. Praising God involves more than just the prayers we say or the things we believe; it includes the way we *practice* our faith on a daily basis.

What we pray is incredibly important, because it both shapes and reflects what we believe. And what we believe is incredibly important, because it both shapes and reflects how we live. Prayer changes us, in deep and meaningful ways.

As a priest, I have had the precious gift of praying with people as they age and when they are dying. Again and again, I have prayed with someone who suffers from dementia or Alzheimer's or a person who is non-responsive, who doesn't seem aware of what is going on or is unable to respond in any way. Yet when I start the Lord's Prayer, more often than not, that non-responsive, largely non-verbal person will begin praying along. The words might be mumbled or difficult to decipher. She might be a few beats behind me or say only certain phrases. But even if he's forgotten nearly everything else, he remembers the Lord's Prayer. Prayers that we pray often and repeatedly become so much a part of us that we remember them on an instinctive, visceral level.

Prayer changes our brains and our behavior. What we say and do on Sunday informs and shapes how we act and think on Thursday and Monday and every other day. When we spend our time in prayer focused on gratitude, we become more grateful people. When we pray for peace, we begin to act more peacefully. Our prayers become a deep and meaningful part of us, words that are truly learned "by heart," being taken into ourselves and shaping us.

For Reflection

✳ What is your favorite prayer, and why is it your favorite?

✳ Do certain lines from prayers come to mind during your daily life? What are they and when do you think about them?

✳ What does the baptismal promise "to continue in the apostles' teaching and fellowship, in the breaking of bread, and in the prayers" mean to you? How have you lived up to that promise in your life? How could you do better?

✳ What are some of the gifts of scripted, common prayer like those in *The Book of Common Prayer*? What are some of the difficulties with this kind of prayer?

The Sacraments and Sacramental Rites

Chapter 2

The New Life of Grace
Baptismal Beliefs

Heavenly Father, we thank you that by water and the Holy Spirit you have bestowed upon these your servants the forgiveness of sin, and have raised them to the new life of grace. Sustain them, O Lord, in your Holy Spirit. Give them an inquiring and discerning heart, the courage to will and to persevere, a spirit to know and to love you, and the gift of joy and wonder in all your works. *Amen.*

—*The Book of Common Prayer*, p. 308

Prayer—our conversation with God, both spoken and silent—is an important way to experience God in our lives. But it is not the only way. In the Episcopal Church, sacraments loom large. In the sacraments, we experience grace, which our prayer book defines as "God's favor towards us, unearned and undeserved; by grace God forgives our sins, enlightens our minds, stirs our hearts, and strengthens our wills" (858). While God's grace absolutely comes in infinite ways, even outside the church, we know that the sacraments are "sure and certain" means of grace.

The classic definition of sacraments says they are "outward and visible signs of inward and spiritual grace." In other words, sacraments are an external manifestation of something that happens internally. To put it another way, they are earthly signs of heavenly activity. For example, when we baptize someone, the outward sign is water, but inside, the person is changed.

It's important to emphasize that the sacraments are not the only way to receive grace; the grace of God's love and blessing comes to us in our daily lives in many ways. At the same time, however, when we partake in the sacraments, we can be confident of receiving God's grace. Furthermore, sacraments are not mere symbols. In the Holy Eucharist, the bread and wine are not simply reminders of Jesus' last meal with his friends, but they become Jesus' Body and Blood. We can be confident that Christ is truly present in the eucharist, and that in receiving Holy Communion we receive God's grace.

Anglicans don't always agree on the number of sacraments. During the Reformation period in the 1500s and 1600s, our forebears focused on two sacraments: baptism and eucharist. Later on, in the nineteenth century especially, Anglicans began to talk about seven sacraments. Today, we often divide the sacraments into two categories. The dominical sacraments (taught by Jesus) are baptism and eucharist. And the five ecclesial sacraments (taught by the church) are confirmation, healing (unction), reconciliation (confession), marriage, and ordination. Our *Book of Common Prayer* is somewhat inconsistent but usually calls the first two "sacraments" and the last five "sacramental rites." In terms of our theology though, all seven are clearly sacramental: They are outward and visible signs of inward and spiritual grace.

Holy Baptism

Baptism is the first sacrament. It is the first one Jesus taught. We may think of baptism as the sacrament of birth, because baptism is often carried out with infants. But we should look at baptism in a broader context, as the sacrament of beginning for all new Christians. Even adults begin their new life and journey as disciples of Jesus Christ at their baptism.

Jesus did not invent baptism. He took an existing practice and completely redefined it. In the ancient world, as is the case today, many religions made use of ritual baths. In Jesus' time, many Jews understood baptism to be a cleansing, a way to wash away sins. Some sects even understood baptism to be part of rituals for entry; baptism was required for membership.

In the New Testament, the famous practitioner of Jewish baptism was John the Baptist (hence the name!). John spent his days calling people to be transformed and to be prepared for the Messiah who was to come soon. He spoke of his own practice of baptism, saying, "I baptize you with water for repentance" (Matthew 3:11a). But John added an important teaching: "one who is more powerful than I is coming after me; I am not worthy to carry his sandals. He will baptize you with the Holy Spirit and fire" (Matthew 3:11b).

Jesus adopted the idea of a cleansing ritual required for entry into a community. And just as John had promised, Jesus' baptism added new dimensions, starting with his baptism by John in the Jordan River.

> Then Jesus came from Galilee to John at the Jordan, to be baptized by him. John would have prevented him, saying, "I need to be baptized by you, and do you come to me?" But Jesus answered him, "Let it be so now; for it is proper for us in this way to fulfill all righteousness." Then

he consented. And when Jesus had been baptized, just as he came up from the water, suddenly the heavens were opened to him and he saw the Spirit of God descending like a dove and alighting on him. And a voice from heaven said, "This is my Son, the Beloved, with whom I am well pleased." (Matthew 3:13-17)

At his own baptism, Jesus was blessed by God's presence for all to see. This dramatically introduced the coming of the Holy Spirit in baptism, and Jesus continued to teach this as the way of beginning a new life of faith. From that moment in the Jordan River, Jesus and his followers continued—to this very day—a baptism that is by water and the Holy Spirit.

Soon after Jesus' death, resurrection, and ascension into heaven, the earliest Christians began to teach baptism as an essential part of the Christian life. Saint Paul teaches,

In most Episcopal churches today, our practice of baptism symbolizes the experience with a pouring or sprinkling of water over the person's head instead of full immersion. What is important is that we use water and that we do the baptism in the name of the Triune God: Father, Son, and Holy Spirit. Whether we use a few drops of water or dunk someone in a pool, whether the baptism takes place in an ornate font (a bowl of sorts that holds the water for baptism) or an outdoor stream, the same thing is accomplished: We are made new in Christ.

Do you not know that all of us who have been baptized into Christ Jesus were baptized into his death? Therefore, we have been buried with him by baptism into death, so that, just as Christ was raised from the dead by the glory of the Father, so we too might walk in newness of life. (Romans 6:3-4)

Saint Paul conveys two important ideas. First, baptism is the way to enter into the church, the Body of Christ Jesus. Second, in baptism, we die to our old selves and rise to new life in Christ. This aspect of baptism is perhaps more clear when the person being baptized is plunged under the water and then raised. Whether an infant or an adult, there is something bold about seeing someone symbolically drowned and raised to new life!

Union with Christ

Today when we speak about baptism, we continue to understand it as a complex of interrelated actions. Our prayer book says baptism is "union with Christ in his death and resurrection, birth into God's family the Church, forgiveness of sins, and new life in the Holy Spirit" (858). Let us look at each of these actions.

❖ **Union with Christ in his death and resurrection.** This is exactly what Saint Paul talks about in Romans. We are mystically joined with Christ when we are baptized. The old, sinful self dies. A new person is raised to life, and we receive the promise that we too will be raised at the last day, at the resurrection of the dead.

❖ **Birth into God's family, the church.** Baptism is the entry to the church, to the community of those who have committed themselves to follow Jesus. But it is more than a membership requirement; in baptism, we are adopted into God's family.

❖ **Forgiveness of sins.** To understand this one, we have to back up, all the way to creation. The church understands that humans were all made in God's image, and we humans were made wholly good. Then we were given freedom, and we made poor choices that resulted in the fallenness of humanity, the idea that we are ruined by sin. We have squandered the goodness and freedom that God gave us, and, left to our own devices, we will continue in this fallen, sinful way of living. Through baptism, we are cleansed from this curse of sin. We are made clean and new in baptism.

❖ **New life in the Holy Spirit.** As Jesus was leaving his friends, he promised that God the Father would send the Holy Spirit to abide with Jesus' followers, the church. The entire Book of Acts is the story of Christ's people living with the presence of the Holy Spirit, and it is our story, too!

Though not every Christian will see the complexity of baptism in exactly the same way, baptism is the one sacrament that nearly all Christians recognize as universal. When a baptized person wants to join an Episcopal church, all that is required is a record of their existing baptism. As long as the baptism involved water and was done in the name of the Father, the Son, and the Holy Spirit, it is considered valid. The same is true for Episcopalians who might join another denomination or church. Nearly every church around the world will recognize each other's baptism.

Some Christians reserve baptism as a sacrament only for adults. These Christians usually believe that baptism requires understanding. Episcopalians have a different view of the sacrament, believing that God's grace is present in the sacrament even when we do not understand how or what is happening. Therefore, we baptize people of all ages, including infants, believing that God's grace is surely and certainly present. It is then the responsibility of parents and godparents to raise the child in faith, helping the child to grow into promises made on his or her behalf.

Most of the time, baptisms are performed by clergy in churches, in the community that represents the Body of

Baptismal candidates are always supported by sponsors, whether the candidates are adults, children, or infants. We colloquially call the sponsors of younger children "godparents" but they are really sponsors, just like any other. Sponsors help candidates or their parents prepare for baptism with the intention to "support them by prayer and example in their Christian life." Being a sponsor is not just an honor but a major commitment to a life of Christian mentoring and support. Sponsors answer on behalf of infants who cannot speak for themselves in the baptismal liturgy, and they signify their role in adult and older children's baptisms by presenting the candidates to the priest.

Christ. But of all the sacraments, baptism is the one that can be performed by anyone, anywhere, in an emergency. Talk to nurses, especially in places where babies are born, and you may hear stories of emergency baptism for deathly ill infants. In these situations, all that is required is water and simple words. "I baptize you in the name of the Father, and of the Son, and of the Holy Spirit." Just a dab of water and these words make a person the recipient of every benefit of baptism.

Sometimes babies who have received emergency baptism get well, and the family later wants a public celebration in the church. We have a way of celebrating these baptisms that does not repeat baptism—because baptism is permanent and indelible—but allows the congregation to welcome a child into the church.

For Reflection

✳ How have you experienced inward and spiritual grace through one of the sacraments?

✳ The prayer book mentions four aspects of baptism: "Union with Christ in his death and resurrection, birth into God's family the church, forgiveness of sins, and new life in the Holy Spirit." What is important about each of these emphases?

✳ Our scriptures and liturgies make a strong connection between baptism and death. What are some of the things that we die to in our baptism, and how is our relationship with death changed by the waters of baptism?

✳ Through the waters of baptism, we are raised to the new life of grace. What are some of the qualities or characteristics of this new life?

Chapter 3

The Covenant
They Have Made
Baptismal Practices

Father in heaven, who at the baptism of Jesus in the River Jordan proclaimed him your beloved Son and anointed him with the Holy Spirit: Grant that all who are baptized into his Name may keep the covenant they have made and boldly confess him as Lord and Savior; who with you and the Holy Spirit lives and reigns, one God, in glory everlasting. *Amen.*

—*The Book of Common Prayer*, p. 214

Every journey begins somewhere, and every Christian's journey in the church begins with Holy Baptism. While God may very well be working in our lives before we are baptized, it is this sacrament that unites us with Christ and his church. Another way to view Holy Baptism is to see it as the gateway to all the other sacraments. Holy Baptism is usually celebrated on Sunday mornings so the whole church community can join in the grand occasion. Much of the service is similar to every other Sunday service, but there are some differences. In this chapter, we will explore some of the features unique to a service of Holy Baptism, and then we'll talk about some of the "stuff" that we use during the baptism. As you read this chapter, we encourage you to follow along in the service for Holy Baptism; it begins on page 299 of the prayer book.

After the usual words at the beginning of a Sunday service, a special set of responses for baptism are said or sung.

Celebrant	There is one Body and one Spirit;
People	There is one hope in God's call to us;
Celebrant	One Lord, one Faith, one Baptism;
People	One God and Father of all.

These words come from the fourth chapter of Saint Paul's Letter to the Ephesians. Paul wrote to the Ephesians to teach about the unity of the entire church—of all people—in Christ. In baptism, all our distinctions—sex, nationality, race, and so on—become less important than our unity in Christ. By placing these words at the beginning of the service, we are reminded that the newly baptized will soon be full members of Christ's body, the Church.

The readings and the sermon then continue as if at a regular Sunday service. The next departure from the usual service comes just after the sermon. The priest invites the candidate(s) for baptism to be presented.

If the baptismal candidate is an infant, the sponsors (godparents) and parents answer questions on the candidate's behalf. Otherwise, older children and adults answer for themselves. Every priest and parent will have a bit of terror when a child is asked the question, "Do you desire to be baptized?" Although young children can be unpredictable, we must ask the question! We can only proceed if the answer is yes, because Christians have long taught that baptism is not to be offered coercively, but only to the willing.

In the early centuries of the church, baptism was reserved to bishops, and local priests did not perform baptisms. Bishops were the primary officiants because baptism is a sign of entry into the larger, universal church rather than simply entry into the local church community. Part of a bishop's role is as a symbol of the unity of the universal church; every bishop ordained in the Episcopal Church has been ordained by the laying on of hands by other bishops who can trace their ordinations back to the very first apostles (this is called apostolic succession). So the bishop connects us to the wider church around the world and to the church through the ages, from the earliest apostles, through our history, and to the present day.

As the church grew and expanded, it became impractical for all baptisms to wait until the bishop's visit, and local priests were given the authority to baptize new believers. We keep the presence of the bishop in baptism by using the oil of chrism, which is always consecrated by a bishop, as a sign of the connection of baptism to the wider church.

Today baptisms are most often performed by priests, unless a bishop is present, or by a deacon or others in certain circumstances.

Next, if the candidate is an infant or child, the celebrant asks the parents and sponsors two questions. "Will you be responsible for seeing that the child you present is brought up in the Christian faith and life?" and "Will you by your prayers and witness help this child to grow into the full stature of Christ?" To both questions, the answer is "I will, with God's help." We won't succeed at either goal if we don't rely on God's help.

The first question comes because we are baptizing infants who cannot answer for themselves. We do this because others are making promises on their behalf. Sponsors and parents are agreeing to a lifetime commitment of raising the child in the Christian faith. This is one reason why it is important for parents and sponsors to be active, practicing followers of

Jesus. Without that, there's little hope that this promise to God, made in front of a congregation, will be kept.

The second question highlights a critical point. Raising the child in faith is not just about knowledge and facts; it is about transformation. The promise is to "help this child to grow into the full stature of Christ"—which is also a good reminder that we're never quite done. None of us will ever become exactly like Christ. But we can try to be more and more like him, offering perfect love. It is important to note that we pledge to show the child (and others) how to be like Christ through "prayers and witness." That is, we teach and others learn through both our prayers and our actions. We must live our lives in a way that shows others who Christ is and how to be like him, and we must be people of prayer. These are the promises we are making. They are a tall order, which is why we say, "I will, with God's help."

In baptism, we are turning toward Christ. To turn toward one thing means to turn away from another, so next, the candidates, parents, and sponsors renounce Satan.

Question	Do you renounce Satan and all the spiritual forces of wickedness that rebel against God?
Answer	I renounce them.
Question	Do you renounce the evil powers of this world which corrupt and destroy the creatures of God?
Answer	I renounce them.
Question	Do you renounce all sinful desires that draw you from the love of God?
Answer	I renounce them.

It isn't fashionable to talk about Satan and the power of evil these days, but it is essential. Look at the front page of any newspaper and the feeds of any social media channel or have honest conversations with people about their deepest struggles. Evil powers are real. We Christians should not be afraid of them because we know that on Easter, Jesus utterly defeated the worst evil imaginable. We should be confident that we can defeat evil, which is why we should not be afraid to look it in the face. In the service of baptism, we consciously acknowledge the reality of evil and then actively turn away from it.

> *Question*   Do you turn to Jesus Christ and accept him as your Savior?
>
> *Answer*   I do.
>
> *Question*   Do you put your whole trust in his grace and love?
>
> *Answer*   I do.
>
> *Question*   Do you promise to follow and obey him as your Lord?
>
> *Answer*   I do.

Just as we turn away from Satan and evil power, we turn toward Jesus Christ and the power of love. These are big promises. Putting our "whole trust" in "grace and love" is easier said than done! To trust in Christ's love and grace is to know that we are loved no matter what we do, that Jesus is with us in whatever we face. To accept him as our Savior is to know that our salvation will not be found in power, money, prestige, family, or friends but only in Jesus Christ. To "follow and obey" acknowledges that we don't have the answers, but that we find our direction, our compass, our hope in our Lord Jesus Christ. The depth and radical nature of these promises takes a lifetime to understand and fully embrace.

The celebrant addresses the next question to the whole congregation. Each person in the congregation is asked, "Will you who witness these vows do all in your power to support these persons in their life in Christ?" The answer should be, "We will." This question is brief but important. We who are the church promise to support those who are baptized. We promise to help them grow into the full stature of Christ. There are no asterisks or exceptions about us helping only when it is convenient or when we feel like it. Indeed, we promise to support these persons for their entire lives, to do all in our power. *All in our power.* The service of baptism is full of big promises!

Baptismal Covenant

We then join in renewing our Baptismal Covenant. This set of eight questions-and-answers affirms our faith in God the Father, God the Son, and God the Holy Spirit, and then we commit to a life of Christian faith and discipline.

First we are asked to restate our faith in God as three persons: Father, Son, and Holy Spirit. We state our faith using the Apostles' Creed, which has been associated with baptism since the early church. In the first centuries of the church, when Christians were often persecuted, unbaptized persons were dismissed from the liturgy before creeds were recited. During that period, the very first time people could hear or recite the creeds was at their baptism. The Nicene Creed is normally used for regular Sunday celebrations of Holy Eucharist; the Apostles' Creed is more ancient and associated with baptism.

> *Celebrant*   Do you believe in God the Father?
>
> *People*   I believe in God, the Father almighty, creator of heaven and earth.
>
> *Celebrant*   Do you believe in Jesus Christ, the Son of God?

People   I believe in Jesus Christ, his only Son,
                    our Lord.
               He was conceived by the power of
                    the Holy Spirit
                    and born of the Virgin Mary.
               He suffered under Pontius Pilate,
                    was crucified, died, and was buried.
               He descended to the dead.
               On the third day he rose again.
               He ascended into heaven,
                    and is seated at the right hand
                    of the Father.
               He will come again to judge the living and
                    the dead.

Celebrant   Do you believe in God the Holy Spirit?

People   I believe in the Holy Spirit,
                    the holy catholic Church,
                    the communion of saints,
                    the forgiveness of sins,
                    the resurrection of the body,
                    and the life everlasting.

The Apostles' Creed summarizes some of the basic teachings of our faith. We profess that God the Father has created everything. We profess that God the Son was born, crucified, raised to new life, and will come again as judge. We profess faith in God the Holy Spirit, in the communion of the saints, and in the grace of having sins forgiven. We profess our trust in God's promise of eternal life and our commitment to the catholic church. The word catholic here (and throughout our liturgies in the prayer book) means universal—the one, worldwide church of Jesus Christ.

Baptismal Promises

After we pray the Apostles' Creed, we ask and answer five questions. These are called the baptismal promises. In these promises, we make extraordinary, impossible commitments that we will never manage to get totally right, especially on our own. Our hope of fulfilling these promises is possible only through God who works in us. That is why we answer, "I will, with God's help."

We promise to continue in the apostles' teaching and fellowship, in the breaking of bread, and in the prayers. We are saying that we will participate in Christian worship, attend classes to learn about our faith, join in the celebration of Holy Eucharist, and pray daily, both as a community and as individuals. To live out this promise, we need to put worshiping with a Christian community at the top of our priority list, not a do-it-when-I-feel-like-it activity. This baptismal promise comes from the Book of Acts, when the earliest Christians found great joy in committing to follow Jesus in community. We too will experience great joy when we make our community of Christ-followers the priority.

We promise to persevere in resisting evil, and, whenever we fall into sin, to repent and return to the Lord. We are saying we will actively turn away from those things that we know to be evil, even if they are alluring. And we are promising to do what is necessary to be reconciled with God and with one another when we sin (not if, but when). Our world is full of things that take us away from God (money, power, selfish desires). In this promise, we acknowledge these things and say we will resist them. We also admit that we're going to get this wrong and promise that we will try again. Our faith gives us as many do-overs as we need. What we promise here is to try our best.

We promise to proclaim by word and example the Good News of God in Christ. We are saying that we will share our faith, share the gospel, share the message of Jesus with anyone and everyone. We will proclaim it both with words and with the example of our lives—not just one or the other. This promise might be hard for Episcopalians: We are called to talk about our faith with other people— perhaps even strangers! We will look at the important topic of evangelism in Chapters 25 and 26.

We promise to seek and serve Christ in all persons, loving our neighbor as ourselves. We are saying that we will look for Jesus in all we meet, even when it might be hard for us to see him. We will serve others, whether we feel like it or not, as though they were Christ himself. This is very easy to say and very hard to do. Christian love is not the same as being nice, and it has nothing to do with convenience. We are promising that we will speak the truth in love when others need to hear it, that we will help strangers just as much as we help family, and that we will make room for the needs of others, always.

We promise to strive for justice and peace among all people and respect the dignity of every human being. We are saying that we will work for justice and peace. And we will make our own best effort to respect every human being, whether we look like them or not, whether we agree with them or not, whether we think they deserve it or not. Think of the people who are most challenging for you: terrorists or others who wish you harm, very rich people, very poor people, liberals, loud people, conservatives, introverts, or whomever. We Christians are called to respect and to treat with dignity every single person on this planet as a beautiful being who bears God's image.

After reminding ourselves of the very challenging Christian life we—and those who are being baptized—have signed up for, we pray. These lovely prayers invite God to be known to the newly baptized and to gradually open our lives and hearts to God's presence.

Water

Finally! We get to the water, the main symbol of baptism, the outward and visible sign. Baptism almost always takes place with a font, which might be an elaborately carved stone basin on a fancy stand, a wooden stand with a brass bowl, a simple table with a glass bowl, or even a built-in pool that people can wade in—or something else. Baptisms can even take place outdoors, in a stream or a lake.

The celebrant blesses the water using a prayer that merits our attention: It speaks of the sacred purpose of water from the beginning of creation and throughout salvation history. The prayer recalls the fundamental purpose of baptism, and it ends with praise to God.

> We thank you, Almighty God, for the gift of water. Over it the Holy Spirit moved in the beginning of creation. Through it you led the children of Israel out of their bondage in Egypt into the land of promise. In it your Son Jesus received the baptism of John and was anointed by the Holy Spirit as the Messiah, the Christ, to lead us, through his death and resurrection, from the bondage of sin into everlasting life.

> We thank you, Father, for the water of Baptism. In it we are buried with Christ in his death. By it we share in his resurrection. Through it we are reborn by the Holy Spirit. Therefore in joyful obedience to your Son, we bring into

his fellowship those who come to him in faith, baptizing them in the Name of the Father, and of the Son, and of the Holy Spirit.

Now sanctify this water, we pray you, by the power of your Holy Spirit, that those who here are cleansed from sin and born again may continue for ever in the risen life of Jesus Christ our Savior. To him, to you, and to the Holy Spirit, be all honor and glory, now and for ever. *Amen.* (306)

Then the candidates are presented by name to the minister who will baptize them. Candidates are baptized, starting with their name, and then with the same phrase Christians have used for hundreds of years: "*N.*, I baptize you in the Name of the Father, and of the Son, and of the Holy Spirit." We never change these words, because baptism in the name of the Father and the Son and the Holy Spirit is universally recognized. If we failed to use those words, some Christians would say that the baptism isn't valid.

This point is an important one, because the two invariable things about baptism are water and these words. We can use any kind of water; we don't need a fancy font or special water. My liturgy professor said that in an emergency, we could even use our own spit! But we need water. And we must say the words, "*N.*, I baptize you in the Name of the Father, and of the Son, and of the Holy Spirit."

Several years ago I was presiding at a baptism in Ecuador where most of the congregation spoke Spanish or Quechua, a language of indigenous people in Ecuador. I spoke Spanish for most of the service, but when it came to the baptism, I wanted to use Quechua, the native language of the boy who was being baptized. I practiced for hours. But when the time came, I very quietly said the words again in English. I was worried that I might have said them wrong, and I wanted to make sure that the boy's baptism "stuck!"

After the actual baptism when water is poured over the head, we say a prayer over the newly baptized. Then the celebrant anoints the newly baptized with oil. This oil, called chrism, has been blessed by a bishop and through this blessing, is a symbol of connection to the universal church. The minister places the oil on the baptized person's forehead and makes the sign of a cross, saying, "N., you are sealed by the Holy Spirit in Baptism and marked as Christ's own for ever. *Amen.*"

Following the anointing (or sometimes the baptism itself, depending on which option one chooses), the celebrant offers a lovely prayer that encapsulates the baptized person's new life of grace-filled living.

> Heavenly Father, we thank you that by water and the Holy Spirit you have bestowed upon these your servants the forgiveness of sin, and have raised them to the new life of grace. Sustain them, O Lord, in your Holy Spirit. Give them an inquiring and discerning heart, the courage to will and to persevere, a spirit to know and to love you, and the gift of joy and wonder in all your works. *Amen.* (308)

After the anointing, the entire congregation welcomes the newly baptized, using these words: "We receive you into the household of God. Confess the faith of Christ crucified, proclaim his resurrection, and share with us in his eternal priesthood" (308). Once we are baptized, we have been claimed by Christ forever. Nothing we do or say can take away the spiritual mantle of Christ that we have received in baptism. After the anointing, the entire congregation welcomes the newly baptized. Then we share in the Peace of Christ. For the first time, the newly baptized person shares this sign of peace as a member of Christ's body, the church.

The rest of the service unfolds like a regular service of Holy Eucharist, though it is a very special occasion. For the first time, the newly baptized person, regardless of age, will receive Holy Communion. Even infants who are baptized can be communicated with a tiny drop of wine. I used to tell parents that if they were willing, this is a time to wake up their sleeping babies and let them partake of communion. As part of Christ's body, these babies, along with all of us, are nourished by Christ's presence in the sacraments. When people are baptized and receive Holy Eucharist in the same service, it shows the indissoluble connection between these two great sacraments.

Baptism is how we get into the family of Christ. The sacred meal, Holy Eucharist, is what we as a family do together.

For Reflection

✳ Read Matthew 3:13-17, and then think about our current practice of baptism. What is similar between Jesus' baptism and those in our day? What is different?

✳ Some people are baptized as infants and others as adults. What are some of the gifts of each of these experiences of Holy Baptism?

✳ Thinking about your life and actions, what does it mean to renounce Satan and evil powers and sinful desires? What does it mean to turn to Jesus Christ and put your whole trust in his grace?

✳ Which of the baptismal promises is most difficult for you to live out in your practice of the Christian faith?

✳ What's your favorite moment in the baptismal liturgy and why?

Chapter 4

A Wonderful Sacrament

Eucharistic Beliefs

God our Father, whose Son our Lord Jesus Christ in a wonderful Sacrament has left us a memorial of his passion: Grant us so to venerate the sacred mysteries of his Body and Blood, that we may ever perceive within ourselves the fruit of his redemption; who lives and reigns with you and the Holy Spirit, one God, for ever and ever. *Amen.*

—*The Book of Common Prayer*, p. 252

The Holy Eucharist is the sacrament that Episcopalians experience most often. In nearly all congregations, Holy Eucharist is celebrated every Sunday. But do we know what we are doing? Is it possible we take this "routine" sacrament for granted? Author Annie Dillard once suggested that we should wear crash helmets when we celebrate the Holy Eucharist because the power we are unleashing in the sacrament is so great. Since we don't always take the eucharist seriously, Dillard provocatively wonders if there's a chance God will smite us one day for neglecting our worship and its power.

The word eucharist comes from a Greek word that means thanksgiving. In this sacrament, we give thanks to God, offering to God our gifts from what God has given us. The centerpiece of the eucharistic service is called the Great Thanksgiving.

I don't think God is going to smite us, and I don't think it's necessary to wear crash helmets. Still, Dillard's point is well taken. In the Holy Eucharist, we are summoning the presence of the Word made flesh among us, the Christ who was present at the moment of creation. We Episcopalians believe that Jesus Christ becomes truly present in the bread and wine. That is nothing to yawn through or mutter by rote.

In the Beginning

As we contemplate this power and this mystery, let's step back and start at the beginning. Along with Holy Baptism, Holy Eucharist is one of the two great sacraments instituted by Jesus himself. The story of the first eucharist—the last meal Jesus ate with his friends, the disciples—is pretty familiar to most. We can find it in all four gospels; here is the version from Matthew:

> While they were eating, Jesus took a loaf of bread, and after blessing it he broke it, gave it to the disciples, and said, "Take, eat; this is my body." Then he took a cup, and after giving thanks he gave it to them, saying, "Drink from it, all of you; for this is my blood of the covenant, which is poured out for many for the forgiveness of sins." (Matthew 26:26-28)

From the earliest days of the church, this sacred ritual was the centerpiece of Christian gatherings. As early as two decades after Jesus' death and resurrection, Saint Paul wrote to the church in Corinth:

> For I received from the Lord what I also handed on to you,
> that the Lord Jesus on the night when he was betrayed
> took a loaf of bread, and when he had given thanks, he
> broke it and said, "This is my body that is for you. Do
> this in remembrance of me." In the same way he took
> the cup also, after supper, saying, "This cup is the new
> covenant in my blood. Do this, as often as you drink it,
> in remembrance of me." For as often as you eat this bread
> and drink the cup, you proclaim the Lord's death until he
> comes. (1 Corinthians 11:23-26)

Saint Paul wanted the followers of Jesus in Corinth to honor
this holy meal. He was concerned that those first Christians
wouldn't honor Jesus as they gathered.

> Whoever, therefore, eats the bread or drinks the cup of
> the Lord in an unworthy manner will be answerable for
> the body and blood of the Lord. Examine yourselves,
> and only then eat of the bread and drink of the cup. For
> all who eat and drink without discerning the body, eat
> and drink judgment against themselves. (1 Corinthians
> 11:27-29)

There was danger that they would be too casual—that they
would not discern Christ's presence or that some would eat
before others, creating a hierarchy at precisely the moment
when Jesus is calling all into mutual obedience in community.
But that's not all. Saint Paul warns people to eat before they
come to the celebration. You see: This isn't an ordinary meal
at all. We don't gather to eat bread that sustains our earthly
bodies but rather to eat the bread from heaven that sustains
our souls.

Saint Paul and Annie Dillard are right to remind us to be
mindful of the (literally) awesome power of what we're
doing. But at the same time, we shouldn't act as if we must

understand everything about it—that we must have a degree in eucharistic theology—before we can fully partake and receive the sacrament.

Several years ago, a new family showed up at the church I was serving, and they were worried that their children "might not be ready" for Holy Communion. When I asked about this, they said that the kids might not understand what we're doing. I hastily responded that, even as a priest with several theology degrees, I didn't claim to understand this profound mystery. Further, the presence of shelves and shelves of books on the eucharist (and more to be written still) is evidence that we might not have it totally figured out. Approaching the sacrament with childlike wonder might be the best model for all of us.

Another time, I was preparing a whole family for baptism, including some young school-aged children. The children had been coming to church for months with their parents. Because they weren't baptized yet, they had been receiving a blessing at the altar rail instead of the consecrated bread and wine. As the date of baptism drew closer, I asked one of the children if he was ready to receive Holy Communion. "Yes!" came the enthusiastic reply. Then I asked him if he knew what to expect when he received the bread and wine for the first time. "It's Jesus!" Perhaps we as adults overthink the eucharist; some children understand it in profound and clear ways—and can teach us a thing or two.

The Presence of Christ

As Episcopalians, we believe that Jesus Christ is really and truly present in the bread and wine as they are blessed and shared by the priest and people. In the eucharist, we offer to God "our selves, our souls and bodies" (336). And in the eucharist, God blesses us with the presence of Christ himself, both in the sacred elements and in the gathered community.

Over the years, Christians have disagreed mightily on exactly how Christ is present in the liturgy. From these varying ideas have come different practices in how Christians celebrate the eucharist. Some Christians believe that the bread and the wine are mere symbols, and that eucharist is but a recollection of the Last Supper. Some Christians believe that the substance of the bread becomes the Body of Christ, literally, and that it only continues to appear as bread. Anglicans have not been keen to adopt dogmatic positions, simply saying that the consecrated bread is the Body of Christ and leaving it at that—although it's not hard to find Anglicans with various positions on this issue.

One way to understand what we're doing is to think about some of the names people use for this sacrament. The Catechism in our prayer book says this: "The Holy Eucharist is called the Lord's Supper, and Holy Communion; it is also known as the Divine Liturgy, the Mass, and the Great Offering" (859).

> The Catechism is a summary of the Episcopal Church's teaching on key topics. Found on pages 844-862 of *The Book of Common Prayer*, the Catechism is presented in question-and-answer format so that it is easy to explore and reference. The answers in the Catechism are meant to be a starting point for deeper reflection and teaching. The responses in the Catechism offer beautiful, succinct summaries of Episcopal teaching, with answers deeply grounded both in the Bible and in the precise words of *The Book of Common Prayer*.

❖ **Eucharist** comes from a Greek word that means thanksgiving because the entire meal is our offering of thanks to God for the many blessings we receive and because, in Holy Communion, we receive Christ himself and we are grateful.

❖ **The Lord's Supper** reminds us that our gathering is a remembrance of Christ's last meal with his friends, the night he shared one last meal with his disciples.

❖ **Holy Communion** emphasizes how we relate to God as he dwells in us and we in him. The sacrament also helps us discover that the many members of Christ's body are made one—as we gather, we commune with one another as well as with God.

❖ **Divine Liturgy** is a name one might expect to find in an Eastern Orthodox tradition, but we Anglicans use it as well. Divine means that what we are doing is a heavenly thing, not an earthly thing. We are, as Saint Paul says, setting our minds on things above. The Divine Liturgy reminds us that we do not gather to deny the pain or needs of the world but rather to offer our prayers and our lives for the deepest needs of the world and all people.

❖ **Mass** is a way of describing Holy Eucharist that some Episcopalians might expect to find in use primarily among Roman Catholics. However, Mass is one of the ways our prayer book suggests we might refer to eucharist, and it is a good reference word. Mass comes from the same Latin word as mission, meaning to send. The word Mass came into being because of the importance of the dismissal— the sending forth—at the conclusion of the service. When we call our service the Mass, we are reminding ourselves of the importance of going out into the world to do the work we have been given to do.

❖ **The Great Offering** is rarely used but is also an important and valid description of this sacrament. In ancient Jewish worship—which Jesus knew and practiced—the pattern was daily prayer and weekly sacrifice. In the temple, burnt offerings were made each week to God, both to give an offering of thanks and to make recompense for sin, among other things. Christians adopted this weekly pattern, and today we keep the discipline of daily prayer and a weekly sacrifice. However, ours is a different kind of sacrifice of praise. Our prayer book says this beautifully: "And we earnestly desire thy fatherly goodness to accept this our sacrifice—one of praise and thanksgiving, whereby we offer and present unto thee, O Lord, our selves, our souls and bodies" (342). In other words, in the act of expressing our profound gratitude to God for all our blessings, we offer back to God our very selves, as well as the visible gifts of money, bread, and wine.

In fulfilling Christ's command to remember him in blessing bread and wine, we experience his presence and are nourished to do his work. This prayer from *The Book of Common Prayer* encapsulates nicely what we're doing during Holy Eucharist.

> Almighty and everliving God,
> we thank you for feeding us with the spiritual food
> of the most precious Body and Blood
> of your Son our Savior Jesus Christ;
> and for assuring us in these holy mysteries
> that we are living members of the Body of your Son,
> and heirs of your eternal kingdom.
> And now, Father, send us out
> to do the work you have given us to do,
> to love and serve you
> as faithful witnesses of Christ our Lord.
> To him, to you, and to the Holy Spirit,
> be honor and glory, now and for ever. *Amen.* (366)

In our celebrations of the eucharist, we are fed by word and sacrament—the scriptures are read, and we feast on Christ's presence in bread and wine. In this act, we see Jesus Christ, but the gathered community is also reminded that we are the Body of Christ. As Saint Augustine famously wrote about Christians who eat the bread and drink the wine: "Be what you see; receive what you are." We see Jesus Christ, and we receive his body, because the church—the gathered community—is the Body of Christ.

For Reflection

✳ Our prayer book gives six names for Holy Eucharist, reminding us it "is called the Lord's Supper, and Holy Communion; it is also known as the Divine Liturgy, the Mass, and the Great Offering." What does each name tell us about what is happening? Do these names make a new connection to the eucharist for you?

✳ The author makes the claim that infants and children should receive communion, even if they don't understand it well. Do you agree with this claim? Why or why not?

✳ We believe that in the Holy Eucharist, the bread and wine become the body and blood of Jesus. What are some of the liturgical practices in your church that help point you to this mystical reality?

✳ If your next-door neighbor called over to you on a Sunday morning as you were getting ready to leave and said, "I'm curious why you go to church to receive Holy Communion every week," how would you respond?

Chapter 5

Be Known to Us in the Breaking of Bread
Eucharistic Practices

Be present, be present, O Jesus, our great High Priest, as you were present with your disciples, and be known to us in the breaking of bread; who lives and reigns with the Father and the Holy Spirit, now and for ever. *Amen.*

—*The Book of Common Prayer*, p. 834

A few years ago, I was in Tanzania on Ash Wednesday. Throughout the day, I was busy with work. When evening came, I wanted to attend an Ash Wednesday service, so I headed to the Anglican cathedral in Dar es Salaam.

I was warmly welcomed and found a seat in the packed church. The opening hymn wasn't in my language, but I sang along, trying my best to pronounce the words sung to a familiar tune. Even though the entire service was in Swahili, I was able to follow along, from the opening prayers, readings, sermon, prayers, blessing, administration of ashes, and offering to the Holy Eucharist and final prayers. Not a single word was intelligible to me, but I knew what was happening at every moment.

Despite being in a strange city and hearing the service in a strange tongue, I felt very much at home. This is because the service was structured like all of the Ash Wednesday services I have ever attended. The vestments, the furnishings, the music, and the ritual movements were familiar.

Over the years, I have attended Anglican services of Holy Eucharist on six continents and in many languages, and I've always been grateful for the gift of our common prayer, of a shared experience that transcends time, race, location, and culture. While plenty of differences exist among these places, the commonality is deeper. Anglican Christians, along with many other Christians, see a great gift in using prayers that reflect our global and ancient church. Our prayers are rooted not just in our own preferences but also in the wider church. Thus, when we pray, we are taking part in a tradition that is bigger than ourselves. Our prayers are united with those of Christians through time and space.

In addition to the words and prayers, music is another place of common ground and a central part of our Christian worship. The prayer book allows any part of the service to be said or sung, and it is common to add hymns or songs to the service and to sing certain parts of the liturgy. Though the style of music or instruments may vary greatly—guitar, drums, pipe organ, trumpets, folk music, English cathedral music, Gregorian chant—there is a venerable history of music being used to adorn and enrich our prayers.

We will look at some of the common elements that are almost always included in celebrations of the Holy Eucharist. Details may vary, but the shape and contour of the service will generally match what you see here.

You might like to follow along in *The Book of Common Prayer*, starting at page 323 for Rite I ("thee" and "thou" language) or page 355 (more contemporary language).

Postures for Prayer and Worship

Traditionally in the Episcopal Church, we use one of three main postures for worship. We sit for instruction, we kneel for prayer, and we stand for praise. These days, kneeling is becoming somewhat less common, but the rule still holds. In places where kneeling has passed out of favor, standing, which is also a traditional and ancient posture of prayer, is substituted. These different postures are ways of using our whole bodies in our prayers. Service leaflets often give guidance about local customs, but when in doubt, just watch what others do.

It is pretty common for people to sign themselves with a cross. To make the sign of the cross, people move their hand from their forehead, to their lower chest, to the left shoulder, to the right shoulder, and usually back to the center of the chest. Some people use four fingers extended, while others prefer to join their first two fingers and thumb as a reminder of the Holy Trinity. It is common to cross oneself during mentions of the Holy Trinity and when the priest pronounces absolution or forgiveness. In some congregations, there will be many more occasions of crossing. When in doubt, watch others, and it's never wrong to ask the priest or someone else why they are crossing themselves at particular moments.

In some congregations, people use additional postures or gestures. Genuflecting—touching the right knee to the ground—is a devotional gesture to acknowledge Christ's presence, used when people enter or exit the church and at other times. Note that this is quite different from a curtsy in that a genuflection lowers the knee until it touches the ground briefly. People may make a simple bow, inclining the head, at the mention of Jesus' name or when the Holy Trinity is invoked. Some people will use a profound bow—lowering the upper half of one's body to about a 45-degree angle or more from the ground—during the singing of the *Sanctus* ("Holy, holy, holy") in the eucharistic prayer or in place of a genuflection.

Gather in the Lord's Name

The first part of the service is the gathering. The people of God assemble for prayer and praise. The gathering itself can be seen as a symbol of the eucharist. Just as many grains are kneaded together into one loaf of bread, so too are many individuals knit together into the one Body of Christ.

As people enter the church, many will pray after they settle into chairs or pews so that they can prepare their hearts and minds for worship. Our prayer book has a really good prayer for this purpose:

> O Almighty God, who pours out on all who desire it the spirit of grace and of supplication: Deliver us, when we draw near to you, from coldness of heart and wanderings of mind, that with steadfast thoughts and kindled affections we may worship you in spirit and in truth; through Jesus Christ our Lord. *Amen.* (833)

As the prayer says, our purpose in gathering is to worship God, not to see friends. That's what coffee hour is for! The worship service itself is meant for us to focus our whole being on worshiping God.

The service usually begins with some kind of procession. Perhaps a cross will lead the ministers into the church, signifying how we all follow the banner of Christ. Processions might also include torchbearers (acolytes), choir, altar servers, a gospel book-bearer, or assisting clergy. Once the priest and the other assisting ministers are in place, the service begins with a response between priest and people that varies by season. For example, the priest may say "Blessed be God: Father, Son, and Holy Spirit," and the people respond, "And blessed be his kingdom, now and for ever. Amen." During Eastertide, this will instead be "Alleluia. Christ is risen," with a response of "The Lord is risen indeed. Alleluia." And during seasons such as Lent or Advent, the priest will say "Bless the Lord who forgives all our sins," and the response is "His mercy endures for ever." There are other possibilities in some of the supplemental liturgical books, also authorized for use in the Episcopal Church.

The priest may then offer this ancient prayer:

> Almighty God, to you all hearts are open, all desires known, and from you no secrets are hid: Cleanse the thoughts of our hearts by the inspiration of your Holy Spirit, that we may perfectly love you, and worthily magnify your holy Name; through Christ our Lord. *Amen.* (355)

This lovely prayer with its themes of cleansing is called the Collect for Purity. The idea is that we rely on God's power in the Holy Spirit to help us make ourselves ready for worship and to be aware of the importance of what we are doing.

Next comes one of several very old Christian worship songs. While the congregation might speak these words, they are certainly hymns. During seasons or occasions when we focus on our sinfulness and our need of God, we might say "Lord, have mercy" or *Kyrie eleison.*

The words *Kyrie eleison* are Greek. This hymn was introduced into Christian worship when many Christians spoke Greek. Ever since, it has been customary for worshipers to sing these words in Greek or in their own language. "Lord, have mercy. Christ, have mercy. Lord, have mercy." It is a simple yet stirring plea.

Other times, especially when we focus on celebration, we might sing "Glory to God in the highest" or *Gloria in excelsis Deo.* Many parts of the service have Latin names, because when they were introduced, Christians were speaking Latin. It's perfectly fine to use the names from our own language! In any case, *Gloria in excelsis Deo* is inspired by the Gospel of Luke when the angels sang at Christ's birth.

Glory to God in the highest,
   and peace to his people on earth.
Lord God, heavenly King,
almighty God and Father,
   we worship you, we give you thanks,
   we praise you for your glory.
Lord Jesus Christ, only Son of the Father,
Lord God, Lamb of God,
you take away the sin of the world:
   have mercy on us;
you are seated at the right hand of the Father:
   receive our prayer.
For you alone are the Holy One, you alone are the Lord,
you alone are the Most High,
   Jesus Christ,
   with the Holy Spirit,
   in the glory of God the Father. *Amen.* (356)

This hymn of praise is meant to join our voices with the angelic witnesses and to enlist our voices in praising the Holy Trinity: God the Father, God the Son, and God the Holy Spirit.

Finally, we might sing the *Trisagion*, or thrice-holy hymn. This hymn is at least 1,500 years old. Much like the *Kyrie eleison*, this hymn is about imploring God's mercy.

Holy God, Holy and Mighty,
Holy Immortal One,
Have mercy upon us. (356)

The exact details of origin for these three hymns are not as important as the fact that in our regular Sunday worship today, we are praying as people have prayed for centuries or even millennia.

Next the leader greets the people: "The Lord be with you." This comes from the book of Ruth (2:4) when a man named

Boaz greets people with these words. Our response is always "And also with you" or "And with thy spirit" depending on whether we are praying with contemporary (Rite II) or more traditional (Rite I) prayers.

Then the leader may pause, leaving a moment of quiet for people to offer silent prayers. Then the Collect of the Day is said. A different collect is appointed for each day or occasion being celebrated. Here's an example from the first Sunday after Christmas Day:

> Collect is a funny word. In church, when we say it, the emphasis is on the first syllable (COLL-ect). This is a special kind of prayer in which the leader brings together (collects) the individual prayers of the gathered community.

> Almighty God, you have poured upon us the new light of your incarnate Word: Grant that this light, enkindled in our hearts, may shine forth in our lives; through Jesus Christ our Lord, who lives and reigns with you, in the unity of the Holy Spirit, one God, now and for ever. *Amen.* (213)

This prayer gathers the themes of the readings and points us toward our celebration of Christ's incarnation and how it can bear fruit in our lives. The Collect of the Day, as it raises up themes for our celebration, concludes the portion of the liturgy in which we are gathering. Next come the scripture readings.

The Word of God

When Jesus' followers gathered for eucharist, they heard scripture read and someone responded by offering teaching. In Jesus' time, a scroll was read, and the reader would simply pick up where the last gathering left off. In our time, a lectionary (a fancy word for a list of readings) tells us which passages of scripture to read.

Normally, we will hear readings from the Old Testament, from the letters of the New Testament, and from the gospels. In addition, we sing or say a psalm or a portion of a psalm. Sometimes there is just one reading plus a gospel, but there is always, without exception, a reading from the gospels, time to hear directly from Jesus and his followers. Our lectionary appoints readings for a three-year cycle. If you come to church every Sunday for three years, you will encounter nearly all of the New Testament and a good amount of the Old Testament. (Some of the most challenging and interesting parts of the scripture are omitted, so there's no substitute for picking up a Bible and reading it yourself, if you want the full story!) You can find the lectionary starting on page 887 of the prayer book.

The scriptures are typically read from a lectern, or reading stand. Our task is to listen carefully, and then when the reader finishes with "The Word of the Lord," or a similar phrase, to respond in gratitude for the scriptures, "Thanks be to God."

Many churches have a special procession for the gospel reading, bringing the book into the midst of the people accompanied by torches and perhaps even incense. By moving into the center of the congregation, the procession symbolizes the way in which the gospel—the Good News of God in Jesus Christ—came into our world and continues to do so. The gospel is read by a deacon when one is present, or otherwise by a priest.

After the readings, our prayer book requires a response to the scriptures in a sermon. The preacher comments on the readings and helps us make connections with our own lives. Sermons are not just Bible studies in which we scrutinize the scriptures with critical eyes, though the sermons may take us deeply into scripture. Sermons are not merely essays on what is happening in the world, though no good preacher will ignore the world outside the church. Rather sermons are meant to draw us into the sweeping narrative of God's love found in the scriptures and to help us find our place in that grand story.

Following the sermon, we say a creed. This will almost always be the Nicene Creed, a summary of the Christian faith that is more than 1,600 years old. By reciting these words together, we place ourselves in a beautiful and slowly moving river of Christian theological tradition. Regardless of the issues we face in our lives and in our world, the church throughout all time and all places proclaims the same ancient faith rooted in the saving work of God the Father (in creation), of God the Son (in our redemption), and in God the Holy Spirit (in sustaining us). Chapter 13 explores the creeds in more detail.

Pray for the World and the Church

From ancient times, it has been customary for gathered Christians to pray for their own needs and the needs of the world. So it is that when we gather for Holy Eucharist, we too pray for not only those things that are important to our local community or to ourselves but also for the whole world. *The Book of Common Prayer* specifies a list of concerns for which we invariably pray:

> The Universal Church, its members, and its mission
> The Nation and all in authority
> The welfare of the world
> The concerns of the local community
> Those who suffer and those in any trouble
> The departed (with commemoration of a saint when appropriate) (383)

We may pray using one of the forms in the prayer book, or perhaps a member of the church will have written prayers. But whatever words we use, we pray for the church and the world. If you would like to read the six suggested forms for the Prayers of the People, they can be found on pages 383-395 of the prayer book. The Prayers of the People may be led by a lay person or a deacon, one of the few moments in our liturgy where the priest participates rather than leading.

We also pray for God's forgiveness of our own sins. After we ask for forgiveness and pray for change in our lives, the priest will pronounce God's forgiveness. This kind of confession is often called the general confession, as it is said by all people, covering all our sins. Some people will want to avail themselves of what is sometimes called private confession—where one confesses privately to a priest—outside of the liturgy. See Chapter 7 to learn more.

Exchange the Peace

In the Gospel according to Matthew, Jesus teaches about the importance of reconciliation prior to making our offerings to God. He says, "So when you are offering your gift at the altar, if you remember that your brother or sister has something against you, leave your gift there before the altar and go; first be reconciled to your brother or sister, and then come and offer your gift" (5:23-24). Because of this teaching, the church began the custom of passing the Peace of Christ before we make our offerings to God and receive the Holy Eucharist. The priest announces, "The peace of the Lord be always with you." We respond in words—often people will say, "And also with you." Then we respond by action, sharing a sign of Christ's peace. In our day, this is usually a handshake, but the ancient practice was a chaste kiss on the cheek. A hug is also a traditional and venerable way to pass the peace; many who pass the peace with a hug gently grip the arms of the other person near the shoulder. This preserves the symbol of a sign of peace while avoiding bodily contact that could make some people feel uncomfortable.

Too often, the passing of the peace becomes a conversational free-for-all in which friends catch up on weekend news. There is spiritual danger in this practice, because we neglect the opportunity for reconciliation at our own peril. When we pass the peace, we should make a special point first to share peace with those from whom we are estranged. A second priority is strangers or guests. Only then should we greet friends, because we have no need for reconciliation with them. In other words, the Passing of the Peace is for reconciliation, not for catching up with our buddies.

It is poignant to see a first-time guest in a congregation standing awkwardly while people who know each other well chat at this moment in the liturgy. At precisely the moment when all should be reconciled, we divide into insiders and outsiders and neglect our guests. In our world of estrangement and division, we need every bit of practice at reconciliation and unity we can muster.

Prepare the Table

After the peace, an offering is collected. It is common for this to be an offering of money only, whether cash or checks. In some places in the world, the offering also might consist of food or other gifts. Whatever is collected from the people, all our gifts—including our gifts of bread and wine for Holy Eucharist—are presented and placed on the altar. In this action, we also offer our very selves to God, trusting that God will transform our lives so that we might live according to God's purposes for us.

If there is a deacon in a congregation, the deacon will set and prepare the table. The bread and the wine are carefully placed and prepared for their consecration in the eucharistic prayer to follow.

Make Eucharist

The priest and other ministers gather at the altar. The celebrant (the priest who says the prayer of consecration) leads the gathered community in the eucharistic prayer. In the Episcopal Church, we may choose from nine authorized prayers: two traditional language prayers (Prayer I on page 333, Prayer II on page 340), four modern-language prayers (Prayer A on page 361, Prayer B on page 367, Prayer C on page 369, Prayer D on page 372), and three experimental prayers that make use of expansive language for people (avoiding many male pronouns, for example); these are found in a book called *Enriching Our Worship 1* (Church Publishing, 1997). All nine of these prayers have some common elements:

The prayers may be sung or said.

The priest begins with a traditional set of greetings and responses, for example, "Lift up your hearts."
"We lift them to the Lord."

The prayers unite our voices with saints and angels of all time and all space.

The prayer includes Jesus' words of institution to bless the bread and the wine. These words come directly from the scriptures.

The prayers include an invocation for the Holy Spirit to descend upon our gifts and upon the gathered community.

The prayers end with an AMEN. It is in all capital letters, the only word so indicated in *The Book of Common Prayer*. The people are meant to boldly say Amen to conclude the prayer—it is our way of saying "let it be so" to the words that have come before.

After the eucharistic prayer, the congregation joins in saying the Lord's Prayer ("Our Father, who art in heaven…").

The Lord's Prayer

According to the prayer book, the Lord's Prayer is always said at every public service of the church. In saying this prayer, we are not merely repeating a prayer by rote, but we are praying as Christ taught us—for the things he taught us to pray for.

The prayer book offers two versions of the Lord's Prayer: traditional and contemporary. Both are fully acceptable options.

Traditional

Our Father, who art in heaven, hallowed be thy Name, thy kingdom come, thy will be done, on earth as it is in heaven. Give us this day our daily bread. And forgive us our trespasses, as we forgive those who trespass against us. And lead us not into temptation, but deliver us from evil. For thine is the kingdom, and the power, and the glory, for ever and ever. *Amen.*

Contemporary

Our Father in heaven, hallowed be your Name, your kingdom come, your will be done, on earth as in heaven. Give us today our daily bread. Forgive us our sins as we forgive those who sin against us. Save us from the time of trial and deliver us from evil. For the kingdom, the power, and the glory are yours, now and for ever. *Amen.*

Break the Bread

Immediately after the Lord's Prayer, the priest breaks the consecrated bread. At this point, the bread has become the Body of Christ, and so this breaking of Christ's body reminds us poignantly of the sacrifice Jesus made for us in his death. Some churches use leavened or unleavened baked bread. Others use wafers that are compressed bread pieces. These wafers don't look much like bread, but they are made of wheat flour. The wafers are often used for convenience, since "real" bread can leave crumbs. In any case, the priest will break the loaf or a larger wafer. The priest's wafer is not larger because the priest is more important, but rather it is bigger so that the whole gathered community can see the action of breaking. After the bread is broken, silence will be kept. This is one of the only places where *The Book of Common Prayer* orders silence. We might constructively use this time for spiritual preparation to receive eucharist, perhaps repeating the words of Saint Thomas when he realized he was seeing Jesus Christ himself: "My Lord and my God" (John 20:28).

Share the Gifts of God

The priest and the ministers at the altar receive communion as the people begin to come forward. Everyone in the congregation is invited to come to the table. Those who do not receive Holy Communion are given a blessing by the priest. In the Episcopal Church, all baptized Christians are invited to receive bread and wine, regardless of age or denomination. Baptized infants may receive Holy Communion with a tiny drop of wine. The fullness of Christ's presence is found in either the bread or the wine, so one can receive either or both. In the Episcopal Church, opportunity is always given to people to both eat the bread and drink from the chalice.

If someone is not baptized, she or he may still approach the altar, where the priest will offer God's blessing. Those who are unable to move from their place because of a mobility issue can usually make this known to an usher, who will direct the priest and an assistant to bring Holy Communion to the worshiper.

After communion has been administered to all who will receive, the priest or the deacon cleans vessels and clears the table. Any leftover bread or wine is reverently consumed immediately or set aside to be consumed after the service. Because we believe that the bread and the wine have been consecrated and are now the Body and Blood of Christ, we treat them with utmost care; they are never discarded. Wine is consumed or poured onto the ground, and bread is consumed. Sometimes bread or wine are kept in the church, in case a sick person is in urgent need to receive Holy Eucharist during the week. The place where the blessed bread and wine are kept or reserved is called an aumbry or tabernacle. It is usually a small metal or wooden box that is kept locked. A candle—a symbol of Christ's presence—burns whenever the aumbry or tabernacle contains the body or blood of Christ.

Once the bread and wine have been consumed or cleared away, the people join together in a post-communion prayer of thanksgiving and hope for God's continued work in our lives. Then the priest pronounces a blessing on the people— or, during Lent, says a prayer over the people.

Lastly, the deacon or the priest sends the people out with the dismissal. This is a very important part of the service, because the dismissal sends us into the world to carry out the work that has been made possible by the sustenance we have received in Holy Eucharist. Our response to the dismissal is "Thanks be to God." In these words—the last words of the service—we give thanks not only for the worship we have experienced but also for Christ's abiding presence in our lives as we go forth into the world to do the work he has given us.

Regardless of form or style in the eucharistic service, Jesus Christ is made known to us in the breaking of the bread. In worshiping as Christians have worshiped for hundreds of years, we too hear God's word in scripture; we too offer our prayers for our community and our world; we too offer our gifts to God; we too are nourished by Jesus Christ's Body and Blood; and we too know the transformation of God's saving grace at work in our lives. Thanks be to God, indeed.

For Reflection

✳ Have you ever attended Holy Eucharist in a different country or in a different church tradition? If so, how did that experience compare with worship in your church? What was the same and what was different?

✳ What is your favorite moment in the eucharistic liturgy and why?

✳ Christians often talk about the importance of word and sacrament in our worship. Our liturgy includes lots of scripture and a sermon. How can you put your encounter with God's word to work in your life?

✳ What are some of the liturgical connections between gathering on Sunday to be nourished by Christ in the sacraments and the experience of doing God's work in the world throughout the week?

Chapter 6

Grow in Grace through the Years
Confirmation and Marriage

Holy Spirit, open our eyes, our ears, and our hearts, that we may grow closer to you through joy and through suffering. Be with us in the fullness of your power as new members are added to your household, as we grow in grace through the years, when we are joined in marriage, when we turn to you in sickness or special need, and, at the last, when we are committed into the Father's hands.

—*The Book of Common Prayer*, p. 569

If you go into any Episcopal Church and check the prayer books in the pew, you'll usually find a well-worn section of pages starting around page 300. This section contains the "main" services of the church—Holy Baptism and Holy Eucharist. These are the two sacraments of the church that are for *all* people, and so we use them most frequently when we gather for worship. But *The Book of Common Prayer* also includes many important liturgies and prayers that make up our common life.

The section following Holy Eucharist is called "Pastoral Offices" and includes many of the sacramental rites instituted by the church through the guidance of the Holy Spirit. These sacramental rites include rites of passage, like confirmation and marriage, as well as liturgies for the sick and dying. The rites encompass times of great joy as well as those of pain and grief, a reminder that God in Christ wants to walk with us through all the moments of our lives—the beginning and the end, the highs and the lows, the everyday and the once-in-a-lifetime. Although these liturgies are less frequently used than the services for Holy Eucharist or Holy Baptism, they are no less important. They are a means of grace, connecting us to God and to one another in the midst of some of the defining moments of our lives.

The Rite of Confirmation

As we explored in earlier chapters, Holy Baptism is the great sacrament of Christian initiation; in the waters of baptism we are made Christ's own and become full members of his body, the church. But baptism is not, of course, the end of the life of faith. It is the entry into Christ's body, the beginning of life in the church, a first step on the journey. At baptism, the church both celebrates our entry into the Body of Christ and looks forward to the moment when, as more mature Christians, we will stand before Christ and the church and affirm for ourselves those commitments we made or that were made for us at our baptism.

Confirmation is our chance to "express a mature commitment to Christ, and receive strength from the Holy Spirit through prayer and the laying on of hands by a bishop" (860). Those baptized as adults have already made a deliberate decision to commit to Christ, so confirmation is a reaffirmation of faith and a commitment to the Episcopal Church. Those baptized as infants had parents and godparents who made big, important vows and promises on their behalf. As teenagers or adults, they are given the opportunity to decide if they want to make those big, important vows and promises to God for themselves. In baptism God welcomes us into the family of faith, and our parents and godparents promise to instruct us in what it looks like to take part in that family. In confirmation, we take the baton of our faith formation for ourselves, both accepting the gift of grace from God and vowing to try, with God's help, to live into those promises, taking our place in the Body of Christ.

Confirmation, a mature affirmation of faith, is accompanied by the laying on of hands by a bishop. As you may recall from Chapter 3, bishops in the early church performed all baptisms. As the church grew, this became logistically impossible, and priests were given the authority to baptize new believers. But the connection of bishops to new Christians is vital; this is why bishops preside at all services of confirmation. Bishops can trace their consecration back to the apostles of Jesus—something called "apostolic succession." In this way, confirmation connects us to the worldwide church through the bishop, the symbol of our unity, and to the communion of saints, past, present, and future. This reminds us of the way in which we are connected to the wider sphere of the church, beyond our local community. So the Rite of Confirmation performs two functions: It allows those who have been baptized at a young age to claim the promises of their baptism for themselves, and it connects all members of the church through the symbol of our unity, the bishop.

The Service of Confirmation

In many respects, the liturgy for confirmation echoes the service of baptism. Confirmation begins with the same opening acclamation and the assertion of the unity of the Church: "There is one Body and one Spirit" (413). It continues in the usual manner, with the collect, scripture lessons, and the sermon.

After the sermon, the candidates for confirmation are presented to the bishop, who asks them a series of questions that harken back to the promises of their baptism: "Do you reaffirm your renunciation of evil? ... Do you renew your commitment to Jesus Christ?" The congregation is then asked the same question that is posed in the baptismal service: "Will you who witness these vows do all in your power to support these persons in their life in Christ?" (416). The congregation answers, "We will," a reminder that Christian community is an important part of the life of faith, not only for infants being baptized but also for all people of all ages!

The service continues with the congregation renewing their own baptismal promises. The prayers for the candidates are the same as those used at baptism. Again, this grounds the service of confirmation in baptism. We are reminded of the commitments that were made on our behalf by others, and we are reaffirming those promises for ourselves.

Next comes the laying on of hands by the bishop. The bishop places his or her hands on each person being confirmed and says a prayer for each one, invoking the Holy Spirit and asking God to strengthen and sustain the person being confirmed.

Reception and Reaffirmation

Anyone who has made a mature commitment of faith in another Christian fellowship (such as adult baptism or confirmation in the Roman Catholic, Orthodox, or many Lutheran churches) is considered to be both baptized and confirmed by the Episcopal Church, so long as they were confirmed by a bishop of their church. People in that situation who wish to make a public affirmation of their faith and commitment to the responsibilities of their baptism in the presence of an Episcopal bishop can choose to be received into the Episcopal Church. In this event, the bishop lays hands on each candidate for reception and says, "We recognize you as a member of the one holy catholic and apostolic Church, and we receive you into the fellowship of this Communion" (418).

Occasionally, someone who is already confirmed or received experiences a deeper conversion to Christ and wishes to reaffirm his or her baptismal promises. This might be for a person returning to the church after a period of absence or unbelief or for someone who has had a particularly transformative spiritual experience that he or she wishes to express in the context of worship with the community. In this situation, the bishop lays hands on the person and says the prayer for reaffirmation: "N., may the Holy Spirit, who has begun a good work in you, direct and uphold you in the service of Christ and his kingdom. *Amen*" (419).

After the bishop has laid hands on each person being confirmed, received, and reaffirmed, the bishop says a concluding prayer over all the candidates. The service then continues with the Peace and Holy Eucharist.

Confirmation: Why? (or Why Not?)

Nearly every priest or parent has heard the question at least once: "Do I *have* to be confirmed?" The question is sometimes posed by a teenager facing his or her parent's expectations, sometimes by a new member checking out what membership in the church means, or sometimes by a couple seeking to be married in an Episcopal church. The short answer is no ... and yes.

The Book of Common Prayer says that confirmation is "expected" rather than required. The canons (the laws governing the church) require confirmation for a few individuals: those being ordained, deputies to General Convention, and those appointed to many church-wide offices. But confirmation is not "required" for most Episcopalians. In the Episcopal Church, you don't have to be confirmed in order to be married (although at least one member of the couple must be baptized), to be buried, or to receive communion.

For most people, confirmation is not required in order to be a member of the Episcopal Church. But confirmation is expected, because it is something that mature Christians can and should *want* to do. Much as with marriage, couples who love one another *want* to stand up and make vows and promises in front of family and friends, so too a Christian, loving God very much, ought to *want* to stand up and make vows and promises to God in front of family and friends. Confirmation is one way that we, as mature Christians, commit to a life of faith. It doesn't mean that we have everything figured out, or that we will fulfill those vows and promises perfectly, any more than a couple seeking marriage has their relationship all figured out or will fulfill their vows and promises perfectly. But confirmation means that we are promising to try, to strive, to commit to God, who has, in our baptism, committed to us.

The Celebration and Blessing of a Marriage

A wedding is a celebration of great joy, and the marriage service is filled with beautiful words and turns of phrase. But in the Episcopal Church, a wedding is much more than a party, a photo opportunity, or even a celebration. Marriage is "a solemn and public covenant ... in the presence of God" (422), and it is a sacramental rite, an outward and visible sign of God's inward, spiritual grace.

So what does that mean, and what does that look like in the Episcopal Church? There are a few things we can learn from this description. Civil government sees marriage as a legal contract—an agreement made between two parties. A civil marriage is really about and between the two people being married. And in the Episcopal Church, all marriages must conform to the laws of the state in regard to that contract. But Christian marriage is not merely a contract; it is also a covenant: a sacred promise that involves not only the two people being married but also God and the gathered community, a union that both echoes and reflects the union between Christ and the church.

We see this in the iconic opening words of the marriage service: "Dearly beloved: We have come together in the presence of God to witness and bless the joining together of this man and this woman in Holy Matrimony" (423). These words, repeated often in movies, books, and TV shows, say a great deal about how the church understands the sacramental rite of marriage. The service begins not by naming the two people getting married but by naming the gathered community, "dearly beloved." The opening line also reminds us that we gather "in the presence of God." The opening address continues with the role that marriage has played through the history of God's covenant with humanity, articulating that marriage exists for "mutual joy; for the help and comfort given one another in prosperity and adversity; and, when it is God's will, for the procreation of children and their nurture in the knowledge and love of the Lord" (423).

Next, the celebrant asks whether there is any reason why the couple may not be lawfully married. This is a moment to reflect on the seriousness of marriage and also a reminder that this marriage is a legal contract as well as a spiritual covenant. Then the service continues with the declaration of consent. Both parties declare their consent, and then the congregation makes their promise to uphold the couple in their marriage, underscoring that the community is not merely there to witness the service but to help the couple uphold those vows in the days and weeks and years to come.

According to the canons of the Episcopal Church, all those seeking marriage in the Episcopal Church must sign the following Declaration of Intention: "We understand the teaching of the church that God's purpose for our marriage is for our mutual joy; for the help and comfort we will give to each other in prosperity and adversity; and, when it is God's will, for the gift and heritage of children and their nurture in the knowledge and love of God. We also understand that our marriage is to be unconditional, mutual, exclusive, faithful, and lifelong; and we engage to make the utmost effort to accept these gifts and fulfill these duties, with the help of God and the support of our community."

This declaration is a beautiful summation of what the Episcopal Church believes marriage is for, and what the characteristics of a Christian marriage should be. By signing this declaration, every couple acknowledges the gift and the duty of these promises and commits to seek the help of God and the support of the community in fulfilling them.

Vows and Blessing

After the optional presentation (where a parent or loved one presents one or both members of the couple), the collect, readings, and a homily, the service continues with the vows. The couple take one another's right hand and promise "to have and to hold from this day forward, for better for worse, for richer for poorer, in sickness and in health, to love and to cherish, until we are parted by death. This is my solemn vow" (427). The couple may exchange rings or other symbols as an outward sign and reminder of their vows. The priest blesses the rings (or other symbols) before they are exchanged and then pronounces the couple husband and wife.

The service immediately moves into the prayers, either continuing with the Lord's Prayer, if there is no communion, or the prayers found on page 429. These lovely prayers are offered not only for the couple being married but also for those witnessing the vows and even the wider community.

Then the couple kneel, and the priest blesses their marriage. After the blessing, everyone stands and the priest offers the peace. The newly married couple greet each other (sometimes with a kiss), and then people throughout the congregation exchange the peace.

If the service does not include communion, the wedding party leaves the church at this time; otherwise, the service continues with Holy Eucharist. At the offertory, the newly married couple may present the offerings of bread and wine, a lovely way for them to offer thanksgiving for the blessings of this day and symbolically share their abundance with all of those gathered. The newly married couple receive communion first, after which all baptized Christians are welcome to receive.

Marriage in the Episcopal Church

Over the past decades, a conversation has been happening across the United States and throughout the Episcopal Church about the meaning and definition of marriage—particularly when it comes to same-sex couples. On June 26, 2015, the United States Supreme Court ruled that same-sex couples have the equal right to civil marriage throughout the United States. On July 1, 2015, the General Convention of the Episcopal Church passed two resolutions. One was a change to Canon 18: Of Celebration and Blessing of a Marriage, that removed all gendered language in reference to marriage, which opened the door for same-sex marriage. A second resolution authorized for trial use two liturgies for same-sex marriage. Trial use means that these liturgies can officially be used in congregations while they are being considered for future inclusion in *The Book of Common Prayer*.

General Convention passed these resolutions by an overwhelming majority, proclaiming the Episcopal Church as a welcoming and affirming place for all people, regardless of sexual orientation, and opening the sacramental rite of marriage to same-sex couples. The resolutions passed by General Convention are clear that the normative teaching of the church is that same-sex marriage is legal and covenantal. At the same time, the decision was not unanimous, and some Episcopalians do not support same-sex marriage. To accommodate the wide and deeply held views on this issue, the Episcopal Church made provisions for those who disagree with offering the rite of marriage to same-sex couples.

Currently, *The Book of Common Prayer's* liturgy still includes gendered references and refers to marriage as "between a man and a woman." For the moment, the Episcopal Church has two distinct sets of liturgies: the Celebration and Blessing of a Marriage in *The Book of Common Prayer* and the liturgies that are authorized for trial use. This is, in part, because it takes two successive General Conventions (a total of six years) to change text in *The Book of Common Prayer*. It is likely that process will begin soon, but it has not happened yet.

For the purposes of our discussion of the rite of marriage, we use the liturgy in *The Book of Common Prayer*. But it is important to note that one of the liturgies for same-sex marriage is very similar to the one in the prayer book, with pronouns and gendered references changed or removed. Any discussion in this book of Celebration and Blessing of a Marriage would apply equally to that trial option.

After a post-communion prayer, a blessing, and a dismissal, the couple, the wedding party, and the attendees leave the church, often accompanied by joyful music. The wedding service has ended, and the marriage is begun.

This is an important part of the Episcopal Church's understanding of marriage. The sacrament of marriage does not take place at a wedding, it begins at a wedding. The sacrament of marriage is enacted in the ongoing relationship—when a couple wrong one another, and then forgive; when a couple choose to take in a stranger and offer hospitality; when a couple show forth God's love by loving one another "for better for worse."

The service is just the beginning; the sacrament will be lived out in ways large and small in the coming days and months and years. It is an important beginning, because the prayers and promises should shape the reality of the relationship that is to come. It is a powerful beginning, because we believe that marriage is a sacramental rite, a rite in which the couple "receive the grace and blessing of God to help them fulfill their vows" (861). But it is only a beginning, a first step into a sacrament that lasts a lifetime.

For Reflection

✳ If you have been confirmed: How did you prepare for your confirmation? What was it like? What impact does being confirmed have on your life?

✳ Some priests require all confirmands to make an appointment with them prior to confirmation to explain why they want to be confirmed. What are some reasons a person might want to be confirmed? Why might a person not wish to be confirmed?

✳ *The Book of Common Prayer* says that the purpose of marriage is "mutual joy; for the help and comfort given one another in prosperity and adversity; and, when it is God's will, for the procreation of children and their nurture in the knowledge and love of the Lord." How is this similar to or different from what culture portrays as the purpose of marriage?

✳ The wedding ceremony is only the beginning of the sacrament of marriage, which lasts a lifetime. In a marriage between two people, what are the "outward and visible signs," and what are the "inward and spiritual graces"?

Chapter 7

Both in Mind and Body

Confession and Healing

Almighty and merciful God, in your goodness keep us, we pray, from all things that may hurt us, that we, being ready both in mind and body, may accomplish with free hearts those things which belong to your purpose; through Jesus Christ our Lord, who lives and reigns with you and the Holy Spirit, one God, now and for ever. *Amen.*

—*The Book of Common Prayer,* pp. 228-229

Throughout the gospel narratives, Jesus heals those he encounters. His healing addresses more than bodily health: Jesus forgives sin, healing the soul. Jesus heals emotional distress. Jesus heals relationships and communities, bringing people back into reconciled life with one another and with God. Jesus' life and ministry teach us that God's desire for people is health and wholeness.

Chapter nine of the Gospel of Matthew gives us an idea of what the healing of Jesus looks like. First, Jesus forgives the sins and heals the body of a paralytic. Then Jesus eats with tax collectors and sinners and describes that act of community as a kind of healing, saying that "those who are well have no need of a physician." Next Jesus heals a woman of a hemorrhage, brings a young girl back from the brink of death, and heals two blind men. Then Jesus casts out a demon, healing the mind of a man who had been possessed and thus restoring him to speech.

At the end of this chapter in Matthew, Jesus asserts that the world's need for healing is vast, and he prays that his followers will be laborers in the harvest. Later, Jesus will entrust his ministry of healing and reconciliation to his disciples. Over the centuries, the church has taken this calling very seriously. As Christians, we strive to live this ministry of healing and reconciliation by offering prayers, forgiveness, and compassion to one another. Two sacramental rites in the Episcopal Church—reconciliation of a penitent and unction of the sick—serve as outward signs of our participation in and experience of God's reconciliation and healing.

Reconciliation of a Penitent

Embedded in the rites of the church is an awareness that we will never perfectly execute our desires—that is, we want to be good and kind, but we sometimes fail. We desire to be good neighbors and compassionate people, but sometimes we miss the mark, letting jealousy, anger, or frustration govern our actions. In baptism and confirmation, we promise to persevere in resisting evil, and, whenever we fall into sin, repent and return to the Lord (304). In the marriage service, we pray for the couple that they might have "grace, when they hurt each other, to recognize and acknowledge their fault, and to seek each other's forgiveness and yours" (429).

In both instances, we promise to repent and seek forgiveness not if, but when. Even in the midst of dedicating ourselves to God, we recognize that we are going to fail in the promises that we make. And when we inevitably fail or flounder, we vow to take action, to repent and return to the Lord. The Christian life is an unfolding and ongoing practice of seeking forgiveness, from one another and from God.

Reconciliation of a Penitent is the sacramental rite whereby we seek and receive that forgiveness. People often express surprise when they learn that the Episcopal Church has a service of confession, exclaiming, "I thought that was only for Catholics!" Others resist the idea of reconciliation by saying, "We say the confession in church every Sunday, so I'm covered; I don't have to do that."

The Episcopal Church's approach to the rite of Reconciliation of a Penitent is that all can, some should, none must. In other words, no one is required to participate in the liturgy in order to receive Holy Eucharist or to be married or buried. No one *must* partake in this sacrament. We can be reconciled in many ways: by the way we offer and receive forgiveness with others and the way that we offer corporate confession of sin in our worship services. Reconciliation of a Penitent is not the only way to confess our sins and be forgiven, and as long as we are confessing and seeking forgiveness in other ways, we don't *have* to participate in the rite of reconciliation.

But to dismiss this sacrament because it isn't required diminishes its power and importance. Reconciliation of a Penitent is not a requirement that we have to check off in order to receive other sacraments or to be in right relationship with God. Instead, reconciliation is an opportunity, a chance to name before God and someone else the things for which we're sorry or ashamed or that burden our conscience. And then in return, we hear from God and from another person the truth that we are forgiven and loved and reconciled. There's a difference between "have to" and "need to/should." Perhaps the right question to ask is not, "Why should I do the rite of reconciliation?" but instead "Why *shouldn't* I do the rite of reconciliation?"

Deeper Apologies, Deeper Forgiveness

When my daughters were younger, I often found myself saying: "Apologize to your sister!" This would elicit a mumbled and less-than-heartfelt apology. "Say it like you mean it!" I would instruct, and a half-sincere "I'm sorry" would follow. I lectured and cajoled, attempting to convince my children to actually *be* sorry, rather than just *saying* sorry. But it felt like an uphill battle.

Then, one day, a friend and her children were visiting. One child hurt the other's feelings, and my friend pulled her girls aside. She sat them down face to face and said, "You need to make a real apology to your sister." And lo and behold, the instigator apologized sincerely, promising to try to act differently in the future and asking how she could make it better. I was amazed.

I immediately asked my friend to teach me how to do that. And she taught me a "five-finger formula for real apologies." Instead of simply saying sorry when a wrong occurs, you stop, look the person in the face, and say:

> I am sorry for...
>
> That was wrong because...
>
> Next time I will...
>
> What can I do to help? (or How can I make this right?)
>
> Will you forgive me?

It's simple but brilliant. Instead of just mumbling "I'm sorry," a real apology includes naming clearly what you did, reflecting on why it was wrong, promising to change the behavior in the future, trying to make amends, and actively asking for forgiveness.

We now use the five-finger formula in our family, and it really works—not just for kids but for all ages! It's a way to take responsibility for our actions and bad choices, to reflect meaningfully on why those things are wrong, to seek ways to change our actions in the future, and to actively ask for and seek out forgiveness.

Reconciliation of a Penitent is the church's version of the "five-finger formula" for apologies. Sometimes our corporate confession of sin in the liturgy, or even our own personal prayers of confession, can become rote, like the mumbled "sorry" of a child who knows she or he is supposed to apologize but doesn't really mean it. And sometimes our confessions aren't rote, but they are rushed: We don't have (or take) time to really reflect on what we have done wrong, why it was wrong, and how to amend our lives going forward. The rite of reconciliation allows us to take the time to work through our apologies with God in a thoughtful and deliberate manner.

Getting Ready for Reconciliation

In order to prepare for confession, you first need to find a confessor to offer the rite. This is normally either a priest or a bishop, because they are empowered by the church to offer absolution: that is, to declare on behalf of God that a person's sins are forgiven. But a lay person may hear confession and offer a declaration of forgiveness, provided in the rite, in lieu of absolution. Some people prefer to make their confession to a priest they don't know; in that case your priest would be glad to help you find someone to hear your confession. Other people are grateful to make confession in the context of ongoing relationship; they feel that the sacred conversation is more natural when they know and have experience with their confessor. Who you choose to hear your confession is a matter of personal preference.

There are some wonderful books that you can read to prepare further for confession. Hillary D. Raining's *Joy in Confession: Recovering Sacramental Reconciliation*, published by Forward Movement (2017) and Martin Smith's *Reconciliation: Preparing for Confession in the Episcopal Church* (1985) are both excellent resources if you would like to learn more.

Your priest may have suggestions for how you can prepare for confession. Many people find it helpful to write out their confession before the service itself. This can give you the opportunity to reflect on what you want to bring to God as well as keep you from being overwhelmed by nervousness in the moment.

A Sacred Conversation

If you have never experienced the rite of reconciliation, you might worry about what it's like. Your only experience with confession may be what you have seen in the movies: a mysterious action that involves sitting in a booth with a priest hiding behind a screen.

But in the Episcopal Church, the rite of reconciliation doesn't usually take place in a confessional booth. Although a few Episcopal churches have and use confessional booths, the normal practice is for the penitent (the person desiring the sacrament of reconciliation) and the confessor (the priest or bishop hearing confession) to sit together, either in the church building or a chapel, or even in an office. The two people might sit on either side of the altar rail, so that there is a place to kneel when appropriate, or they might even sit face to face in chairs. The point is that the rite is not simply scripted words but a sacred conversation.

The Book of Common Prayer provides two forms for reconciliation, following a similar formula, but with different wording and emphasis. Starting on page 447, both forms begin with an opening prayer followed by a prayer that includes space for the penitent to enumerate particular sins.

At the heart of both rites is the chance to name aloud the things for which you are seeking God's forgiveness. Saying these things out loud can be scary; we would rather avoid our sins than face them head on. But there is also great power in shining the light of truth into the dark places of our lives. Shame feeds on silence and secrecy. When we enumerate our sins aloud and ask specifically for forgiveness, we can set down the weight of sin and shame that we've been carrying and allow God to take away those burdens.

Next the priest offers counsel, direction, and comfort; this is also incredibly important. Talking through some of the things that we have named can bring relief, and our confessor can help us think through problems and how we might face them. This is where it is helpful to think of the rite as a sacred conversation. In the course of this conversation, the priest may offer a "psalm, prayer, or hymn to be said, or something to be done, as a sign of penitence and act of thanksgiving" (446). This is a way of acknowledging that the act of reconciliation involves more than just words; sometimes action for restoration is needed. Any action that is suggested is emphatically not punishment; it is a sign of penitence and an act of thanksgiving. These prayers or actions are the outward and visible sign of the inward work of forgiveness and reconciliation that is being done between us and God.

After we have named our sins, talked about them with our confessor, and engaged in or committed to any acts of penitence and thanksgiving, the priest offers absolution, the sure and certain assurance of God's forgiveness. The absolution from the rite of reconciliation is slightly different from the general absolution we receive in our Sunday worship. In this rite, the words of absolution are specific, focused on the particular acts or failures you have named aloud and directed to you, personally, rather than the gathered congregation. This can help us hear the assurance of forgiveness in a new and powerful way. After absolution, the rite ends with a dismissal, sending the forgiven penitent out into the world in peace.

The secrecy of reconciliation is not, hopefully, a license for abuse. The space in the rite when a priest offers "counsel, direction, and comfort" is a moment when, if a crime had been committed, the priest could encourage the penitent to report himself or herself and offer to go with the person to the authorities immediately. A priest would presumably withhold absolution until true repentance, including taking responsibility for one's actions, had been made.

The dismissal is the end of the matter. Confession has been made, God's forgiveness is offered, and the penitent can depart in peace. The content of a confession is "not normally a matter of subsequent discussion" (446). The person who hears your confession will not hold on to it. When God offers forgiveness, that forgiveness is complete, as though the slate has been wiped clean. And the "secrecy of confession is morally absolute." You don't have to worry about your confessor telling other people what you said during the reconciliation or even speaking to you about it again.

Unction

The rite of reconciliation is one of the ways that we can experience healing and wholeness of the soul, feeling fully restored to right relationship with God. But Jesus was also frequently involved in physical healing of the body. Out of this central part of Jesus' ministry arose the practices of prayer, anointing, and laying on of hands. Even in the New Testament, we hear stories of early groups of Christians engaged in these practices:

> Are any among you suffering? They should pray. Are any cheerful? They should sing songs of praise. Are any among you sick? They should call for the elders of the church and have them pray over them, anointing them with oil in the name of the Lord. The prayer of faith will save the sick, and the Lord will raise them up; and anyone who has committed sins will be forgiven. Therefore confess your sins to one another, and pray for one another, so that you may be healed. The prayer of the righteous is powerful and effective. (James 5:13-16)

Praying, anointing, and laying hands on the sick is a practice the church has engaged from the earliest times until this day. The sacramental rite in which we do this is called unction, meaning simply "to anoint." Anointing is the act of pouring or rubbing oil on a person.

Some people connect the practice of unction with extreme unction, otherwise known as "last rites." This type of prayer and anointing is done when a person is nearing death, and it is an important expression of the rite of unction. But, as is clear from the passage from James, anointing is not reserved exclusively for the deathbed; it is for any time of sickness. Thus *The Book of Common Prayer* contains two different rites that both contain elements of unction—one for all the sick and one especially for the time of death.

Ministration to the Sick

As a priest, I pray a lot; I sometimes joke that it's my job to pray. I'm always the one at family gatherings asked to offer the blessing, I lead the liturgies of the church on a regular basis, and I often have the joy of praying with and for people in all stages and circumstances of life. But my prayers are the most fervent and faithful in times of sickness: when someone I love is suffering or when I, myself, am in pain. When we find ourselves sitting in the doctor's office, getting a diagnosis, or holding the hand of a loved one in a hospital bed, our prayers take on a renewed urgency and importance. These times of sickness and struggle often draw our most desperate prayers.

We can, of course, offer prayers in our own words—our heartfelt cries to and conversations with God. But sometimes we cannot find the words to pray on our own, and we need the ancient prayers of a liturgy to give voice to our faith and fears. At other times, we desperately desire companions in our prayer—we want our priest to pray with and for us as well as the company of all the saints joining their prayers to ours. For times such as these and many more, the Episcopal Church offers unction, also known as Ministration to the Sick.

Found in *The Book of Common Prayer* on pages 453-457, Ministration to the Sick can be used both for visiting people in hospitals and homes and for regular administration at church in a formal service of healing. Anyone who wants the sacramental rite can call the church and the clergy would be glad to come, pray, anoint the person with oil, and offer communion. If you find yourself far from home, simply call a local Episcopal church; any priest would be honored to come and offer this sacramental rite.

Whether this rite takes place in a home, hospital, or church, Ministration to the Sick contains the same three parts:

ministry of the word, laying on of hands and anointing, and Holy Communion.

The ministry of the word begins with readings and prayers, grounding the experience in biblical stories of anointing and healing. After the confession and peace, the service continues with the laying on of hands and anointing. The priest lays hands upon the sick person while praying. Just as a priest touches the bread and wine during eucharist or the water at baptism, a priest touches the person receiving prayers during this sacrament. A priest may also use oil to anoint the sick person, making the sign of the cross. The oil serves as a physical sign of the spiritual grace. "As you are outwardly anointed with this holy oil, so may our heavenly Father grant you the inward anointing of the Holy Spirit" (456).

After anointing, the service may continue with Holy Communion. If the rite takes place in a home or hospital, the service of communion may be omitted. When the anointing is used at church, it is usually in the context of Holy Eucharist:

Oil for anointing is used in both the service of Holy Baptism and in Ministration to the Sick, but the oil used in the two rites is different. The anointing oil used at Holy Baptism is oil of chrismation and must be blessed by the bishop; the oil is then used at individual baptisms as a sign of connection to the wider church. The anointing oil used in Ministration to the Sick is oil of unction and can be blessed by either a priest or a bishop. Traditionally olive oil is used, sometimes mixed with certain scents or spices. The particular oil is not specified, only the prayers that are used to bless it.

Feasting together in Christ's Body and Blood is the ultimate sacrament of healing. In fact, The Book of Common Prayer notes that "when the Laying on of Hands or Anointing takes place at a public celebration of the Eucharist, it is desirable that it precede the distribution of Holy Communion and it is recommended that it take place immediately before the exchange of the Peace" (453). This sounds very particular, but there's a reason behind this instruction—it intimately links prayers of healing with forgiveness. This is a reminder that forgiveness of sins and reconciliation—the healing of the spirit and soul—are inextricably linked to physical health and healing. The service then continues with eucharist, a reminder of the healing and wholeness we experience every time we share in communion, of how we are brought into right relationship with God and with one another. By ending with communion, the service builds to a climax with Holy Eucharist being the final and most important moment.

The service of Ministration to the Sick includes the following notation: "If the sick person cannot receive either the consecrated Bread or the Wine, it is suitable to administer the Sacrament in one kind only. If a person desires ... to receive the Sacrament, but, by reason of extreme sickness or physical disability, is unable to eat and drink the Bread and Wine, the Celebrant is to assure that person that all the benefits of Communion are received, even though the Sacrament is not received with the mouth" (457). This is an important reminder, not only in times of sickness, but for anyone who is unable, for whatever reason, to eat and drink the Bread and Wine of communion.

Personal Prayers

Nestled between the formal rites for the sick and those who are dying is a small "library" of prayers for times of sickness (458-461). These pages include beautiful prayers available for all different circumstances: for an operation, for sleep, for doctors and nurses, and many others. These prayers are not limited to use in the liturgy—they are great for use in personal prayer. They are even appropriate to be saved and shared with loved ones, to be included in a mailed card, or to be left after a hospital visit.

Ministration at the Time of Death

It may seem strange to think of death as part of a healing rite, yet that is exactly what Christians believe—that death is a kind of healing. In death we are gathered to God and restored to fullness in body, mind, and spirit, in that place where there is no sorrow or sighing, but only life everlasting. So it is that *The Book of Common Prayer* includes a liturgy at the time of death as part of its healing services. The focus of these prayers is not a last-ditch effort to save a person *from* death but a way to accompany a person *through* death. Healing in these prayers is seen not as a bodily deliverance from illness but as salvation and peace.

The service begins on page 462 with a reminder that the church should be present, with prayers and ministry, when someone dies. Every priest is grateful to pray with families, no matter where or when. This is what the church is for, and you can always call and ask for a priest's presence and prayers at any time of the night or day.

This sacramental rite begins with an opening prayer, then moves to a litany that is said with responses, the Lord's Prayer, and a concluding collect and commendation. The service ends with a commendatory prayer that will be said again in the burial service. All of these prayers connect life in this world with life in the world to come, a reminder that death is not an enemy to be fought but a force that has already been vanquished by Jesus Christ, who ushers us in to eternal life.

This rite exists as a service of healing for the community as well. As family and friends pray with and for the one who is dying, they can hopefully also experience healing and receive some measure of the peace that only Christ can give.

Taken together, these sacramental rites of the church—
Reconciliation of a Penitent and Ministration to the Sick as
well as at the time of death—reflect the many circumstances
and situations that might need healing. They also remind
us that healing looks different for various people and in a
variety of circumstances.

We are healed when we are forgiven of sin and brought back
into relationship with God and one another. We are healed
when we recover from sicknesses of body, mind, and spirit.
And we are healed when, in our final days, we enter into life
everlasting with Jesus Christ. Our healing is a lifelong journey,
as we seek again and again the sacraments of reconciliation
and unction, asking God to be present and bless us, even in
the midst of sin and sickness, and ultimately to bring us to
wholeness and health.

For Reflection

✳ Confession is perhaps the least understood and practiced sacrament in the Episcopal Church. What are some of the reasons that people might be resistant to it? What are some of the benefits that a person who receives the sacrament might experience?

✳ Have you ever given or received a sincere apology that led to the repair of a relationship? What was that like? How might that same experience impact our relationship with God?

✳ *The Book of Common Prayer* and the scriptures make a connection between healing of soul and healing of the body. How might acts of confession or reconciliation heal us, as individuals and as communities?

✳ Healing doesn't always look like full, perfect restoration to bodily health. What are some of the other forms that healing can take?

✳ Our prayer book provides prayers for the time of death. How might offering these prayers benefit the dying person or gathered family members?

Chapter 8

For the Benefit of Your Holy Church

Ordination

Almighty God, the giver of all good gifts, in your divine providence you have appointed various orders in your Church: Give your grace, we humbly pray, to all who are called to any office and ministry for your people; and so fill them with the truth of your doctrine and clothe them with holiness of life, that they may faithfully serve before you, to the glory of your great Name and for the benefit of your holy Church; through Jesus Christ our Lord, who lives and reigns with you, in the unity of the Holy Spirit, one God, now and for ever. *Amen.*

— *The Book of Common Prayer*, p. 256

Who is the most important person in the church? If you attend church on a regular basis, you might think that the most important person is the priest: She does most of the talking, leading the prayers and preaching the sermon. Perhaps you think the deacon has the prime position, because when the deacon reads the gospel, we all turn and face him. Or you might think the most important person is the bishop: She wears the fanciest clothes, sits in the most elaborate chair, and has authority over the priests. Or maybe you think the most important people are the members of the church: After all they are the most numerous people by far, and they are the ones who carry out much of the church's ministry and help keep the doors open with their pledges and contributions.

In 1 Corinthians 12, Paul describes the church as a body with many members, each member having an important, integral part in the whole:

> Now there are varieties of gifts, but the same Spirit; and there are varieties of services, but the same Lord; and there are varieties of activities, but it is the same God who activates all of them in everyone. To each is given the manifestation of the Spirit for the common good ... For just as the body is one and has many members, and all the members of the body, though many, are one body, so it is with Christ. For in the one Spirit we were all baptized into one body—Jews or Greeks, slaves or free—and we were all made to drink of one Spirit. Indeed, the body does not consist of one member but of many. If the foot would say, "Because I am not a hand, I do not belong to the body," that would not make it any less a part of the body. And if the ear would say, "Because I am not an eye, I do not belong to the body," that would not make it any less a part of the body. If the whole body were an eye, where would the hearing be? If the whole body were hearing, where would the sense of smell be? But as it is, God arranged the members in the body, each one of them, as he chose. If all were a single member, where would the body be? As it is, there are many members, yet one body. The eye cannot say to the hand, "I have no need of you," nor again the head to the feet, "I have no need of you." ... Now you are the body of Christ and individually members of it. (1 Corinthians 12:4-7, 12-21, 27)

The metaphor that Paul uses here is a powerful one. When we choose to follow Jesus, we become a part of something bigger than ourselves: the Body of Christ. And as we explore Paul's metaphor of the body, we learn a few things about the church. The church has a unity; it is "one body." But it also has diversity; there are "many members." In this body, we each have a unique place and an essential role; we need each other. The church is diminished by the absence of any one member; we cannot say to one another, "I have no need of you." And a single member cannot function without the body; no one person can say "because I am not a hand, I do not belong to the body." There is no single, most important member of the Body of Christ; we are all necessary. Each person has unique gifts, skills, and talents that God has given us, and these gifts are to be used "for the common good." In order for the Body of Christ—the church—to work properly, each person must find his or her role in the body, an important part of the larger whole.

From the very beginning, followers of Jesus tried to find their place in the community. Jesus' disciples argued about who would be the greatest and who would sit at Jesus' right hand (Mark 10:35-45). Jesus told them then what Paul would say later: It is not about being the greatest or most powerful but about serving one another and working together for the common good.

After the death and resurrection of Jesus, the church began to form, and it became evident that some system of organization was needed.

> Now during those days, when the disciples were increasing in number, the Hellenists complained against the Hebrews because their widows were being neglected in the daily distribution of food. And the twelve called together the whole community of the disciples and said, "It is not right that we should neglect the word of God in order to wait on

tables. Therefore, friends, select from among yourselves seven men of good standing, full of the Spirit and of wisdom, whom we may appoint to this task, while we, for our part, will devote ourselves to prayer and to serving the word." What they said pleased the whole community, and they chose Stephen, a man full of faith and the Holy Spirit, together with Philip, Prochorus, Nicanor, Timon, Parmenas, and Nicolaus, a proselyte of Antioch. They had these men stand before the apostles, who prayed and laid their hands on them. (Acts 6:1-6)

The apostles laid hands on certain people and prayed for them, in order to set them aside for a particular ministry. This was not about a hierarchy of importance or holiness but about a differentiation of responsibility. Early gatherings of Christians sought out people with the gifts and skills to serve in certain positions—so that all the different aspects of ministry would receive the attention and care they needed.

The idea of ordination—praying for and laying hands on certain people to set them aside for ministry as deacons, priests, and bishops—comes from these early roots. Ordination is not about instilling a hierarchy or limiting the power of ministry to certain people. As the Catechism tells us quite clearly: "Q. Who are the ministers of the Church? A. The ministers of the Church are lay persons, bishops, priests, and deacons" (855). All Christians—lay people, bishops, priests, and deacons—are ministers of the church. Notice how the clergy—bishops, priests, and deacons—are listed in a particular rank, from highest to lowest. And note the position of lay people: first. This is because our church teaching places lay people as the most important ministers in the church. Ordination, then, is about putting everyone in an ordered life. Part of that ordering is giving different roles and responsibilities and, yes, authority, to different members of the body, so that hands can be hands and feet can be feet and eyes can be eyes, and the entire body is enriched.

Orders of the Church

From the time of the New Testament, there have been specific, different ministries within the church; scripture passages such as Acts 15:2-23, 1 Timothy 3:8-13 and 5:17-22, and Titus 1:5-9 give an early sense of what these ministries looked like. By the second or third century, these various descriptions had developed into three distinct orders (or types) of ordained ministry in the church: bishops, priests (or presbyters), and deacons.

- **Bishops:** The English word for bishop comes from the Greek *episcopos*, which literally means overseer. Thus the bishop's ministry is one of oversight: leading, supervising, and uniting the church. Bishops in the Episcopal Church are part of the historic episcopate, which means that they can trace their ordinations, through apostolic succession, back to the earliest apostles.

- **Priests (Presbyters):** In the New Testament, presbyter comes from the Greek word *presbyteros*, meaning elder, and indicates a leader of the church. In its earliest usage, presbyter was sometimes used interchangeably with the word for bishop, but as the church began to grow and spread, bishops and presbyters evolved into distinct roles. By the third century, bishops were those with overarching authority, while presbyters were responsible for the teaching and preaching, administration, and sacramental ministry in a particular congregation or area, under the oversight of the bishop. The English word priest is derived from the word for presbyter, and the two terms can be used interchangeably.

- **Deacons:** Deacon comes from the Greek word *diakonos*, meaning servant, and the ministry of deacon is clearly described in the New Testament. Acts 6:1-7 details the selection of the first deacons, and 1 Timothy 3:8-13 describes the qualifications and traits of deacons. These passages, taken together with the tradition of the early church, have shaped our understanding of deacons as people who are especially set aside for a ministry of service, both in their role in the liturgy and in their work on behalf of the poor and oppressed.

Orders of Ministry

The Episcopal Church recognizes three distinct orders of ordained ministry within the church: bishops, priests, and deacons. Each order of ministry has a unique role in the church. Bishops are tasked with the responsibility to "guard the faith, unity, and discipline of the Church" (517). They also "carry on the apostolic work of leading, supervising, and uniting the Church" (510). The bishops' roles as leaders and guardians are held in tension: They are called to guard the historic faith and are sometimes cautious with respect to change and innovation, especially when the change at hand might be divisive. Yet as leaders, bishops also are called to boldly proclaim the gospel, challenging and stirring up the conscience of their people. As guardians and leaders, bishops are also called to live as servants, following the example of Jesus who came, not to be served, but to serve.

Priests are called "to proclaim by word and deed the Gospel of Jesus Christ ... to love and serve the people among whom [they] work, caring alike for young and old, strong and weak, rich and poor ... to preach, to declare God's forgiveness to penitent sinners, to pronounce God's blessing, to share in the administration of Holy Baptism and in the celebration of the mysteries of Christ's Body and Blood, and to perform the other ministrations entrusted to [them]" (531). These roles are clearly sacramental, rooted in the experience of worship, though certainly not limited to the realm of liturgy. The role of the priest is rooted in community; priests work *among* the people of a particular church. Yet the role of priests is not passive; they are entrusted with the call and the power to proclaim the gospel, preach, declare forgiveness, pronounce blessing, and perform other expressions of ministry.

Both bishops and priests are called to be servants, as the ordination services tell us again and again. Yet deacons are called to a special ministry of servanthood within the church: "interpret[ing] to the Church the needs, concerns, and hopes of the world ... At all times, [their] life and teaching are to show Christ's people that in serving the helpless they are serving Christ himself" (543). The focus of deacons is ministering to the needs of those who are most often forgotten—by the world and by the church—and relentlessly reminding all Christians of their baptismal vow to seek and serve Christ in all persons.

The church laws, known as the canons, include specific instructions about how people are chosen, trained, and equipped to serve as bishops, priests, and deacons. The process for seeking ordination is clearly laid out in these guidelines, but our prayers for ordination reveal most clearly what we hope bishops, priests, and deacons will do, and who we hope they will be in the context of our common life. The last of the sacramental rites in *The Book of Common Prayer*, ordination is "the rite in which God gives authority and the grace of the Holy Spirit to those being made bishops, priests, and deacons, through prayer and the laying on of hands by bishops" (860-861).

Ordination Rites

All three services of ordination follow a similar structure, though each contains unique prayers and features suited to their particular ministry (the services begin on page 509 in *The Book of Common Prayer*). After beginning with the opening acclamation and collect for purity, each ordination service includes:

❖ **The presentation:** This is when members of the church, including both priests and lay people, present the ordinand (the person being ordained) to the bishop and certify that she has fulfilled the requirements of the canons in order to be ordained. The ordinand is then required to sign the following declaration: "I solemnly declare that I do believe the Holy Scriptures of the Old and New Testaments to be the Word of God, and to contain all things necessary to salvation; and I do solemnly engage to conform to the doctrine, discipline, and worship of The Episcopal Church."

❖ **The litany for ordinations:** Prayer for one another is one of the most important things we do as Christians. The litany for ordinations, which may be said or sung, includes a few prayers for the ordinand but is largely focused on praying for the whole church and for the world (548-551).

❖ **The liturgy of the word:** Each service includes suggestions for appropriate readings of scripture, which are followed by the sermon and the Nicene Creed.

❖ **The examination:** The bishop begins the examination with an address that articulates the unique character of each order of ministry. Then the ordinand is asked a series of questions that echo the baptismal promises but also are specific to how those promises are lived out in ordained ministry.

❖ **The consecration:** The ordinand kneels before the bishop while those gathered sing a hymn invoking the Holy Spirit. The bishop says a prayer of consecration, then lays hands upon the head of the ordinand. After a final prayer and the people's loud "Amen," the ordinand is vested according to his order—that is, bishops receive the accoutrements of the office, such as a bishop's hat, called a mitre, and a pastoral staff, called a crozier, which reminds the bishop that she or he is a shepherd to a spiritual flock.

Priests and deacons receive stoles. Deacons traditionally wear the stole diagonally across their bodies, while priests wear the stole around their neck with the sides hanging in front. The newly ordained receive a Bible as well.

❖ **The peace and celebration of Holy Eucharist:** The service continues with the eucharist. The newly ordained person(s) takes part in the liturgy as befits the order (administering the bread or wine, saying the blessing, dismissing the people).

The beautiful prayers of the ordination services have a lot to teach us and articulate a vision for the church and those ordained to serve it. As we read through the services and reflect on the prayers and promises, we find:

❖ Each ordination service articulates a distinct view of ministry, but they are also all interdependent. Deacons are reminded that they assist bishops and priests, priests are instructed to "labor together" with the laity and fellow ministers, and bishops are called to "encourage and support all baptized people in their gifts and ministries." The ordination services remind us that all of us together are the Body of Christ and that we rely on one another to faithfully live out Christ's call in the world.

❖ One of the most frequently repeated words in the services of ordination is "servant." The Episcopal Church is clear that those who are ordained—as bishops, priests, or deacons—are set apart in order to serve the church, not rule over it. They are called to be leaders, but not lords. This is a delicate, and often difficult, balance.

❖ In ordination, we endow our leaders—bishops, priests, and deacons—with authority. That authority is not to be taken lightly, as it is a sacred trust and responsibility.

In turn, those being ordained take vows of loyalty and obedience (things we don't much like to talk about in today's world) and make specific promises about how they will live their lives and exercise their ministry. There is mutual obligation here: Ordinands commit themselves to the community, and the community places itself under the authority of those being ordained.

❖ The entire Body of Christ has an integral role in the ordination services. Those who are being ordained are selected and presented for ordination by representatives of the community. In an echo of the baptism and marriage services, all of those present at the ordination service commit to uphold the person being ordained in her ministry. And at the end of the Prayer of Consecration, the prayer book directs "The People in a loud voice respond **Amen.**" This is the only place in *The Book of Common Prayer* where it describes the volume we should use in making a response, an indication that the role of the community is particularly important here. In ordination, we, the church, ask God to empower the person being ordained with authority. We commit to uphold these persons in their ministry. And we consent, with our loud Amen, to the descent of the Holy Spirit upon the ordinand.

Despite some of the differences in the ordination service for bishop, priest, and deacon, the rite points us to the foundation of the Episcopal Church, the idea that life and liturgy are intimately linked. In ordination, we call bishops, priests, and deacons not only to functions with the church's services but also to a way of life that reflects who they are ordained to be. This is true, in fact, of all of our liturgy and life: as it is in our worship, so it is in the world. The roles that each order of ministry plays in our worship reflects their roles in the world.

In the liturgy, deacons serve at the table of eucharist, guide the people in prayer, and dismiss the people into the world, because deacons are servants who pray and send people out to seek and serve Christ. In the liturgy, priests celebrate the sacraments, pronounce blessing, and declare forgiveness, because priests are sacramental people who communicate God's blessing and forgiveness in the world. In the liturgy, bishops ordain, confirm, and lead when they are present because bishops are people of leadership and unity, drawing distinct congregations together into the greater body of the Episcopal Church. And in the liturgy, lay people read the lessons, administer the chalice, and carry the cross and torches because laity are called to communicate Jesus Christ, in word and deed, in ways big and small, in their daily lives in the world.

Our ordination liturgies proclaim what Paul tells us in Corinthians and what Acts tells us about the beginning of the church: We are one body, with many members. Each member of the church has an important, integral role to play. And we can and must allow all people—laity, bishops, priests, and deacons—to exercise their particular gifts in the service of both the church and the world.

For Reflection

✳ According to the prayer book, "The ministers of the Church are lay persons, bishops, priests, and deacons." What are the roles and responsibilities of each, in the church and in the world?

✳ How do you see each order of ministry exercised in liturgy?

✳ Look at the vows for the ordination of a priest on pages 531-532 of *The Book of Common Prayer*. What do you notice about the scope of these vows? Are any of the vows surprising?

✳ Think about the last bishop's visitation at your church. What are some of the ways that you could see the bishop's ministry exercised, in liturgy or otherwise?

Marking Time

Chapter 9

Accept the Prayers of Your People

The Daily Office and Daily Prayer

> Almighty and eternal God, ruler of all things in heaven and earth: Mercifully accept the prayers of your people, and strengthen us to do your will; through Jesus Christ our Lord. *Amen.*
>
> —*The Book of Common Prayer*, p. 394

Prayer was a fundamentally important part of Jesus' life and ministry. Jesus began his earthly ministry by heading into the desert to fast and pray (Luke 4:1-13), he spent his last night on earth praying in the garden of Gethsemane (Mark 14:32), and throughout his ministry, Jesus would take time to go off "by himself to pray" (Matthew 14:23).

And prayer wasn't just something that Jesus did himself; he also encouraged his followers to pray. Jesus tells his listeners stories about "their need to pray always" (Luke 18:1), and he even spends time teaching his followers how to pray (Matthew 6:5-15).

Following the example and words of Jesus, Paul instructs Christians to "pray without ceasing." The early Christians took these words to heart, continuing the Jewish practice of regular prayer at certain hours of the day and night. From this practice of regular prayer arose the tradition of the Divine Office, or Liturgy of the Hours, a set of seven liturgies spaced through the day so that prayers were offered throughout the day and night. By the fifth century, communities of monks and nuns set themselves aside so that they could dedicate their lives to praying the Divine Office. This tradition of prayer continues today, with religious communities offering nearly constant prayer.

At every moment of every day, people of faith are praying with and for you and me. Thanks be to God for these monks and nuns around the world committed to a life of prayer. For some, the continual prayer that Paul describes is a reality through the centuries and an incredible example of lived faithfulness.

But what about the rest of us? Not all of us are called to a life set apart exclusively for prayer (though if you think you might be, please pick up the phone and call your nearest monastery, because you are a gift and sign to the world!). But is continual (or even daily) prayer the exclusive purview of the "professionally religious"?

Thomas Cranmer, the author of the first *Book of Common Prayer*, didn't think so. He believed that daily prayer should be available to all people, not just priests or those who lived in monasteries. In fact, that's why *The Book of Common Prayer* is called "common," not because it is ordinary, but because it is a way of prayer available to all people—it is prayer held in common. Cranmer wanted to make daily prayer accessible to everyone, so he simplified the monks' prayer cycle into two Daily Offices, morning prayer and evening prayer. In our prayer book, we have more recently added Noonday Prayer and Compline. Instead of the full Divine Office—prayers every three hours throughout the day—the prayer book's Daily Office offers a simplified version of four services of prayer: Morning Prayer, Noonday Prayer, Evening Prayer, and Compline.

In simplifying the hours of prayer, Cranmer did something radical. He tried to take "continual prayer" and make it something that wasn't just for religious "professionals" but for everyone. One of the great gifts of *The Book of Common Prayer* is that it offers patterns of prayer that anyone, priest or lay person, monk or mechanic, nun or nurse, can use. If you adopt the habit of praying throughout the day, you will discover the great gift of this rhythm. At times, when we wander or stray from God, the next prayer time affords an opportunity to draw near again to God, to get back on the right path.

This idea is so central to the Anglican and Episcopal ethos that all of our successive *Books of Common Prayer* have included the Daily Offices. These liturgies are intended for private and public prayer: People can gather for the Daily Office in churches or in homes, families can pray them together, or individuals might read the offices on their own as part of their personal prayer discipline.

The word office comes from the Latin *officium*, meaning literally service or duty. In modern usage, an office is simply another word for a scripted set of prayers and can be used interchangeably with words like service, liturgy, or rite. All of these words are different ways of talking about the various sets of prayers contained in *The Book of Common Prayer*. In the Anglican tradition, we call these rites the Daily Office because these are the offices that we are meant to do on a daily basis, which sets them apart from rites like Holy Baptism and Holy Eucharist, offices that we use weekly or occasionally.

When you open your prayer book to the Daily Office (pages 35-146), it can seem confusing. There are two rites, Rite I and Rite II. There are a bunch of different services: Morning Prayer, Evening Prayer, Noonday Prayer, An Order of Worship for Evening, and Compline. And within each service, there are lots of different options. It can be overwhelming. But once you take a moment to look at the different pieces, you begin to see a structure and an order, a rhythm that is the same throughout. So let's walk through the different options.

The first choice you have, when you look at the Daily Office, is whether you want to pray Rite I (pages 36-73) or Rite II (pages 74-146). With only a few small differences, the Rite I and Rite II versions of Morning and Evening Prayer are the same services, just in different language. Rite I is the more traditional and formal language of "thee" and "thy." The prayers use words like "vouchsafe" and "inestimable." The

To get a sense of the difference between Rite I and Rite II, compare the two versions of A Prayer of St. Chrysostom:

Rite I: Almighty God, who hast given us grace at this time with one accord to make our common supplication unto thee, and hast promised through thy well-beloved Son that when two or three are gathered together in his Name thou wilt be in the midst of them: Fulfill now, O Lord, the desires and petitions of thy servants as may be best for us; granting us in this world knowledge of thy truth, and in the world to come life everlasting. *Amen.* (59)

Rite II: Almighty God, you have given us grace at this time with one accord to make our common supplication to you; and you have promised through your well-beloved Son that when two or three are gathered together in his Name you will be in the midst of them: Fulfill now, O Lord, our desires and petitions as may be best for us; granting us in this world knowledge of your truth, and in the age to come life everlasting. *Amen.* (102)

Rite I liturgy reads more like Shakespeare than a *New York Times* bestseller. Rite II translates some of the language into words that are more contemporary and easier to understand. Rite II retains much of the imagery and poetry of the older language but sounds more like the way that you might speak in regular conversation.

The choice of whether to use Rite I or Rite II is a personal one. Some people find the language of Rite I difficult to understand, awkward, and off-putting. They find Rite I hard to pray, and they connect to God more easily through Rite II language. Other people find that the poetic beauty of this language, different from everyday speech, connects them more deeply with the mystery of God. Rite I feels like prayer to them. When you are just starting out with the Daily Office, you should use whichever form feels right to you. Read through a few of the prayers or responses in each form, and then choose the one that best helps you to connect with God in prayer. Then, after you've been praying that way for a while, consider changing it up. You might be surprised by what you hear in a new way when you use a different rite! You will probably always have a favorite, but learning to experience and appreciate new ways of prayer is an important part of the spiritual life.

For this book, we look more in depth at Rite II, the common usage for the Daily Office in most Episcopal churches today. These offices are spaced throughout the day so that, if you pray all of them, you would be praying throughout the day. But even if you don't pray all of them, the different offices provide an opportunity to find a practice that works in your context; the prayers are suited to whatever time of day you are able to make the space for daily prayer.

All of the offices (Morning Prayer, Noonday Prayer, Evening Prayer, and Compline) follow a similar structure, though each has unique prayers and features suited to its time of day. Every office includes:

1. **Opening sentences:** These might include a seasonal sentence of scripture, an opening versicle (short sentence said or sung) and response between the leader and the congregation, or both. The opening sentences help set the tone of worship, focusing our attention on God and reminding us of key themes in the seasons of the church year.

2. **Psalms:** Psalms, the prayer book of the Bible, is the heart of the offices. If you pray the offices daily, using the appointed psalms, you will go through the entire psalter (the book of Psalms) in a month. (People may also choose a cycle of reading the psalms that lasts seven weeks and skips some psalms). Some of the offices have introductory sentences or an invitatory (invitational) psalm that is said or sung before the psalms appointed for the day. In saying the psalms, we engage in a tradition of prayer that stretches back to the beginnings of the Bible, and our voices join with the faithful through the centuries. The psalms give expression to the full range of human emotion— joy and sadness, fear and celebration, love and loss— and put all of those emotions in the context of God's action in the world and in our lives.

3. **Readings:** All of the offices have readings from the Bible. Each day has a schedule of psalms, an Old Testament reading, an epistle reading, and a gospel reading.

4. **Canticles:** All of the offices have canticles that are to be sung or said after each reading. Canticles are hymns, poems, or songs of praise taken directly from the Bible. In saying or singing the canticles, we enter into the biblical story, joining our voices and prayers

with Miriam and Moses as they cross the Red Sea, with Isaiah as he proclaims the prophecies of God's comfort and salvation, and with Mary as she receives the good news of Jesus' birth from Gabriel. In praying the canticles, we hear echoes between the events of the Bible and events in our own time and learn of God's constant presence in both.

5. **Prayers:** All of the offices include the Lord's Prayer and a series of additional prayers. There are suffrages (verse-and-response prayers), collects (thematic prayers) specific to the time of day or appointed for certain days, and closing prayers. There are also times for people to offer their own prayers of intercession

The way that the church determines which scripture passages are read is guided by lectionaries (schedules of readings). Having a set schedule of readings harkens back to the early church, and while different communions may follow different lectionaries, many traditions have a set of appointed readings for weekdays and Sundays.

The Book of Common Prayer has two different lectionaries. One is the lectionary for Sundays, found on pages 888-931. Called the Revised Common Lectionary, these readings are arranged in a three-year cycle, so that we hear the same portions of the Bible once every three years. But there is also a Daily Office lectionary, so that we can hear different lessons in our daily prayers and go deeper in our study of the Bible. The lectionary (or schedule of readings) for the Daily Office is found on pages 934-1001 of *The Book of Common Prayer.* The Daily Office lectionary is a two-year cycle; if you read the lessons every day, then you will read most (though not all) of the Bible over the course of two years. The appointed lessons are designed to be divided up among the day, so that you have readings for every office. For example, if you say Morning Prayer and Evening Prayer daily, you might read the Old Testament and epistle readings during Morning Prayer and save the gospel lesson to read during Evening Prayer.

and thanksgiving. The inclusion of both traditional suffrages and collects alongside times for unscripted prayer allows us to join our own thoughts and conversations with God with the prayers that have been prayed by faithful Christians through the ages. This time of prayer is an opportunity to talk with God and listen to God in holy conversation.

6. **Concluding versicle and response**: The offices close with a dismissal, and there is often a concluding sentence of scripture. The dismissal reminds us that we are grounded in prayer and then sent out into the world to both worship and serve God in all that we say and do.

You may have heard of a service in the Episcopal Church called Evensong but if you look in *The Book of Common Prayer*, you won't find that service named anywhere. That's because Evensong is Evening Prayer but with all or most of the prayers sung, either by the choir or by the congregation. Singing Evening Prayer in this way is a longstanding Anglican tradition, and many churches use the form of Evening Prayer from the 1662 prayer book (*The Book of Common Prayer* still in use in the Church of England). While the content is similar to our current prayer book, the language is more formal and traditional.

Morning and Evening Prayer are the two main pillars of the office: They are the longest services and the ones most widely used by individuals and communities. In addition to the core pieces described above, Morning and Evening Prayer include the Apostles' Creed and an option for the Confession of Sin.

As you see in this section of *The Book of Common Prayer*, there are numerous options within the prayer services. You can select the opening sentences from a variety of options for each season; you can choose which canticles to say in response to each reading, select the collects you'd like from an array of choices, and choose whether to include or omit the optional parts. The different options can be overwhelming at first. But praying the Daily Office is like any new skill—it takes time to learn, yet eventually, it becomes second nature. The key to the Daily Office, like any discipline, is practice. The more you pray it, the more you learn the rhythm offered by these prayers, appreciating the variety while finding comfort in the things you pray again and again.

If you want to pray the Daily Office, start by familiarizing yourself with the service. Sit down and take time to read about the Daily Office in *The Book of Common Prayer*. Read the words in italics (called the rubrics): They give instructions, from which parts are optional to what actions to take at various points in the liturgy. To pray the Daily Office, all you need is *The Book of Common Prayer* and a Bible, but you may want to use bookmarks or ribbons to mark the readings, psalms, and canticles for each day to make the process easier.

The Daily Office is a wonderfully Anglican way to pray: It is an important part of our heritage and a way

If you find the options in the prayer book a little confusing, and you'd like an easier way to try the Daily Office, a number of resources present the offices in easy and accessible ways. If you'd like to pray the Daily Office any time, anywhere, Forward Movement's website (prayer.forwardmovement. org) or the *Forward Day by Day* app both include the Daily Office, with the prayers automatically filled in for the day and time you are praying. Or, for those who like physical books, the *Daily Office Book: Two Volume Set* by Church Publishing includes the liturgies of the Daily Office and the full readings for each day in a portable set. Phyllis Tickle's *The Divine Hours* has a version of daily prayer for each season of the church year, simplified and easy to pray.

that we connect through time and space to other believers who have prayed and are praying in these same forms. But the Daily Office is not the only way to pray using *The Book of Common Prayer*. The prayer book offers hundreds of wonderful resources for prayer. They include:

❖ **Daily Devotions for Individuals and Families:** Found on pages 136-140 in *The Book of Common Prayer*, these devotions follow the basic structure of the Daily Office but in a much shortened form. Praying these simple devotions only takes a few minutes each day and can be a way for families or individuals to root themselves in the tradition of prayer.

❖ **Grace at meals:** Saying a prayer before eating is one of the easiest ways to begin a prayer practice. If you do it every time, all of the sudden you are praying three times a day! Simply begin by making a commitment to pray at every meal, every time—whether you are eating at home or in a restaurant, whether your meal is a long sit-down dinner or a quick muffin as you race out the door. *The Book of Common Prayer* includes options for graces on page 835, or you can use a family grace or other prayer of thanks.

❖ **Prayers for the sick:** We often find ourselves in need of prayer when someone we love is sick. In those circumstances, it can be hard to know what to say—or what to pray. On pages 458-461, *The Book of Common Prayer* has a variety of options for different circumstances: prayers for before an operation, for a sick child, for sleep, and many more.

❖ **Prayers and Thanksgivings:** The back of *The Book of Common Prayer*, from pages 809-841, offers a section of prayers and thanksgivings. These pages are a compendium of prayers for all different situations and circumstances. They include prayers for a birthday, for an election, for the poor and neglected, for rain, and dozens of other times and seasons.

❖ **The Collects for the Church Year:** The collects are the prayers that are appointed for each Sunday of the church year; they usually connect to the readings for the day or for the theme of the church season. Many of the collects are good not only for the Sunday that they are written for but also for other times and circumstances as well. You can find the collects in traditional, Rite I language on pages 159-210, and in contemporary, Rite II language on pages 211-261.

Other Ways to Pray

The Book of Common Prayer contains many beautiful prayers and collects that are found within the liturgies of the church. There are so many riches in this prayer book that even those who have been priests for decades can find new and beautiful ways to pray.

But, of course, the forms and prayers from *The Book of Common Prayer* are by no means the only ways to pray! Prayers can come from many sources: You can use scripted prayers from other books or traditions, prayers you've written on your own, or ones you think of in the moment (this is often called "extemporaneous prayer").

In fact, the Catechism in *The Book of Common Prayer* says that "prayer is responding to God, by thought and by deeds, with or without words" (856). That definition covers a lot of ground! You can pray using a set form like the Daily Office or a collect, or you can pray by simply talking to God in an informal way. You can pray with words or without words. You can pray by thought or by deeds. There is no correct or certain posture for prayer. You can pray standing, kneeling, or bowing. You can pray with your eyes opened or closed; you can pray in the silence of your heart or aloud with words. You can pray in a church or you can pray in your bed before you begin the day.

Just about any action, taken with intention, directed toward God, can be a kind of prayer. You can pray by walking or by painting or by singing. Driving your car? Turn off the radio and pray for each person you see (even the ones who cut you off) as well as those on your prayer list. Doing the dishes? Thank God for all the blessings that make that possible (the food you ate, the hands that grew and prepared it, the warm water, etc.) Wash the dishes as though you are washing Jesus' feet.

The important thing is not how you pray but that you pray and strive to make prayer a part of your daily life. God receives the same amount of joy from any and all prayers, whether they are offered by a monk who prays for hours on end or by a desperate person who wakes up in the morning and just says "help."

Prayer is not a once-a-week action, something we do only when we gather in church on Sundays. Prayer is meant to be a daily discipline, something we do frequently and regularly. It is also something that gets easier, more instinctive and more ingrained, the more often that you practice. Whether you use the Daily Office, Daily Devotions, extemporaneous prayer time, prayer walks, or any other kind of prayer, the form that your prayers take is less important than the frequency. God wants to be engaged with us on a regular, daily basis. A key way to deepening our relationship with God is by committing to some form of daily prayer. And there's no time like the present—give it a try!

For Reflection

❋ Have you ever been to a public service of Morning Prayer, Evening Prayer, or Evensong? What was that experience like? How did that compare to the experience of Holy Eucharist?

❋ In praying the Daily Office, we participate in an ancient tradition and join with Christians all around the world who are praying the same form. How might this expand our horizons of prayer beyond ourselves and deepen our relationships with God and one another?

❋ Read A Prayer of St. Chrysostom on page 114 of *Walk in Love* or compare the versions on pages 59 and 102 of *The Book of Common Prayer*. What does this prayer say to you? Which version of the prayer (Rite I or Rite II) do you prefer and why?

❋ Think about your own habit of daily prayer. Are there ways to improve or expand this practice?

Chapter 10

All Times Are Your Seasons

The Church Calendar and the Liturgical Year

Almighty God, all times are your seasons, and all occasions invite your tender mercies: Accept our prayers and intercessions offered in this place today and in the days to come; through Jesus Christ, our Mediator and Advocate. *Amen.*

— *The Book of Common Prayer*, p. 572

525,600 minutes—how do you measure, measure a year? In daylights, in sunsets, in midnights, in cups of coffee. In inches, in miles, in laughter, in strife … How do you measure a year in the life?

The question posed by the hit Broadway musical *Rent* is a good one: How do you measure a year? In childhood, most of us measure our time by holidays. Every day is a countdown, to our birthdays or Christmas or summer vacation.

My children love Halloween. It's not actually the candy (although they enjoy that also!); it's the costumes. From the moment they wake up on November 1, they start talking about what they're going to be next year. The pumpkins are still on the front step, most of the candy is still waiting to be consumed, and this year's Halloween costume still has plenty of wear. But they are so excited that they can't wait for it to happen all over again. For the entire year, they imagine and plan and scheme. They change their minds about what they are going to wear approximately 500 times, but not a week goes by that they aren't dreaming of next year's Halloween.

As we get older, the way we measure time usually shifts (although I know some adults who still count down to their birthdays or favorite holidays). Many of us measure our time by the simple secular standard of New Year's Day, the day when our calendar flips from one year to the next, the day when we change the date on our checks. Those in agriculture may also measure time by growing seasons, rainfall, and sun. A tax accountant orients the year around April 15. And a teacher uses the beginning of the school year as a starting point and the first day of summer vacation as the countdown clock.

How we measure time says something fundamental about how we think, what we value, and what we work toward and long for. The way that we measure our time says something about what really matters to us.

The Calendar of the Church Year

The Calendar of the Church Year appears near the beginning of *The Book of Common Prayer* (15-33). Before we learn about how to become a Christian through Holy Baptism or how to worship in our weekly celebrations of Holy Eucharist or how to pray on a daily basis, we are told about how Christians measure time.

In the Christian life, we measure our time not by things we achieve or things we need to do. We measure our time by what God has already done for us in the birth and resurrection of Christ Jesus. Our church year is oriented around two special days: Easter, the Sunday of the Resurrection; and Christmas, the Feast of Our Lord's Nativity.

Now, that probably makes sense. Most people know the two big holy days of Christianity are Christmas and Easter, right? But what you may not know is that we orient *all* of our time in relation to them.

Our new year doesn't begin on January 1. Rather, the church's new year begins on the First Sunday of Advent, which is always four Sundays before Christmas Day. This start of the Christian year calls us to orient our days and our years around the birth of Jesus. As Christians, our year begins as we wait with expectation and excitement for the birth of Jesus.

The other critical date of the Christian year is Easter, the day we celebrate the resurrection of Christ. Unlike Christmas, which always falls on December 25, Easter doesn't have a set date. It is determined in an ancient fashion based on when the first full moon occurs after the spring equinox on March 21. Thus the actual date of Easter changes from year to year, ranging anywhere from March 22 to April 25. (The prayer book actually includes a table on pages 882-883 that lists the date of Easter for every year between 1900-2089).

From Easter Day, the Feast of the Resurrection, all the rest of our time is measured and counted. Ash Wednesday, the beginning of Lent, is always 46 days before Easter Day. The Day of Pentecost, which marks the end of Easter season, is always 50 days after Easter Day. And "the sequence of all the Sundays of the Church Year depends upon the date of Easter Day" (15).

Everything about our time as Christians hinges on the resurrection of Jesus, and together with Christmas, these two primary dates are the linchpins of a rich cycle of feasts and holy days that flesh out our church year.

Seasons

Celebrating Christmas and Easter is only the beginning. Although these are the two primary days in the Christian year, they are by no means the only important days. The fullness of the Christian faith is felt when we live into all the cycles and seasons of the church's calendar and discover the riches they hold. The church has seasons of the year, and just like our secular seasons of winter, spring, summer, and fall, each church season is distinct. As Ecclesiastes (and the musical group the Byrds) remind us, there is a "time for every season," and each year we return to these seasons, as they offer comfort in familiarity and opportunity for deeper and richer spiritual growth.

The church has seven seasons: Advent, Christmas, Epiphany, Lent, Holy Week, Easter, and the Season After Pentecost (which is sometimes called Ordinary Time). While oriented around the compass points of Christmas and Easter, each season has a different emphasis that helps focus our spiritual life. There are times for waiting and times for celebrating, times of darkness and times of light, times of pain and times of deep joy. Being a Christian is not about being happy all of the time, and it is not always easy. The changing seasons of

There are a variety of ways that we can observe the different seasons in our church year through our worship. Often, *The Book of Common Prayer* offers specific suggestions of prayers that are particularly suited to a certain season. Sometimes certain words or phrases help set a season apart. For instance, during the penitential season of Lent leading up to Easter, we fast from the word "alleluia" in our worship —a reminder that the joy of Easter is yet to come. In addition, churches often use certain liturgical colors to decorate the sanctuary for particular seasons. These colors are not specified in *The Book of Common Prayer* but instead come through tradition (some ancient, some more recent). For this reason, different churches may choose to use different colors. **Purple** is used to designate both penance and preparation; it is often used during Lent and Advent, times of repentance and preparation. Some communities use **blue** for Advent, in order to differentiate from the season of Lent and mark Advent as a time of both preparation and hope. Other communities use **Lenten array**, a kind of simple burlap with deep red and black accents, to set Lent apart as a time of simplicity. **Red** is associated with sacrifice and the Holy Spirit and typically used for Palm Sunday, Pentecost, the feasts of apostles and martyrs, and ordinations. **White** and **gold** are used to indicate great joy and celebration. They are used for Easter, Christmas, baptisms, funerals, and the feasts of saints who were not martyrs. **Green** is associated with our growth in faith and is used during the Season after Pentecost, the longest part of the church year, and for any other time in which another color is not appointed.

the church year remind us that there is room for all of our experiences in the Christian journey.

Advent, the beginning of the new year of the church, is a time of waiting, preparation, and expectation. Like the winter season, it is a time of deepening darkness, when we contemplate shadows and silence even as we wait for the dawning of the light from on high, Jesus. Many churches use an Advent wreath as a visible symbol of this idea, lighting an additional candle each week of Advent, culminating in the Christ candle on Christmas Day. The Old Testament readings of Advent are from the prophet Isaiah, who prophesies about the coming of the Messiah, and the gospel readings are typically those from the story of John the Baptist, the cousin and forerunner of Jesus who tells us to prepare the way for Christ's coming into the world.

The **Christmas** Season begins with the Feast of the Nativity of our Lord (Christmas Day), but Christmas is not simply one day. The season of Christmas is twelve days (remember the famous song!) and concludes on January 5. Christmas is a time to worship at the manger throne, to celebrate the newborn Jesus, and to give thanks for the Word made flesh.

The Feast of the Epiphany (January 6) is the day when we remember the arrival of the magi or wise men who followed a star to worship Jesus. It begins the Season of **Epiphany**, which lasts until Ash Wednesday. Epiphany is the season when we remember the revelation of Jesus to the world and to individuals. During this season, we hear stories of the way that the Light of Christ spreads to the ends of the earth.

> Every Sunday is a feast day celebrating Christ's Resurrection, even during Lent. This is why today we do not count Sundays as part of Lent. If you have given up some kind of food for Lent, for example, you can eat it on Sundays.

The Season of **Lent** is a time of discipline and self-denial that begins on Ash Wednesday and lasts until Holy Saturday, for a total of forty days, not including Sundays. The forty days of Lent remind us of the forty years the Israelites spent wandering in the wilderness and the forty days Jesus spent in the wilderness tempted by Satan. The devotion of Lent is meant to be a time of preparation, not punishment. We follow the example of Jesus, who prepared for his earthly ministry with a time of prayer and fasting. We engage in disciplines and devotions that draw us closer to him, so that we are ready to walk with him toward Jerusalem and the cross. During Lent, we often pray the Great Litany (148) or read the Decalogue (Ten Commandments) on page 350.

Holy Week, the week from Palm Sunday to Easter Day, is both the conclusion of the season of Lent and a special time in its own right. During this week, our liturgies help us to walk with Jesus through his final days on earth, from his entry into Jerusalem to his last meal with his friends, through the cross and to the grave.

The Season of **Easter** begins with the Great Vigil of Easter, which takes place sometime between sunset on Holy Saturday (the night before Easter Day) and sunrise on Easter morning. But Easter is too large a celebration to be contained in one day; instead we celebrate the great fifty days, lasting from Easter Day to the Day of Pentecost. It is a time when we rejoice extravagantly. In our liturgy, we add extra alleluias to express our deep joy in the resurrection of our Lord.

The **Season after Pentecost** encompasses all the Sundays after the Day of Pentecost until the end of the church year. The Day of Pentecost, which falls fifty days after Easter, is when we remember the coming of the Holy Spirit among the apostles, described in Acts 2. On the Day of Pentecost, we celebrate the Holy Spirit, which inspired and empowered the followers of Jesus to do the work of Christ in the world. This long season is also sometimes referred to as Ordinary Time, not because it is mundane, but because we count the Sundays using "ordinal numbers"—Second Sunday after Pentecost, Third Sunday after Pentecost, etc. This is a season for growth, a reminder that the long walk of faith isn't always highs and lows but is made up of the stuff of everyday life. The Last Sunday after Pentecost brings us to the end of the church year, then we head into Advent to begin the cycle again.

Year in and year out, we cycle through the church year: from the waiting and anticipation of Advent, to the celebration of Christmas, to the spreading of light at Epiphany, to the contemplation and repentance of Lent, into the extraordinary joy of Easter, and through the long season after Pentecost, the "ordinary time" of our church year. In all of these seasons we are focused, not on ourselves, but on the birth, life, death, and resurrection of Jesus Christ.

These different seasons keep us from getting "stuck" in one image of God. In the church year, sometimes we remember and worship and celebrate the baby Jesus born in the manger, and sometimes we remember and worship and celebrate the broken Jesus, hanging on the cross. We don't get to pick which Jesus we like best; we don't get to remake Jesus in our image or package Jesus in the way that is simple and safe for us. Instead, the church year invites us to walk with Jesus through all the moments and seasons of his life—and all the moments and seasons of ours.

Feasts, Fasts, and Holy Days

While the seasons give us a general rhythm to our year, within these seasons are specific feasts and fasts, holy days that Christians are called to mark in order to learn more about our faith and ourselves.

The church calendar provides five kinds of special days to observe and celebrate:

> Principal Feasts
> Sundays
> Holy Days
> Days of Special Devotion
> Days of Optional Observance

The seven Principal Feasts of the church are the most important days of the year. You've already heard about four of them: Easter, Christmas, Epiphany, and Pentecost. The other three are: Ascension Day (forty days after Easter Day, marking the conclusion of Jesus' earthly life and ascension into heaven); Trinity Sunday (the Sunday following the Day of Pentecost, celebrating the gift of God's threefold nature: Father, Son, and Holy Spirit); and All Saints' Day (November 1, remembering the multitude of saints whose holiness inspires and encourages us in faith). The church has declared these days have highest importance, and all Christians should strive to observe them.

The second most important category in the church calendar is Sundays. That's right! Every single Sunday is a major holiday in the Christian church. The prayer book explains that "All Sundays of the year are feasts of our Lord Jesus Christ." So it doesn't matter whether it's Easter Day or the middle of Lent, whether it's the First Sunday of Advent or the Twenty-Sixth Sunday After Pentecost, every Sunday is an important holiday, a feast of our Lord Jesus Christ.

In particular, a few moments from Jesus' life are especially important when they fall on a Sunday. The Holy Name, observed on January 1, commemorates the day when Jesus would have been circumcised and named. The Presentation is observed on February 2, forty days after Jesus' birth, which Luke 2:22-40 tells us was when Jesus was presented in the temple, and the Transfiguration, August 6, which observes the day on which Jesus was transfigured on the mountaintop (Matthew 17:1-9, Mark 9:2-8, and Luke 9:28-36).

The fact that Sundays are the second most important holy days (after the Principal Feasts) reminds us that Christianity is a faith that is lived every day, week in and week out, year round, not only on the big days like Christmas and Easter.

The third category of time in the calendar is holy days. These include feasts of our Lord (days that we remember certain important things in Jesus' life), other Major Feasts (days when we remember the apostles, evangelists, other important saints from Jesus' lifetime, and the national feasts of Independence Day and Thanksgiving Day), and fasts (Ash Wednesday and Good Friday).

These holy days are often called red-letter days, because early calendars in *The Book of Common Prayer* were printed with these days in red type. In today's *Book of Common Prayer*, these holy days are printed in bold type. For all of these holy days, *The Book of Common Prayer* provides a collect (or prayer) (pages 185-194, 237-246) and lessons (pages 922-926 and 996-1000) so that we, as individuals and as a community, can remember these important days in our prayers and readings.

Days of special devotion are different from the rest of the calendar in that they are not a single date, but instead a series of days that Christians are called to observe "by special acts of discipline and self-denial." Most of our calendar is marked by feasts, or days of celebration. Days of special devotion, together with Ash Wednesday and Good Friday, give us the other end of the spectrum of time: fasts, or days of discipline and self-denial. Our calendar sets aside all the weekdays of Lent and Holy Week, as well as Good Friday and all the Fridays of the year as days of special devotion.

As Christians, we understand that these days, too, are important for our spiritual formation. They are days of discipline, not in the sense of beating ourselves up, but instead in the true meaning of the word: Discipline is related to the word "disciple" and means to learn or to follow. When we observe the fasts of our church, stepping away from rejoicing to embrace solemnity, we learn something about ourselves and the world. Observing fasts helps us to celebrate our feasts even more deeply. Just as every Sunday is a feast of the Lord's Resurrection, an echo of Easter Day, so too every Friday is a day of special discipline, an echo of Good Friday.

Our calendar is clear: Celebration and resurrection are of primary importance. The feasts of great joy are those listed first in our calendar, and we should orient our time and our lives around them. But our celebration must leave room for discipline and self-denial, for contemplation and solemnity, for the recognition that there is sorrow as well as joy, struggle as well as celebration in the story of Jesus and in the Christian life. The days of special devotion root our time in that awareness.

Days of optional observance round out the final category in the church's calendar. Found on pages 19-30 of *The Book of Common Prayer*, these days commemorate the lives of saints, including early martyrs like Perpetua and her Companions, civil rights leaders like Martin Luther King Jr., and theologians like Thomas Cranmer. Each of these people, and many others, are assigned days so that we remember them, pray for and with them, and can be drawn into deeper life in Christ through their witness.

The days of optional observance are rich, in that we could observe a feast or fast every single day of the year, if we so chose. And these days are

If you want to see the full list of people who the church remembers through the year, you can look in a book called *Lesser Feasts & Fasts*. As of this writing, the most recent version of the official list of approved and optional observances is from 2022. You can purchase the book or download a PDF for free from episcopalcommonprayer.org. For several years, our church had a trial use book called *Holy Women, Holy Men*, but that book is no longer used. You can learn more about saints and our commemoration of them in Chapter 19.

what the title states: they are optional, so that no Christian *must* honor these days in a particular way.

The Christian Calendar

In the cycle of seasons, feasts, and fasts, the church calendar articulates how we, as Christians, approach time.

❖ **The calendar tells us how we think.** Christians are people who orient their entire lives around Jesus Christ; our calendar is focused around the birth, life, death, and resurrection of our savior.

❖ **The calendar tells us what we value.** Christmas and Easter are of utmost importance, the days around which all of our lives should be oriented, but every Sunday is also a major, important holiday, and underscores the importance of the day-in, day-out, lived character of the Christian life.

❖ **The calendar tells us what we work toward.** Or, more importantly, it tells us that our work is not the focus; our lives are lived in grateful response to the work that God has already done in Christ Jesus.

Perhaps most importantly, the Christian calendar tells us what we long for: Our church year begins with Advent, with the season of yearning and expectation for the coming of God into the world in the person of Jesus Christ. Even as we remember the moment when God entered into history in a stable in Bethlehem, we also long for and anticipate the moment when Christ will come again into our lives and into the world, to draw the whole world to himself. This is who we are; this is how we measure time.

For Reflection

✳ What might it look like to orient all of our time and our lives around the birth and resurrection of Jesus instead of around other things?

✳ What is your favorite liturgical season and why?

✳ How is the passage of liturgical time marked at your church? What signs, symbols, or rituals do you observe as a community?

✳ How can all the possibilities of observance—seasons, feasts, fasts, and days of special devotion—deepen our relationship with God?

Chapter 11

Walking in the Way of the Cross

Holy Week and Easter

Almighty God, whose most dear Son went not up to joy but first he suffered pain, and entered not into glory before he was crucified: Mercifully grant that we, walking in the way of the cross, may find it none other than the way of life and peace; through Jesus Christ our Lord. *Amen.*

—*The Book of Common Prayer*, p. 272

As humans we give an immense amount of weight to "last things." The Make-a-Wish Foundation helps terminally ill children to "live their dreams" before they die, working to fulfill a last wish. Prisoners on death row select their last meal and are asked before execution if they have any "last words." When we want to find out what people really value in their lives, we ask: What would you do if this were your last day on earth? We believe, on some deep level, that last things are of ultimate importance and that you can tell a lot about a person based on what they would do in those final moments of life.

Holy Week and Easter, the pinnacles of the church year, are important in part because this is when the Christian community remembers the last week of Jesus' life on earth—his entry into Jerusalem on Palm Sunday, the Last Supper, death on the cross, silence of Holy Saturday, and the celebration of Easter Vigil and Easter Day.

The liturgies of Holy Week are about remembering, not in the sense of thinking about what happened so that we don't forget, but in the sense of re-membering, re-embodying, re-entering into them so that we might live through and experience them anew. Through the liturgies of Holy Week, we are given a yearly opportunity to walk with Jesus through his final days in a real and powerful way.

All of Holy Week is important, but the crux of it is the three holy days—Maundy Thursday, Good Friday, and the Easter Vigil. Together, these days are called the Triduum, which literally means three days. Celebration of the Triduum is one of the most ancient customs of the Christian church, through time, across denominations, and around the world. Though our celebrations might differ, our honoring of these days of holiest importance connects us.

Palm Sunday

The pilgrim Egeria describes an observance of Palm Sunday in the late fourth century. Christians gathered on the other side of the Mount of Olives, in a place called Bethphage, where they read together the story of Jesus' entry into Jerusalem.

They walked to the Mount of Olives and down the hillside into the city.

Egeria tells us that these early Christians waved palm or olive tree branches, sang psalms (especially 118), and shouted the antiphon: "Blessed is he who comes in the name of the Lord!"

Our observance of Palm Sunday, nearly 2,000 years later, follows the same pattern. The service, found in the prayer book on pages 270-273, typically begins with the Liturgy of the Palms, which starts outdoors or in another place away from the church building. In this portion of the service, we commemorate the triumphal entry into Jerusalem, one of the few events described in all four gospels (Matthew 21:1-11, Mark 11:1-11a, Luke 19:29-40, John 12:12-19). We read aloud the story from one of those gospels, and then we re-enact that story as a community, waving our own palm branches while walking into the sanctuary, singing or saying hymns of praise and joy, including the refrain "Blessed is he who comes in the name of the Lord," and often Psalm 118, the very same words Egeria tells us were said in the fourth century.

After entry into the church on Palm Sunday, the service continues as usual until it is time for the gospel. *The Book of Common Prayer* calls this holy day "The Sunday of the Passion: Palm Sunday" because it is a day when we remember not only Jesus' triumphal entry into

The liturgy for Palm Sunday is one of only a few places in *The Book of Common Prayer* where the rubrics (instructions) suggest a specific hymn; usually the hymn selection is left up to the clergy in consultation with the church musician. But on page 271, the prayer book suggests singing "All glory, laud, and honor" during the procession of palms. Found in *The Hymnal 1982*, this hymn has been sung since at least the ninth century as part of the Palm Sunday liturgy. When we sing this particular hymn, we are joining our voices with saints from ages past and continuing a tradition that is 1,200 years old!

Jerusalem but also the rest of the passion narrative: Jesus' betrayal, trial, crucifixion, and death. So on Palm Sunday every year, the passion gospel is either read or chanted. We hear this story on Palm Sunday from either Matthew, Mark, or Luke; on Good Friday we will hear the passion narrative again, but it is always read from the Gospel of John on that day.

The reading of the passion gospel on Palm Sunday and Good Friday is the only time in the year when the gospel can be read by lay people and/or read "in parts," with different people taking specific roles (at other times, the gospel is read in whole by ordained clergy—preferably a deacon, if one is available). The reading of the gospel is not a play or a performance; instead, in this holy drama, everyone is invited to enter into the story. The entire congregation has a role, taking the part of the crowd. And the congregation does not sit passively but instead is instructed to stand at the verse that mentions Jesus' arrival at Golgotha.

In this way, on Palm Sunday, we get a taste of the full narrative of Holy Week, moving from the joy of Jesus' triumphal entry into Jerusalem to the devastation and loss of his death. We experience the very same voices that shouted "Hosanna," shortly thereafter shouting, "Crucify him!" By taking our part in the liturgy, we discover those voices are our own, and we find our place in Jesus' story.

The passion narrative of Palm Sunday is not meant to take the place of the observances in the week to come, especially the three holiest days of the Triduum. Instead, Palm Sunday gives us an overview of what is to come, so that as we continue through the week, we can engage even more deeply with the story.

Holy Monday, Holy Tuesday, Holy Wednesday: The days between Palm Sunday and Holy Thursday are known simply as Holy Monday, Holy Tuesday, and Holy Wednesday. Each day commemorates different events from the last week of Jesus' life. On Holy Monday, we hear from John 12:1-11, which tells the story of the anointing of Jesus at Bethany in a way that prefigures and prepares us for the anointing of his body after death. On Holy Tuesday, we hear some of Jesus' predictions of his death from John 12:20-36. On Wednesday, we hear the story of Jesus predicting his betrayal by Judas (John 13:21-32). These stories from the Gospel of John set the stage for what is to come in Jesus' final days.

On **Maundy Thursday**, we remember Jesus' final meal with his friends before he was crucified; this is often called the Last Supper. In a sense, we recall this event every week when we celebrate Holy Communion. But on Maundy Thursday, we offer a special commemoration of this meal, following the service in *The Book of Common Prayer* on pages 274-275 or *The Book of Occasional Services*, on pages 93-94. In the epistle reading from 1 Corinthians 11:23-26,

In addition to *The Book of Common Prayer*, the Episcopal Church has another official book of liturgies and prayers called *The Book of Occasional Services*. As the title suggests, this book contains forms for services that are used infrequently or "occasionally." Although they are not used often, the prayers in this book are a beautiful part of our tradition; there are lovely liturgies for commissioning lay ministers, for blessing homes, for the anniversary of a marriage, and many more. *The Book of Occasional Services* also includes many seasonal services: from Advent and Christmas lessons and carols to services for Lent and Holy Week, such as stations of the cross, tenebrae (a service of light and shadows typically observed on Wednesday of Holy Week), and instructions for foot washing or an agape meal on Maundy Thursday.

Paul describes the tradition of sharing bread and wine as the Body and Blood of Jesus. As Paul writes, "For as often as you eat this bread and drink the cup, you proclaim the Lord's death until he comes." On Maundy Thursday, we remember not only this moment in Jesus' life, his final meal with his friends, but also his commandment to his disciples and to us to "Do this in remembrance of me."

In fact, the word *maundy* comes from the Latin word for commandment, because Maundy Thursday is the day when we remember Jesus' commandments, the things that Jesus commanded us to do on the night before he died. Matthew, Mark, and Luke all tell similar stories of what Jesus did on that night, and their descriptions of the Last Supper coincide with what we hear from Paul in 1 Corinthians. The Gospel of John tells another story and introduces another commandment. John's version of the Last Supper doesn't talk about the bread and wine. Instead we hear about Jesus kneeling on the floor and washing his disciples' feet. In this ultimate example of servanthood, Jesus sets an example for his disciples and for us, commanding us to wash one another's feet and "love one another as he has loved us."

In many congregations, the Maundy Thursday service continues after the readings and sermon with a ceremony of the washing of feet. Sometimes this is done symbolically: The clergy or other members of leadership wash the feet of a specific number of people (usually twelve), or the clergy wash everyone's feet. But perhaps more appropriately the foot washing should be done by everyone—everyone both washing and getting washed— so that all are participating in and fulfilling Christ's commandment: "So if I, your Lord and Teacher, have washed your feet, you also ought to wash one another's feet" (John 13:14). The liturgical action of washing one another's feet symbolizes that servanthood is something we do for one another—a mutuality where all are served and all are servants.

After the ceremony of washing of feet, the service continues with the Prayers of the People and then Holy Communion. This is the last celebration of Holy Eucharist until the Great Vigil of Easter. Some churches choose to consecrate more bread and wine than is necessary at this service, in order to reserve some of the sacrament for Good Friday. If additional elements are being reserved, they are taken, often by a solemn procession, to a separate chapel or other place out of the main sanctuary. The area where the sacrament is kept is called the Altar of Repose. In some congregations, people remain through the night to pray and keep vigil with the sacrament, as an echo of the disciples who Jesus asked to stay awake and pray with him in the Garden of Gethsemane.

After Holy Communion is concluded, many communities observe the custom of stripping the altar. Members of the congregation remove all decoration and ornaments from the church and veil or cover all visible crosses. This can be done in silence or with a recitation of Psalm 22. As we strip the sanctuaries of their decorations, we are reminded of the moment in the passion story when Jesus is stripped of his clothes. Many communities conclude by washing the altar and extinguishing the sanctuary lamp, the sign of Christ's continued presence among us. These actions prepare the sanctuary for the solemnity of Good Friday and also help us focus on what is happening—Jesus and the cross, rather than all the "trappings."

After the altar is stripped, the ministers and people depart in silence. There is no dismissal or end to the service. This silence invites people to remember that the Triduum services are part and parcel of one another—they are one continuous liturgy telling one continuous story. Maundy Thursday is the first act of the Triduum; the story continues with our re-membering the next day with Good Friday and on Saturday night or Sunday morning with the Easter Vigil.

Good Friday is the day when Christians recall with our prayers and readings the crucifixion of our Lord and Savior on the cross. On this day, the people and ministers enter in silence into a church that is bare of ornamentation following the stripping of the altar on Maundy Thursday. The liturgy on this day, like the church, is "stripped down" to the essentials; it is brief and solemn.

The prayer book service (pages 276-282) begins with an opening collect (prayer) and readings. Then, just as on Palm Sunday, we hear a reading of the passion, this time from the Gospel of John. Once again, the passion may be read or chanted by lay people; different people may take on specific roles and the congregation may participate as the crowd, with all standing at the verse that mentions Golgotha. This repetition of the passion that we heard only a few days prior helps us to hear and interact with the story in a new way. We can notice the things that are the same between the two accounts and ponder those that are different. And we are encouraged to find our own place in the narrative in a different way each time.

After the passion is a sermon and an optional hymn. Then we engage in an extended time of prayer, using the ancient tradition of the solemn collects. In these prayers, we pray for people everywhere: for our own sins and redemption, for the church throughout the world, for all nations and people of the earth, for all who suffer and are afflicted, and for those who do not know God. These prayers remind us that on Good Friday, we do not merely focus on our own grief or sense of loss at the death of Jesus but instead allow that grief to fuel our prayers and actions on behalf of the whole world.

The service of Good Friday can end here, with a hymn, the Lord's Prayer, or a final prayer. But *The Book of Common Prayer* also includes two additional, optional parts of the service: Veneration of the Cross and Holy Communion from the reserved sacrament. Communities can add one or both of these options to their observance of Good Friday.

For Veneration of the Cross, a wooden cross is brought into the church and placed in the sight of the people. The prayer book includes the words to appropriate anthems that can be sung or said, or the congregation can choose another suitable anthem. During or after the anthems, people can offer "appropriate devotions" to the cross. In some communities people kneel before the cross in prayer. Some might choose to touch or kiss the cross, as a sign of devotion. In other communities, people lay flowers at the foot of the cross, similar to how we might put flowers on a grave at a funeral. All of these options are different ways that communities attempt to honor the holy cross of Jesus, by which our Savior redeemed the world.

On Good Friday, we observe the darkest moment in our history: the Lord of Love is tortured and killed on the cross. So why, you might wonder, do we call this day good? Scholars disagree over the answer to this question. Some say that the word for good comes from the words for pious or holy, so the name Good Friday actually means Holy Friday. Others say that the "good" is a corruption of God, and that it was meant to be God Friday, in recognition that it was God's self upon the cross. Still others say that the day is good, in the sense of positive, because even though it involves sadness and suffering, Christ's crucifixion accomplishes the greatest good imaginable—our salvation. Without a clear and easy answer, each of us is called to wrestle with the question: What does it mean to you to call this Friday "good"?

The final option for the Good Friday service is to celebrate Holy Communion—but in an unusual manner. Tradition demands that we do not consecrate the bread and wine on Good Friday as a way of remembering that Jesus was dead, in the grave, absent from our presence on this day. Using

Shortly after the death and resurrection of Jesus, early Christians began venerating the physical places where Jesus spent his last day on earth: from the place of his trial before the Sanhedrin to the location where Simon of Cyrene helped Jesus carry the cross to the spot where he was crucified and then laid into a tomb. Eventually this practice developed into a path of pilgrimage, called the Via Dolorosa, a walk through Jerusalem where the faithful stop to pray at fourteen stations commemorating events in Jesus' final hours.

Over time, those who could not physically travel to Jerusalem yet wanted to take part in walking through these holy moments began a tradition of observing the Stations of the Cross in other places by placing images of the fourteen stations along a path or around their own churches. As an act of devotion, worshipers can travel from one station to the next, stopping at each station to say prayers, listen to reflections or readings, or sing.

The traditional fourteen Stations of the Cross include locations specifically mentioned in the gospels and six stations based on pious legend. Some communities use a Scriptural Way of the Cross, replacing the six non-biblical stations so that all fourteen stations are directly from the Bible. The Episcopal Church's *Book of Occasional Services* includes a liturgy for the Way of the Cross using the traditional fourteen stations. The Way of the Cross is often used on Fridays during Lent. When it is used on Good Friday, it is an addition to, not a replacement for, the Good Friday service in *The Book of Common Prayer*.

the bread and wine set in reserve on Maundy Thursday, the minister conducts a simple service of communion, offering the bread and wine without the traditional prayer of consecration. The community eats and drinks all of the bread and wine that remains, so that there is no sacrament until the bread and wine are consecrated for the first time at Easter.

The Good Friday service concludes with a simple prayer, no blessing or dismissal, and the people depart in silence. In this way, we stay in the solemnity of the occasion. But we are also reminded that Good Friday is not the end of the story of Jesus or of this holy service. Good Friday is the second act of the Triduum, which will continue and conclude with the Great Vigil of Easter.

Consisting of only one page (283) in *The Book of Common Prayer*, the service for **Holy Saturday** is simple and brief. There is no celebration of Holy Eucharist on this day, a stark reminder that Jesus is absent, dead and in the tomb. Instead the service consists of a collect, a few readings, and a short anthem from the Burial Office (pages 484 or 492). The liturgy offers no easy answers or trite statements. Instead the mood of the day is quiet and still, reflective of an old tradition that required silence throughout the day.

The Great Vigil of Easter is the fullest expression of Christian life and joy in our earthly pilgrimage. On this night, we enter into the heart of our faith. Starting on page 285 of our prayer book, the service begins in darkness, a reminder that what is to come emerges from the darkness of Good Friday and Holy Saturday, the cross and the grave. In the darkness, a fire is kindled. This recalls both the creation of light—the first creative act by God—and the light that is brought into the world in the new creation of Jesus Christ. From the new fire, we light the paschal candle, which stands as a symbol of Christ, both in its association with light and in the candle's association with baptism. The deacon carries the paschal candle in procession, stopping three times to acclaim the light of Christ. In some places, members of the congregation have handheld candles that are lit from the paschal candle, spreading the first new fire into the congregation, filling the church with the light of Christ. The paschal candle is taken to the front of the sanctuary, where it will remain throughout the fifty days of Easter.

Next, a minister sings or says the *Exsultet*, an ancient hymn that proclaims the heart of Easter joy: "Rejoice and sing now, all the round earth, bright with glorious splendor, for darkness has been vanquished by our eternal King" (286). This hymn is a raucous celebration of the mighty power exhibited in the resurrection, when light overcame darkness, when love overcame sin, and when life overcame death. Again and again the *Exsultet* proclaims, "This is the night...", a reminder that in this holy moment, heaven is brought down to earth and the past is brought into the present as we celebrate our salvation as though it were the first time.

The service continues with a selection of stories from the Old Testament; at least two or as many as nine are read. The reading from Exodus, when God brings the people out of slavery in Egypt, is always read. The stories remind us of the whole arc of salvation, the way that God has been present

The word paschal comes from the Hebrew word *Pesach*, which means Passover. Every year at the Easter Vigil, we hear the story of Israel's deliverance at the Red Sea (Exodus 14:10–15:1), connecting our deliverance from sin and death in Jesus Christ to God's deliverance of the people of Israel out of bondage in Egypt.

At the Easter Vigil liturgy, we use a large paschal candle, whose flame recalls for us the pillar of fire that led God's people on their journey from captivity to freedom (Exodus 13:21). The final meal that Jesus ate with his disciples, which we call the Last Supper, was described in three of the gospels as a Passover meal, and Jesus himself is often described as the Paschal lamb.

In this way, the Hebrew Passover story in Exodus is seen as a piece of the salvation story that continues in the death and resurrection of Jesus Christ. For Christians, Jesus is our Passover. Just as in the ancient Passover, God's people were marked for deliverance from death, so for Christians, we believe that we are marked at baptism as Christ's own and are thus rescued from death.

with and loved humanity from the beginning of creation. After each reading, the people respond by singing a psalm or a canticle and praying a collect. In this way, we hear what God has done, we offer praise for God's presence in our past, and we pray for God's continued presence and action.

Following the readings is the service for Holy Baptism. The Great Vigil of Easter was once the main day for new Christians to be welcomed into the church through baptism, and it continues to be a major occasion for baptisms. If there are no candidates for Holy Baptism, those present instead renew their own baptismal vows, recommitting themselves on this holy night to the life of faith.

Then comes the moment we've all been waiting for: Easter is joyously proclaimed with the words, "Alleluia. Christ is risen." The people respond, "The Lord is risen indeed. Alleluia" (294). This simple statement proclaims our deepest truth as Christians: the reality of the resurrection of Jesus Christ.

After joyfully proclaiming the resurrection of Jesus three times, the congregation sings one of the canticles of celebration. The service then continues with an epistle reading, psalm, gospel reading, sermon, and prayers of the people. Then the table is set for the first eucharist of Easter, a true thanksgiving in which we recall with gladness Christ's resurrection and are nourished by Christ's Body and Blood to proclaim it to the world.

The Great Vigil of Easter is just the beginning; the celebration of Christ's resurrection continues in the rest of the services on Easter Day. Furthermore, the joy of Easter is so great that it cannot even be contained in one day. Easter Day is only the first day of the Easter Season, which begins the Great Fifty Days of Easter. The paschal candle remains lit and in the front of the church throughout the season, calling to mind the light of Christ that was proclaimed at the vigil and that continues to shine. Throughout the season of Easter, the service begins with the same proclamation of Christ's resurrection that we heard at the Great Vigil: "Alleluia. Christ is risen." In fact, additional alleluias are sprinkled throughout the service of Holy Eucharist during the season of Easter: at the opening, during Holy Eucharist, and at the dismissal. Alleluia is a word of great celebration, a shout of unbridled joy. These extra alleluias are not added at other times of the year, so they serve as a way to set the Great Fifty Days of Easter above and apart as an occasion of deep joy.

The liturgies of Holy Week are not simply a checklist, an obligation that Christians are required to fulfill. Instead they are an invitation to walk more closely with Jesus, to enter into the story of salvation in a unique and powerful way. The patterns of prayer are ancient, and in walking this holy path, we join pilgrims from around the world and through time who have also chosen to walk with Jesus. In Holy Week we move through all of the experiences of Christ's life—from the excitement of Palm Sunday to the pain and suffering of Good Friday and finally to the unparalleled joy of Jesus' resurrection from the dead at Easter. Observing all of the liturgies of Holy Week is our way of standing with Jesus through both the good and the bad, the highs and the lows of life. In so doing we are reminded that God in Jesus Christ stands with us as well—no matter what.

For Reflection

✶ Have you ever experienced the complete Triduum (Maundy Thursday, Good Friday, the Great Vigil of Easter) by attending worship for each of those days? What was that experience like and how did it shape you? (If no one in your group has experienced the Triduum, ask someone to speak with you who has!)

✶ Jesus commands us to wash one another's feet and to remember him with bread and wine—in the same passage. Why do you think we partake of Holy Eucharist weekly but foot washing only occasionally?

✶ Is there a service of Holy Week that is difficult for you? Why is it difficult? What might this discomfort say to you about your life of faith?

✶ Which moment from the liturgies of Holy Week is most powerful and important to you, personally? Why is that moment particularly important?

✶ The church takes the season of Lent very seriously, and many people take on Lenten practices. What might it be like if we took on Easter practices? What kind of Easter disciplines or practices can you imagine?

Chapter 12

Jesus Christ Who Is the Resurrection and the Life
The Burial Office

Merciful God, Father of our Lord Jesus Christ who is the Resurrection and the Life: Raise us, we humbly pray, from the death of sin to the life of righteousness; that when we depart this life we may rest in him, and at the resurrection receive that blessing which your well-beloved Son shall then pronounce: "Come, you blessed of my Father, receive the kingdom prepared for you from the beginning of the world." Grant this, O merciful Father, through Jesus Christ, our Mediator and Redeemer. *Amen.*

—*The Book of Common Prayer*, p. 505

Tucked at the end of An Order for Burial is a great treasure of *The Book of Common Prayer*. It is a note, which reads:

The liturgy for the dead is an Easter liturgy. It finds all its meaning in the resurrection. Because Jesus was raised from the dead, we, too, shall be raised. The liturgy, therefore, is characterized by joy, in the certainty that "neither death, nor life, nor angels, nor principalities, nor things present, nor things to come, nor powers, nor height, nor depth, nor anything else in all creation will be able to separate us from the love of God in Christ Jesus our Lord." This joy, however, does not make human grief unchristian. The very love we have for each other in Christ brings deep sorrow when we are parted by death. Jesus himself wept at the grave of his friend. So, while we rejoice that one we love has entered into the nearer presence of our Lord, we sorrow in sympathy with those who mourn. (507)

This note sets the context for what Episcopalians believe about death and how we honor the dead in our funeral liturgies. These beautiful words remind us that, for Christians, the death of a loved one is a conflicted moment. We experience both immense joy and profound grief. We celebrate the fact that the person who has died has gone into the nearer presence of Jesus. But we also mourn our loss, just as Jesus mourned the loss of his friend Lazarus (John 11:28-37). Our experience of death stands in the midst of this tension: love and loss, joy and grief, celebration and mourning. Episcopal funeral liturgies balance these emotions: They celebrate the resurrected life of the one who has died while at the same time honoring the grief of those who mourn.

The service for The Burial of the Dead is the last service in *The Book of Common Prayer* in the "Pastoral Offices" section of the prayer book. This section includes Confirmation, Marriage, Birth of a Child, Reconciliation of a Penitent, Ministration to the Sick, and Burial. These rites signify for many the milestones of our journey through life. In these offices we are reminded that God in Christ walks with us in life and joy, in death and grief.

Found on pages 468-507, the burial rites have three forms: The Burial of the Dead: Rite One, The Burial of the Dead: Rite Two, and An Order for Burial. All three forms largely follow the same structure.

Notes About the Service

The services begin with a list of rubrics or guidelines for the service. Though these might seem like mundane details, these notes provide important insight into how the symbolic actions in funerals express what we believe about death. One of the first sentences clarifies that death of a member of a church should be reported to the minister of the congregation, and that "baptized Christians are properly buried from the church." Church funerals are not only for those who give money to the congregation or reserved for those who were very active and attended services frequently. All baptized Christians, regardless of age, denomination, or church attendance records, are properly buried from the church. It doesn't matter if the person hasn't been to church in a long time; it doesn't matter if the person who died had a difficult or complicated relationship with faith (don't we all?). The church is here to welcome you home, no matter what.

The notes say that the service should be held at a time "when the congregation has opportunity to be present." This is an important reminder that part of the gift and responsibility of Christian community is to "bear one another's burdens" (Galatians 6:2). The burial service is not a private affair only for the family of the person who has died. It is a service of the church, an opportunity for the Christian community to gather in prayer, both for the person who has died and for the family who is now bereaved.

The notes go on to say that the coffin should be closed before the service and covered with a pall. A pall is a cloth, usually white, that is spread over the coffin. This detail is a reminder that before God we all look the same. It doesn't matter if the person had money for the most expensive coffin or could only afford to be buried in a cardboard box; in death we are all covered in the love of Jesus, dressed in the white of baptism, and carried into the church on the day of our burial as a beloved member of the Body of Christ.

Next, the notes describe the different roles that people take in the service: a priest normally presides, but a deacon or lay reader may lead the service if a priest is not available. The lessons from the Old Testament and epistle should be read by lay persons; this is an opportunity for family members or friends to participate in the service in a meaningful way.

Even before the service begins, it is customary that the celebrant meets the body and goes before it into the church or toward the grave. In fact, *The Book of Common Prayer* includes a lovely series of prayers for "Reception of the Body" on page 466, in which the priest prays both for the person who has died and for those who mourn. By receiving the body and going before it into the church and to the grave, the celebrant offers a reminder that the person who has died does not travel alone; the faithful saints who have gone before are present with the deceased, and Jesus himself leads the way through death and the grave and into life eternal.

After the notes, we turn to the service itself. We will look specifically at The Burial of the Dead: Rite II (pages 491-505), but the theological and pastoral points are similar across both rites.

The Service of Burial

The service begins with everyone standing as the body is carried into the church. During this entrance, one of the anthems printed on pages 491-492, or a hymn, psalm, or other anthem is said or sung. The service continues in a manner similar to a regular Sunday service, with prayers and selected readings from Holy Scripture. The prayers focus on the reality of grief and the importance of our ministry, as the gathered church, to love and support one another in these times. The readings, like the anthems that began the service, help to recall the joy of resurrection, while also striving to comfort those who mourn. In all these things, the focus is on God, not the person who died, and we know and proclaim that there is nowhere we can go that Jesus has not already been, not even to death and the grave. If the service includes communion, a gospel reading must be offered.

After the readings, there may be a homily by a priest, a family member, or a friend. A homily is not a eulogy. Whereas a eulogy is a speech in praise of a person, a homily is a reflection on the scriptures that have been read. This is an important distinction, because while the homily can and should be personal, it is not focused exclusively on the person who died but on the connection between that person's life and the passages from the Bible that have just been read.

The service can continue with the Apostles' Creed. This creed, which is used at baptismal services, reminds us of the connection between death and baptism: Each is an entrance into a new and different life.

Here, the service for burial can take one of two paths. If the burial service does not include communion, then it continues with the Lord's Prayer and the Prayers of the People or other suitable prayers, and then skips ahead to the Commendation and Committal for the ending of the service. If the burial service does include communion, then it continues with the Prayers of the People.

Families, in consultation with their priest, can make the determination whether or not to include Holy Communion as part of the burial service. Sometimes, certain dynamics may make offering communion difficult or divisive. But in most instances, communion is a powerful and important part of the service of burial. After all, in Holy Eucharist we are joined together with angels and archangels and with the communion of saints, all those who have gone before, including the one who we bury this day. Communion means "together with," and sharing communion at a burial in the midst of sadness can be an important way to join together with the one who has died and with the gathered community, supporting one another in grief.

Either way, the service continues with the Prayers of the People, prayers that specifically refer to the death of Jesus' friend Lazarus, brother of Martha and Mary (John 11:1-44). When Lazarus died, Jesus wept so openly that people around him saw it as a sign of his deep love. Then, in the midst of his grief, Jesus raised Lazarus from the dead, restoring him to life. This story, referenced in the prayers, reminds us both of the way that Jesus himself experienced grief and of the power that Jesus has to raise all of us to newness of life.

Then the service continues with the peace and the offertory of bread and wine, just as in a regular eucharistic service. In the eucharistic prayer, the celebrant offers the Preface for the Commemoration of the Dead, "Through Jesus Christ our Lord; who rose victorious from the dead, and comforts us with the blessed hope of everlasting life. For to your faithful people, O Lord, life is changed, not ended; and when our mortal body lies in death, there is prepared for us a dwelling place eternal in the heavens" (382). This preface, like many of the elements of the liturgy, reinforces our understanding of death: As Christians we proclaim that in death our life is changed, not ended. The one who has died continues, even now, in a new life in Jesus Christ.

After Holy Communion, the service continues with a prayer found on page 498, which reminds us that sharing communion is a "foretaste of [God's] heavenly banquet." Then, the celebrant and other ministers take their places at

What is heaven like?

When we think of heaven, many of us envision Saint Peter at the pearly gates, streets paved with gold, and an eternity spent relaxing and doing things we enjoy with those we have loved and lost. Yet most of these ideas about heaven are from popular culture, not from the Bible or our tradition of prayer. The pearly gates and streets of gold come from the Revelation to John (21:21), but they are only a small part of a larger vision full of poetic imagery and metaphor. Neither Revelation nor any other scripture describes heaven as a place focused on our comfort, enjoyment, and leisure. Instead, the Bible says:

- What is most memorable about heaven is the nearness to God's presence, and our activity in heaven will not be playing games but worshiping and praising God (Revelation 7:9-17 and 5:11-14).

- Heaven isn't only about humanity; through Christ all of creation is being redeemed (Romans 8:19-23).

- Jesus speaks mostly about the kingdom of heaven in parables (Matthew 13:24-47). Through metaphor and story, Jesus compares the kingdom of heaven to things that are small yet valuable, things that grow and multiply, things that are ordinary and surprising.

- Jesus repeatedly says that the kingdom of heaven is "near" (Matthew 4:17, 10:7) and "among us" (Luke 17:20). The New Testament continues this understanding, describing heaven as something that is already here, already begun, and to which we currently belong (Ephesians 1:9-10, Philippians 3:20).

The Bible's description of heaven is full of mystery and metaphor, inviting us to think about heaven in new and different ways.

the body for the commendation. The commendation is our sending forth of this person, commending him or her to God. We affirm our belief in God, the God who created us and to whom we return. And we hear the focus on the joy of resurrection even in the midst of the grief of death: "even at the grave we make our song: Alleluia, alleluia, alleluia."

The celebrant faces the body and says the prayer at the bottom of page 499. This prayer names the true identity of each of us: servant, sheep, lamb, sinner, redeemed, saint. We are reminded that the deceased was not perfect but is beloved by God even so, just as we are.

The service concludes with a blessing, and then an anthem or hymn is sung or said as the body is carried from the church. In this way the service ends as it began, affirming our focus on Jesus Christ, who leads each of us through death and the grave and into paradise.

Committal

Even though the service in the church has ended, the burial is not over. The final portion of the burial rite is the committal, prayers that we say as the body of the deceased is placed in its final resting place. The service for committal is brief, with only a few anthems and prayers. It normally takes place wherever the body is being laid to rest: at the graveside if the body is being buried or at the columbarium if ashes are being interred in a niche. In this way, we go with the deceased to the very end of their journey on this earth, lovingly accompanying them with prayers even to the grave. As the body is placed in the grave or the ashes are interred, the celebrant says a prayer commending the person who has died to God and committing them to the earth. The directions specify that "earth is cast upon the coffin," an important connection to the words of scripture that humans were created out of the earth and we return to it. The service concludes with the Lord's Prayer and other prayers, and then the celebrant offers the dismissal.

These final words of the service begin with the very same words that we proclaim at Easter: "Alleluia. Christ is risen. The Lord is risen indeed. Alleluia." In this way we end with a focus on Easter, on joy, on Christ's resurrection from the dead.

Finding Meaning

Now that we understand some of the intricacies of the service of burial, what do they mean? What do we learn about what Episcopalians believe from exploring how we pray in the face of death?

The Episcopal Church's burial rites offer a great deal of room for different practices. Some people prefer to have their bodies preserved and buried in a coffin; others choose to be cremated before burial. Both are completely acceptable in the Episcopal Church. The prayer for committal includes "the ground, the deep, the elements, or its resting place," a variety of options that allow for burial in the ground, burial at sea, or interment in a columbarium. Many churches have a columbarium—a collection of niches, either in the ground or in a wall or bench—where ashes from cremation can be interred on the church property.

Firstly, and perhaps most importantly, our prayers reflect our belief and our feelings in the face of death: a combination of joy and grief, celebration and sadness. When planning funerals, I've often been told by families: "We don't want it to be sad. We want to celebrate our loved one's life." On the other hand, I've encountered families who are so drowned by grief that they are unable to see or experience any joy. The Episcopal service attempts to help people find a middle ground that acknowledges both realities. Yes, we celebrate the joy of resurrection, proclaim alleluias, and affirm that when someone dies, her or his life is changed, not ended. But we also repeatedly pray aloud the reality of our grief and loss, naming that Jesus himself wept at the loss of his friend. It is by holding both of these things in tension, by naming and honoring both joy and grief, that we live out the fullness of our faith and humanity and find the peace that God promises us.

Secondly, we are reminded that, even in the midst of grief and death, we are surrounded by the church, the Christian community. Again and again, the burial service emphasizes the importance of the gathered community. As Christians, it is incredibly important that we show up to funerals, to love and support those who are grieving. Even now, decades later, my father remembers every person who came to his mother's funeral. But just as death is not the end of life, so, too, the funeral is not the end of grief. It is important to remember those who are grieving, not only on the day of the burial but in the weeks and months to come. At burial services, I often remind people to pick a date on the calendar in a week or a month, or a few months, to call and check on those who are grieving.

The burial service, like the other practices in *The Book of Common Prayer*, undergirds our beliefs about death. Each component of the service reminds us that death is a step on the journey and not its end, that it is a time of joy as well as grief. This understanding should make us less afraid of talking about and acknowledging death—our own and those of our loved ones. We live in a death-defying, death-denying culture, where products to make you live longer or look younger clutter our advertisements and our shelves. But as Christians, we are called to be honest about death. Jesus talks about death a lot, and our liturgies acknowledge the reality of death. For a Christian, death is not the enemy but a moment in the continuum of life. When we begin to talk about death honestly, we begin to be freed from fear. And we are also able to plan for and discuss with our families the way we want to live and the way that we hope to die.

Planning Ahead

One of the great gifts that we can give our families is planning our funeral service. People often resist this idea because it sounds morbid to them, but it's important: It helps us acknowledge the reality of our mortality, and it is an incredible help to our families. When someone dies, the family is often paralyzed with grief. Trying to make the many decisions surrounding burial services can be overwhelming. And those who have never talked with their loved ones about death can spin their wheels, wondering: "What would [my mom] want?" "I don't know what hymns [my dad] liked." Grieving is already a wrenching experience without adding the heartache of indecision and uncertainty. And when people participate in a service that was planned in concert

It might seem surprising to talk about writing wills in a book about Christian belief and practice. You might think a will is a legal rather than a religious document. But, in fact, *The Book of Common Prayer* says it is "the duty of Christian parents to make prudent provision for the well-being of their families, and of all persons to make wills, while they are in health, arranging for the disposal of their temporal goods, not neglecting, if they are able, to leave bequests for religious and charitable uses" (445). The act of making a will is a theological act; it helps us to think about all the riches we've been given and how we can share them with God and with future generations. Making a will helps us to face death, clearly and honestly, while we are still in good health and not motivated by fear. And making a will is a gift—a chance to talk with our families and friends about the things that really matter, about our faith and our hopes and our dreams.

with the one who has died, they feel connection and comfort, hearing God's Holy Spirit speaking through the readings and hymns.

Perhaps all that we believe about death, all that has been expressed in the prayers of our burial service, is best summed up by Saint John Chrysostom in the most stirring of all Easter sermons:

> Let no one fear death,
> for the death of our Savior has set us free.
>
> The Lord has destroyed death by enduring it.
> The Lord vanquished hell when he descended into it.
> The Lord put hell in turmoil even as it tasted of his flesh.
>
> Isaiah foretold this when he said,
> "You, O Hell, were placed in turmoil when he
>   encountering you below."
>
> Hell was in turmoil having been eclipsed.
> Hell was in turmoil having been mocked.
> Hell was in turmoil having been destroyed.
> Hell was in turmoil having been abolished.
> Hell was in turmoil having been made captive.
>
> Hell grasped a corpse, and met God.
> Hell seized earth, and encountered heaven.
> Hell took what it saw, and was overcome by what it could
>   not see.
>
> O death, where is your sting?
> O hell, where is your victory?
>
> Christ is risen, and you are cast down!
> Christ is risen, and the demons are fallen!
> Christ is risen, and the angels rejoice!
> Christ is risen, and life is set free!

Christ is risen, and the tomb is emptied of its dead.

For Christ, having risen from the dead,
is become the first-fruits of those who have fallen asleep.

To Christ be glory and power forever and ever. *Amen!*

Source: http://www.thewords.com/articles/chrysostom.htm

For Reflection

✳ If we focus only on the Christian hope of resurrection, then we deny the reality of grief when we lose the ones we love. If we focus only on grief, then we ignore the promise of the Christian hope of eternal life. How does the burial liturgy balance hope and grief? How do we do this in our own lives?

✳ Heaven as described in the Bible is strikingly different from the idea of heaven often portrayed in popular culture. How does the Bible's description of heaven challenge, comfort, or unsettle you?

✳ *The Book of Common Prayer* clearly states that "baptized Christians are properly buried from the church" (468). Why do you think it is important for Christians to be buried from the church instead of another place, such as a funeral parlor?

✳ Have you planned your own funeral? If you have, what is it like? If you haven't, why not?

Basic Beliefs

Chapter 13

Gathered Together in Unity
The Creeds

Grant, O merciful God, that your Church, being gathered together in unity by your Holy Spirit, may show forth your power among all peoples, to the glory of your Name; through Jesus Christ our Lord, who lives and reigns with you and the Holy Spirit, one God, for ever and ever. *Amen.*

— *The Book of Common Prayer,* p. 232

Rules are funny things. To see a list of rules is to see a list of problematic things that people have done. As a way to understand the odd list of rules that appear in Saint Paul's letters to the church, one of my seminary professors offered this example. Suppose that thousands of years from now, archeologists excavated a public swimming pool. The purpose of the large concrete hole in the ground might not be clear, but archeologists would know two things based on the list of rules posted near the hole. It was not a place intended for running or diving. And they would also learn that people both ran and dove, hence the need for the rules against such actions.

Creeds are not laws but rather rules of faith. Creeds are, as the prayer book's Catechism says, "statements of our basic beliefs about God" (851). Why do we have these particular statements? At various times, the church has been racked by controversy, and so its leaders have met to settle basic questions of faith. Thus we have creeds, or summaries of the faith. Creeds speak especially to those matters that were controversial at the time they were written, and most of those controversies were related to belief in the Holy Trinity. Our creeds, therefore, mostly speak about God the Father, the Son, and the Holy Spirit. Many other important items of faith are left out, vital issues such as war and peace, the role of clergy and lay people in the church, protection of the vulnerable, or the sin of great wealth. So we turn to the creeds to find our bearings on who God is, but we also must realize that other very important matters of doctrine are not settled in our statements of faith.

We use two creeds regularly in our worship. On Sundays and Major Feasts, when we celebrate Holy Eucharist, we say together the Nicene Creed. When we say morning or evening prayer, baptize new Christians, or bury the dead, we say the Apostles' Creed.

According to tradition, the twelve articles of faith in the Apostles' Creed were written by the apostles themselves, with each apostle contributing one statement. Scholars today generally believe this is not how the creed arose, but there is wide disagreement as to its age or even whether it is more ancient than the Nicene Creed. The most important thing for us to note is that the Apostles' Creed is deeply connected with Holy Baptism. From very early times, this creed was used as new Christians were baptized. Today we continue this practice by incorporating the Apostles' Creed in our Baptismal Covenant in a question-and-answer format whenever we baptize someone or renew our baptismal promises. The Apostles' Creed is also used when we pray the Daily Office (see Chapter 9), especially in morning and evening prayer. Finally, we use the Apostles' Creed at funerals. Thus the earthly pilgrimage of a Christian begins and ends with the Apostles' Creed.

In this chapter, we will step through the Nicene Creed, because the Nicene Creed is largely an expansion of content similar to what the Apostles' Creed covers. If you are curious about the individual statements or articles of the Apostles' Creed, just look for the corresponding line from the Nicene Creed in the explanation below.

The Nicene Creed is named after Nicea, the place where the church held an ecumenical council (worldwide gathering of bishops) in the year 325. In response to certain divergent beliefs about Jesus, the bishops at that conference ratified the Nicene Creed. This was later modified and extended in 381, and this version is essentially the one that Christians around the world have said for more than 1,600 years and still say each Sunday.

Our creeds teach us about our faith in God. All the major creeds are organized along Trinitarian lines, so there are sections on God the Father, God the Son, and God the Holy Spirit. The creeds generally do not delve into other matters. May Christians fight wars? Who may be ordained or married? These and other important matters of faith are not resolved by the creeds. Instead, the creeds focus on the divinity and humanity of Jesus Christ. They focus on God the Father as creator of all that is. And they articulate the nature and role of the Holy Spirit. Especially in the Nicene Creed, words about the relationship of the Triune God (God in three persons) have been chosen very carefully. All this is designed to help us avoid saying or teaching things that would lead to error. For example, if I overemphasize the humanity of Jesus, then he is no longer God and thus cannot be proclaimed as the savior of the world. Conversely, if I overemphasize Jesus' divinity, then his humanity could be seen as an illusion and thus God has not dwelt among us as the scriptures say.

More than one person has observed that it is a good thing the Nicene Creed comes right after the sermon in our eucharistic celebrations: If the preacher has gone off the theological rails, the creed gets us back on track. The creed does indeed remind us each week of what the church teaches and how we ought to believe, but it is more than that. Coming shortly before our gathering at the altar, the creed can also be understood as a reminder of who God is—Father, Son, and Holy Spirit—as we ready ourselves to feast on Christ's presence. As a corrective against the possible idea that our celebration is all about us, the creed puts us in mind of the eternal nature of Jesus Christ. Jesus is not just a nice guy who shows up when we say some prayers; he is the only-begotten Son of God, loving us and all of creation from before time, redeeming not only those we can see around us but also those in all time and space. The creed reminds us of the big picture, the biggest picture.

People will sometimes wonder about one line or another in the creed. "I'm not sure about the virgin birth." "Is God really almighty?" "What does it mean that Jesus will be our judge?" At times, these questions are whispered furtively, as if no one else in the congregation asks them. But of course, people who take their faith and their intellect seriously will inevitably have serious questions about our faith and our world and our place. Many of these questions have an underlying question, "Do I really have to believe all this stuff we say?"

We can and should use our intellect to probe the depth of our faith—how, why, what, where, when, whom—but we should also be ready to join our voices with those of every generation who have taught the core beliefs of our faith. One way to understand the creeds' function is through the allegory of a yardstick. We can use the creeds to measure what we hear and determine if it represents the teaching of the church. If, God forbid, a preacher says that Jesus did not rise from the dead at Easter, we can immediately reject this as false teaching, because the creeds—universal statements of faith—are so emphatic that Jesus was indeed resurrected from the dead. This does not mean that we cannot ask questions about exactly what happened on Easter morning. In fact, a close reading of the gospels reveals that Jesus' own disciples were confused after Jesus was raised from the dead. Who wouldn't be?!

If you are interested in exploring questions of faith, a good resource is *Faithful Questions: Exploring the Way with Jesus,* which is all about the importance of wrestling with our faith. *Faithful Questions* also offers some guidance on important questions such as who Jesus is or what happens when we pray. This book is published by Forward Movement and is available from Forward Movement or your local bookseller.

The Nicene Creed

So let's take a look at the Nicene Creed. This will necessarily be a very brief survey. For a more detailed treatment, we recommend *The Creed: What Christians Believe and Why It Matters* by Luke Timothy Johnson.

> We believe in one God,
>> the Father, the Almighty,
>> maker of heaven and earth,
>> of all that is, seen and unseen.

The opening of the creed is not too complicated, really. We assert that God the Father made all that is, everywhere. Saying that God made everything has significant implications for how we treat the world we live in, as we'll see in Chapter 21. We might also note that this version of the creed, from Rite II, has us saying, "We believe," which is how the oldest versions of the creed read. Later, much of global Christianity preferred "I believe" and you can still find that version in our Rite I liturgy. While "we" emphasizes our common profession of faith, it avoids personal accountability. To say "we" emphasizes that we are stating not just our own beliefs but saying the beliefs of the whole church. This might help us along sometimes if we personally struggle with parts of the creeds, knowing that we are really articulating the ideal faith of the whole church. On the other hand, when I say "I believe," it reminds me that I take ownership of my own life of faith and beliefs. Try the creed using both voices and consider the advantages or disadvantages of each.

> We believe in one Lord, Jesus Christ,
>   the only Son of God,
>   eternally begotten of the Father,
>   God from God, Light from Light,
>   true God from true God,
>   begotten, not made,
>   of one Being with the Father.
>   Through him all things were made.

Nearly every sermon I've heard about Jesus is about his earthly life. And yet the creed has eight lines about the eternal life of Jesus Christ. Everything in these lines from the creed happened before Jesus was born. To make these claims emphasizes the vastness of God's love for us. To echo Saint John's words, "In the beginning was the Word, and the Word was God" (John 1:1) is to see Jesus not just as a person who lived in the Holy Land 2,000 years ago but as the crux of God's salvation history for all creation and for us.

It may be risky to privilege one phrase over another, but the words "of one Being with the Father" are especially important.

This means that Jesus Christ and his Father are peers and of one kind. In simple, practical terms, to say that Jesus and his Father are of one being prevents us from wrongly saying that Jesus is lesser than the other persons of the Holy Trinity.

Some of the phrases here ("Light from Light") are responses to specific controversies that raged in the ancient Byzantine world when the creed was composed. These words and phrases are well worth exploring in depth, but for now, we can stand back and note how the Jesus of the creed is far vaster than the warm, fuzzy Jesus we sometimes imagine.

> For us and for our salvation
>> he came down from heaven:
> by the power of the Holy Spirit
>> he became incarnate from the Virgin Mary,
>> and was made man.

This set of lines says much about Jesus—and about us. Why did Jesus come to dwell with us? "For us and for our salvation." How was this accomplished? "By the power of the Holy Spirit." And of course, we cannot overlook the gift of Mary in all this. No shy, retiring woman, Mary boldly said "yes" to God's invitation to bear God in Jesus Christ into the world. Because of our awe at God taking on human flesh, it has long been traditional, among some Anglicans, to bow or even genuflect as these words about the incarnation are sung or spoken.

Several years ago, I was teaching a basics class in a congregation, and it occurred to me to ask a question. "Can anyone say what 'incarnate' means?" Silence. No one had any idea. Incarnate is actually a very important word. (And this is a good reminder that we shouldn't idly repeat rote liturgical phrases; we should make sure we know what we're saying!)

Incarnate comes from the same root as *con carne* that you might have seen in a Mexican restaurant's menu. With meat. To say Jesus is God incarnate is to say that Jesus is God enfleshed. This takes away any possible idea that our God is remote from us or somehow does not understand the human experience.

> For our sake he was crucified under Pontius Pilate;
>   he suffered death and was buried.
>   On the third day he rose again
>   in accordance with the Scriptures;

Pontius Pilate was an official of the Roman empire. His story is told in all four gospels, and there are mentions of him elsewhere. It's positively extraordinary that only he and Mary (the Mother of God) are named in the creeds. Only two humans are mentioned; Mary brought Jesus into this earthly life, and Pilate played a key part in ending Jesus' earthly life. By repeating Pilate's name every week, we are reminding ourselves of the historicity of Jesus Christ. Pilate was a real person whose identity and existence are archeologically verifiable. Pilate was a real person, tainted by the same sin and fear that inhabit us all. We invoke his name week after week, grounding Jesus in historical reality and exposing the painful gulf between our sins and fear and God's love and hope.

We profess that Jesus died and was raised to new life. This is one of the central claims of Christianity. Apart from a claim of his resurrection, we might make the mistake of thinking that Jesus is merely a teacher. Without this claim that Jesus really died for us, we might make the mistake of thinking that God's love for us is limited. Dying for another is an ultimate expression of commitment, and Jesus' death proves God's commitment to us and our salvation.

> he ascended into heaven
>   and is seated at the right hand of the Father.

> He will come again in glory to judge the living and the dead,
> and his kingdom will have no end.

Many Episcopalians don't make a big deal about the ascension of Jesus into heaven. Many churches don't even have a midweek service to mark this central event, which occurs on a Thursday forty days after Easter Sunday. In the ascension, Jesus returns to heaven to dwell with God. Perhaps we don't celebrate the ascension more because we are stuck on the mechanics of the event rather than the why of it.

Just before he returns to God, Jesus blesses his followers. He promises that the Spirit will abide with them—and thus with us—as Jesus' ministry continues. The ascension is in some ways the beginning of our own earthly ministry of being Christ's hands and feet in our world, ministering to the world in his name.

The creed then moves into a part about judgment. Comfortable people don't like to think about judgment and consequences. But put yourself in the place of someone born in Darfur or someone whose family was extinguished in the Holocaust or another of the too-many genocides of the last hundred years. Righteous judgment may look very different for those who endure more evil than most of us can imagine.

Universalism—the idea that everyone is judged favorably, that there is universal salvation—works best for those who do not want to face consequences. But the teaching of the gospel is clear: God will one day judge us and all people. The parable of Lazarus and the rich man gives us insight into this judgment (Luke 16:19-31). In the parable, a rich man refuses to help a beggar named Lazarus. When the rich man and the poor man die, the rich man discovers that he is consigned to a life among flames, while the poor man has been taken into paradise. The rich man asks if the poor man can help him, but he is told that he has already enjoyed pleasure in his earthly life and will get no help in eternity. Like the rich man, I have routinely walked past the poor and needy, ignoring their pleas. For me to speak of judgment is to speak of the judgment I will face for failing to honor Christ in the most vulnerable people. Our prayer can and must be for mercy, for ourselves and our whole world.

We will be judged—but by God (and not one another!). Fortunately, God's judgment is above our "pay grade" so we can focus on our own salvation while yearning for God's mercy.

> We believe in the Holy Spirit, the Lord, the giver of life,
>   who proceeds from the Father and the Son.
>   With the Father and the Son he is worshiped and glorified.
>   He has spoken through the Prophets.

The third person of the Holy Trinity, the Holy Spirit, is oft-neglected. We tend to pray to God the Father or God the Son much more frequently than we pray to God the Holy Spirit. Only once a year, on the Day of Pentecost, do most of us turn our gaze fully to the Holy Spirit.

The Holy Spirit is the "giver of life" in that the Spirit was present from the moment of creation and continues to be one of the ways God animates us with God's presence. The creed reminds us, in case we forget, that the Spirit is itself worthy of worship and praise. Finally, the creed emphasizes how the prophets through time have been the Holy Spirit's voice. This is important both because it reminds us that the Spirit is eternal—and not just in our present—and that God sometimes chooses to speak through people. You can read more about the Holy Spirit in Chapter 23.

> We believe in one holy catholic and apostolic Church.
> We acknowledge one baptism for the forgiveness of sins.

This section of the creed has one of the most controversial lines. In the original version of the Nicene Creed, the Spirit was said to proceed from the Father. Period. Several centuries after the creed was ratified, the church in Europe began to insert another phrase, "and the Son." To untangle this controversy would require another book, so we'll just say this. Whether or not "and the Son" is added has an effect on our understanding of the relationship among God the Father, God the Son, and God the Holy Spirit. To say from whence one proceeds is to describe the source of power and being, and this affects the relationship among the persons of the Trinity.

Proponents of each position will make a case that "their" position is the only possible correct one. Anglicans have gradually begun to move toward the more ancient line. The bishops of the Anglican Communion have urged all Anglicans to omit "and the Son" in future prayer books, and, indeed, our own Episcopal Church has omitted the phrase in the *Enriching Our Worship* supplemental worship materials. It's all very complicated, but we mention this because wars have been fought over this and because the language varies somewhat in modern liturgy as this controversy continues to play out, thankfully without bloodshed.

> We look for the resurrection of the dead,
>   and the life of the world to come. Amen.

Here we profess our faith in the church universal. We call the church holy, because we believe that Jesus Christ himself is the head of it, and that we, his disciples, carry on his ministry under the guidance of the Holy Spirit. We call the church catholic, because despite our many differences, nearly every Christian recognizes the baptisms performed by nearly every other Christian. We call the church apostolic because we are bound to teach and to practice the tradition that was handed down to us, continuing all the way back to the apostles.

And we end our recitation of the Nicene Creed with a statement of hope, hope for an eternal life with God.

The creeds are somewhere between rules of faith, doctrinal statements, poems of belief, and aspirational articulations of what we hope all Christians will confess as their faith. The language is meticulously precise and yet comprehensible by anyone. If the creeds seem elusive, give them time. If it seems that you have mastered them, give them even more time and study. Our creeds are gifts: They teach us about our faith, and as we study them, we enrich and expand that very same faith.

For Reflection

✳ Christian practice has varied with statements of the creed; sometimes the creeds have read "I believe" and sometimes "We believe." What are the advantages and disadvantages to each way of reciting the creed?

✳ Every thoughtful Christian will struggle with parts of their faith at times. How does saying a creed help or hinder our struggle with faith?

✳ The creeds address themes of judgment and the end of history, yet these are often not part of our everyday conversations of faith. Why is it important for these things to be in the creeds?

✳ Look at the Apostles' Creed on page 96 and the Nicene Creed on page 358 in *The Book of Common Prayer*. What do you notice is different between the two creeds? Which creed do you prefer and why?

Chapter 14

Written for Our Learning

The Bible

Blessed Lord, who caused all holy Scriptures to be written for our learning: Grant us so to hear them, read, mark, learn and inwardly digest them, that we may embrace and ever hold fast the blessed hope of everlasting life, which you have given us in our Savior Jesus Christ; who lives and reigns with you and the Holy Spirit, one God, for ever and ever. *Amen.*

—*The Book of Common Prayer*, 236

When filling out paperwork for various church conferences, I am often asked to identify my denomination. Typically, a list features the usual suspects: Catholic, Methodist, Baptist, Episcopal, and so forth. Recently, however, I encountered a list that stopped me in my tracks. Asked to identify my denomination, I was given three selections: Catholic, Protestant, or Bible. I stared at the screen for a long while, torn as to how to identify myself. I wanted to simply type, "Yes!" Yes, I am Catholic, Protestant, and Bible! I needed a fourth option: All of the above.

The truth is, Episcopalians are all of the above. We are catholic (a word which, at its heart, simply means universal or available to all). The Episcopal Church's catholic identity is expressed through our bishops and sacraments in a way that connects to the historic beliefs and practices of the church from its earliest beginning and unites Christians around the world today. And we are Protestant, incorporating many of the best ideas of the Protestant Reformation into our beliefs and practices, including our assertion that the Bible contains all things necessary to salvation and our belief that both the Bible and our prayers should be accessible to all people. In fact, the Episcopal Church often finds the *via media*, the middle ground between Roman Catholicism and Protestantism. The via media does not mean "anything goes" but rather the middle way. Being a middle way church means that we embrace the sacramental richness of our Roman Catholic heritage as well as the theological richness of the Protestant Reformation.

But perhaps above all, the Episcopal Church is a Bible church. The Bible plays a central role in our beliefs and practices. Visit any Episcopal congregation on a Sunday and see for yourself: We take reading the Bible very seriously. Our liturgy includes four different readings from the Bible: the Old Testament, the psalms, the New Testament, and the gospel. After the Old Testament and New Testament readings, we proclaim "the Word of the Lord," a reminder that these are not just nice stories but holy, inspired words from God. And the gospel is often given special honor; many churches have a gospel procession, in which the gospel book is carried out into the middle of the church, led by torches and accompanied by singing. The people in the church typically turn and face the gospel book, a sign that we orient our bodies and our lives around the good news of Jesus Christ.

And the readings are not the only places in which we hear the words of scripture; the words of our liturgy come from the Bible as well. Approximately 70 percent of *The Book of Common Prayer* is biblical quotation—not only does the prayer book include the entire book of Psalms, but many of the most beloved and beautiful prayers and responses in the liturgy are also directly from the Bible. Our opening greeting, "the Lord be with you," comes from Ruth 2:4; the Lord's Prayer is from Matthew 6:9-13, the Sanctus or "holy, holy holy," comes from Isaiah 6:3 and Matthew 21:9, and the words said at every Holy Eucharist are from 1 Corinthians 11:24-25. Further, most of the phrases and images from our weekly collects and eucharistic prayers come directly from the Bible. As Episcopalians, the Bible saturates our liturgy: From the scriptures we read to the prayers that we say, the Bible is deeply ingrained in everything that we do.

On pages 582-808, *The Book of Common Prayer* contains the entire book of Psalms, often called the psalter. Singing or saying the psalms as part of individual prayer and corporate worship has been part of Jewish practice for thousands of years and part of Christian liturgy from its earliest days. The version of the psalms in the prayer book comes from the Coverdale translation of the Bible, which has been used in revisions of *The Book of Common Prayer* since its first version in 1549.

In our current, 1979 *Book of Common Prayer*, the psalter is slightly modernized from the original Coverdale version, while retaining continuity with the prayer book tradition. You might notice slight differences between the psalter and the New Revised Standard Version or other Bible translations, but the phrasing and division of the verses makes the prayer book psalter particularly suited to responsive reading and singing. Suggestions for a variety of different ways to sing or say the psalms in worship are included on pages 582-584.

Reading the Bible

The question is not whether Episcopalians read and honor the Bible—we do! The question is instead how Episcopalians read and honor the Bible. We get a glimpse of the answer in a somewhat surprising place—our services of ordination.

Our *Book of Common Prayer* includes three services of ordination: for bishop, priest, and deacon. In each service, the person being ordained makes vows and promises that are specific to the particular ministry. But at the beginning of each service of ordination, all three orders make the same declaration, including this line: "I solemnly declare that I do believe the Holy Scriptures of the Old and New Testaments to be the Word of God, and to contain all things necessary to salvation" (526). This declaration is so important that *The Book of Common Prayer* instructs that it must be provided as a printed document, and every ordinand must sign the declaration during the ceremony, in the sight of all present (527).

So, what does this tell us about how Episcopalians read and understand the Bible? First, the declaration begins with the phrase, "the Holy Scriptures of the Old and New Testaments." This is an important distinction: Many Christians focus heavily on the New Testament, often to the exclusion of the Old Testament. And some Christians give the Old Testament more credence than the New Testament. As Episcopalians, we clearly state that both the Old and New Testaments are Holy Scripture. We don't throw out or dismiss the stories of the Old Testament. God's revelation to humanity begins with Genesis 1:1, and the story of God's great love for us is constant and consistent throughout the Old and New Testaments. The Old Testament is the Bible that Jesus read, knew, and loved. And thus it speaks to us too.

Secondly, we, as Episcopalians, say that the Holy Scriptures of the Old and New Testaments are "the Word of God." We proclaim this same phrase in worship in response to the scripture readings. Quite simply, this means that we believe the Bible is more than nice stories; it is the Word of God. In the Catechism, we explain this phrase further: "Q. Why do we call the Holy Scriptures the Word of God? A. We call them the Word of God because God inspired their human authors and because God still speaks to us through the Bible" (853). The Bible is the Word of God because at the time of its writing, it was inspired by God and because, when we hear these words today, we, too, can be inspired by God. The answer in the Catechism also acknowledges the human component: Human authors wrote the Bible, and human listeners hear these words today. But the words are not *just* human-composed; they are not simply stories written by humans about God, with no involvement from God. They are, in some mysterious way that we can neither quantify nor understand, inspired by God. So the scriptures are both human and holy; they are written and heard by people. And both those who wrote and those who hear were and are inspired by God.

Finally, the vow taken by ordinands proclaims that the Holy Scriptures "contain all things necessary to salvation." This is important: People don't need any additional knowledge beyond the Bible to learn about God's salvation. As Episcopalians, you don't have to have read or prayed *The Book of Common Prayer* or believe some set of ideas promoted by another book or source. The Bible is our primary text. Can we learn about and meet and experience God in other ways and places? Of course we can! But the additional stuff isn't necessary. The basics of the Christian faith are conveyed in the Bible, and Episcopalians aren't required to believe or subscribe to anything that is not in the Bible.

The Bible, Literally

From the liturgy, ordination vows, and Catechism, we see that Episcopalians take the Bible *seriously*. But that doesn't mean that we read the Bible *literally*.

The truth is, no one reads the Bible literally, even people who claim they do. In John 8:12, Jesus says: "I am the light of the world." If we took that literally, it would mean we believe that Jesus glowed, that he emanated light. If Jesus literally glowed, the disciples never needed light and candles; they could just stand Jesus in the middle of the room and use him to read by! Obviously, Jesus didn't mean this phrase literally. He meant us to hear these words as a gripping image so that we might understand Jesus and his presence in the world in a new way through the metaphor of darkness and light.

There are no literalists of the scriptures. Every reading of the Bible requires us to interpret what we are reading, to decide how we understand the images that the Bible uses, to sift through what is metaphor and what is factual description, what is imagery, and what is command. But even though we don't take every word of the Bible literally (again, no one does!), we do absolutely take the Bible seriously. And we believe that the Bible is both real and true. We believe the Bible contains real stories about real people who had real experiences of God in the real world. And we believe that the Bible is completely, deeply true. The Bible tells us truth about ourselves, about the world, and about God. Often that truth is told through metaphor and poetry that is not literal, and we might have to wrestle with its meaning in order to fully understand what God is saying to us.

Understanding the Bible seriously rather than literally is hard. We do this work, in part, by learning more about the Bible so that we can better understand and interpret it. For instance, it might help in our understanding if we recognized the Bible not as a single book, but a library or collection of sixty-six books bound in one volume.

The Old Testament, sometimes called the Hebrew Bible, is made up of three main sections: the Torah or Pentateuch, the Prophets, and the Writings.

❖ **The Torah** (also called the Pentateuch) includes the first five books of the Bible: Genesis, Exodus, Leviticus, Deuteronomy, and Numbers.

❖ **The Prophets** include both the major prophets, like Isaiah and Jeremiah, and the twelve minor prophets, the shorter prophetic books such as Micah and Habakkuk.

❖ **The Writings** include historical writings, such as Chronicles, poetic writings like the Psalms, and wisdom writings like Proverbs and Song of Solomon.

The New Testament is composed of four sections.

❖ **The Gospels** are Matthew, Mark, Luke, and John.

❖ **The Book of Acts** tells the story of the early churches and the work of the Holy Spirit.

❖ **The Epistles** feature the letters of Paul and other early Christian missionaries.

❖ **The Revelation to John**, the final book of the Bible, is the account of John's mystical vision of God's final judgment.

Additionally, Anglicans also include the Apocrypha, a collection of books between the Old and New Testaments (called intertestamental books). These books have been included in some editions of the Bible since the fifth century and were written at the same time as many of the other books in the Bible. The Roman Catholic and Anglican churches both include the Apocrypha in the Bible, although it is not given the same status as the Old and New Testaments, which are agreed upon across denominations. Still, passages from the Apocrypha are occasionally read in worship as part of our lectionary, and our church agrees that the Apocrypha are helpful for instruction and learning.

The books of the Old Testament, the New Testament, and the Apocrypha were written by different people in different places in different times in different languages. Some of the books were written in Hebrew, some in Greek, some in Aramaic. Not only are the languages different but so too are the genres. The Bible is not all one kind of writing. Some books are history, some are poetry, some are law, some are prophecy, some are narratives, some are letters or epistles. Different kinds of writing occur even within the same book! From one verse to the next, the Bible can change between poetry and prose, between comparison and command.

All of these variations, including style, tone, and authorship, require careful reading to begin to understand and interpret the Bible. So how do Episcopalians read the Bible? One of the collects in *The Book of Common Prayer* gives us a template for how to understand and interpret the Bible. It says:

> Blessed Lord, who caused all holy Scriptures to be written for our learning: Grant us so to hear them, read, mark, learn and inwardly digest them, that we may embrace and ever hold fast the blessed hope of everlasting life, which you have given us in our Savior Jesus Christ; who lives and reigns with you and the Holy Spirit, one God, for ever and ever. *Amen.* (236)

This prayer offers a pattern for how we can and should read the Bible as Episcopalians: It begins with a reminder that the holy scriptures originate and are grounded in God. God caused the Bible to be written. And God did so "for our learning." The Bible was written by God for us. The Bible is fundamentally about relationship; it is a conversation, a communication, between God and humanity. Further, the Bible exists so that we might learn more about God and more about ourselves, about our history and who we are today, about those who have followed God and those who have failed, and about what we are called, as followers of Jesus, to take up and what we are called to lay down.

Learning about God

Believing that the holy scriptures are from God, for us, and written so that we might learn, we encounter the next challenge: How do we undertake this learning? The collect names six specific ways that we can engage the Bible in order to meet God.

Hear: We usually think of the Bible as a book that we read, but this collect reminds us that the first way that we encounter the Bible is by *hearing* it. Before these words were written down, much of the Bible was an oral tradition, stories told through generations so that people would remember the mighty deeds of God. There is a reason that we say the Bible "speaks."

Each week, when we gather together as a community, we hear the Bible read aloud in our service of Holy Eucharist. It is important, as much as we are able, to try to hear the words rather than read them from our bulletins or Bibles. Reading is an individual activity, each person individually focused on her own paper. Listening is a communal activity, the entire community focused on one voice, proclaiming aloud the Word of the Lord. The different voices of the lectors, who read aloud the lessons in worship, remind us of the different voices

Hear

The collect reminds us that the first—and primary—way that we encounter the scriptures is to *hear* them in community, in our worship, read aloud and proclaimed as "the Word of the Lord."

Tips for hearing scripture:

- Put down your bulletin and try to listen actively instead of reading. This can be uncomfortable or difficult but keep trying. You can always go home and read the biblical text later; this is the time to try to *hear* it.

- If you struggle with hearing, sit in a place that makes hearing easier, perhaps toward the front. If your church offers assisted listening devices, use them.

- Practice active listening. Really try to focus on what is being said. Close your eyes if that helps you to listen better.

of the authors of the Bible. Listening to the Bible read aloud can help us hear things that we might otherwise miss or be struck by a familiar reading in a new way.

Even struggling to hear, or hearing imperfectly, can help teach us about the beauty and difficulty of the Bible. Which words did you hear, even if you didn't hear all of them? Where did your mind go, if you struggled to keep focus? How can you discipline yourself so that you can both listen and hear better? How does hearing the Bible in community change the way that you understand it?

Read: Of course, hearing scripture read aloud in worship is not the *only* way that we encounter the Bible. We are also able to read the Bible, for ourselves, as individuals. In our modern world, it is easy to forget how extraordinary and radical this is. For centuries, very few people were able to read the Bible since most of the population was illiterate.

And even fewer people were able to afford copies of the Bible, since the Bible was written out by hand on precious materials

> **Read**
>
> To read the Bible, you need a Bible that you can read. If you already have a Bible that you love—read it! If you struggle to read or understand your Bible, try a different Bible. Some people like a translation like *The Message*, which is a modern-day rendering of scripture. Other people enjoy a study Bible, such as the New Interpreter's Study Bible, which includes helpful notes and summaries so that you can learn more about the Bible. If you have a hard time wading through the Bible, try *The Path*! Using excerpts from the New Revised Standard Version, *The Path* presents the narrative arc of the Bible from Genesis to Revelation and is published by Forward Movement.

that were incredibly expensive. For a long time, reading and interpreting the Bible was a privilege reserved for the wealthy and educated elite. Reformers and missionaries have fought and died so that we can have access to read the Bible, in our own homes, in our own languages. Thanks to their work, in our time, everyday people can hold in their hands and read for themselves the Holy Word of God.

We are expected not only to hear short sections of the Bible read aloud once a week in worship but also to read the Bible ourselves, every day. It is not an either/or proposition but a both/and. We *both* hear the Bible read aloud in worship, *and* we read the Bible for ourselves. We go home during the week and read the same scriptures that we heard on Sunday, perhaps noticing different aspects by reading them on paper that we might have missed in hearing them. We can and should read other parts of the Bible: the context around the passages we heard, in order to fit them into a larger narrative, or other parts of the Bible that we do not hear read aloud in church. It is not enough simply to hear the scriptures read aloud in church on Sunday. We are called to a next step, a deeper engagement—to read the Bible for ourselves, as well.

Mark

Some people like to literally mark in their Bibles, making notes in the margins, highlighting or underlining key words, and writing observations and questions. Another way to be sure you are paying attention to a biblical text is to read it more than once. Read the text the first time and see what word or phrase stands out to you. Read it again and see what else you notice. Read it a third time and see how the text is speaking to you. Coming back to the text again and again is a way to be more deeply attentive to what it says and to what God is saying to you through the words.

Mark: Next we are reminded that we don't just read or listen to the scriptures casually or carelessly. We are instead reminded to mark them. Mark, in this sense, means to notice or pay careful attention to something. We shouldn't just skim over the Bible in order to check off "read the Bible" from our to-do list. Instead we are called to give close attention to what we are reading and to notice things that are interesting or confusing, uplifting or upsetting. Reading the Bible with this kind of care and attention is more demanding than simply scanning through the words, but it is also more rewarding. With this deliberate practice of marking scripture, we begin to notice new things in the Bible—and hear the words speaking to us more powerfully.

Learn: Next, our collect tells us that we are called to learn the scriptures. This is the next step in the process of scriptural engagement. It would be all too easy to hear or read the Bible, say to ourselves, "Huh, that's interesting," and then stop there. But we are called to more than that. We are called to learn, to change, to grow in response to what we hear and read in the Bible. Learning, in its most simple definition, means to "to gain knowledge or skill by studying, practicing, being taught, or experiencing something."

When we increase our frequency of reading and engaging the Bible, we gain more knowledge about the Bible and become more skilled interpreters of the sacred text. We learn by reading the Bible again and again ... and again and again, always discovering something new. We read the words of the Bible, and then we study them, looking more deeply into the Bible for patterns and connections. We can also put the words of the Bible into practice, learning through experience.

Too often, Christians, perhaps especially Episcopalians, have been taught that "Sunday school" is only for children, and confirmation is graduation from learning in church. Nothing could be further from the truth. Learning is a lifelong endeavor. We are called, as Christians, to constantly learn more about our faith, discovering new ways of understanding the scriptures and connecting to God. The Bible is rich enough that we can learn new things every time we read it, and we can hear God speaking to us in new and different ways.

Learn

Most churches have formation opportunities for adults, as well as children. Attend formation on Sunday mornings ("Sunday school") or sign up for a weekday Bible study, book group, or other formation class. We can learn a lot, not only from the Bible but also from one another, when we remember and treat Christian formation as a lifelong endeavor.

Many wonderful resources are available for learning from the Bible on your own. A good study Bible is a great start. Commentary series can help you go even deeper into God's word. Check out the resource section at the end of this book or ask your priest for suggestions.

Inwardly Digest: Encountering the Bible is not just a head exercise, a cerebral process of thinking and evaluating. The fifth command of our collect, to inwardly digest the scriptures, reminds us that encountering the Bible is a

Inwardly Digest

This step is, perhaps, the hardest, because it's not an intellectual exercise. To inwardly digest the Bible, we are called to be changed, to be transformed, by it. When we read the Bible, we cannot merely ask ourselves, "What have I learned?" We instead must ask ourselves, "How am I being called to change?"

Digesting takes time; we have to return to the Bible again and again, to gnaw on it. Inwardly digesting means returning to old passages of the Bible and seeing if they speak to us in new ways.

One way to take the Bible more deeply into yourself, to inwardly digest it, is to memorize it. Pick a favorite verse or verses from the Bible. Read that section again and again every day, until you have learned it by heart. Then pick another one and add it. Soon you will have digested many bites of scripture, and they will empower and nourish you.

whole-body activity. In our worship on Sundays, we take in the literal food of communion: The bread and wine become the Body and Blood of our Lord Jesus Christ, feeding us in body and soul. We are also fed on the Word of God. Throughout the Bible, we are told that the words of scripture have a nourishing quality, that they taste like honey (Psalm 119:103). Pastor Eugene Peterson, in his wonderful work *Eat This Book*, explores the words of God to the prophet Ezekiel, when God commands Ezekiel to "eat this scroll" (Ezekiel 3:3). Peterson uses this as a metaphor for the way that Christians are called to interact with the scriptures, the Bible, by taking the words into ourselves, gnawing on them like a dog at a bone, chewing them over and over to see what new nourishment they might offer, what last remnants might cling to the bone. That idea is precisely what our collect proclaims, that we are called not only to hear, read, mark, and learn the Bible but also to inwardly digest it. When we eat something, we take it into ourselves, and it becomes our sustenance and substance. The Bible is meant to act that way in us. We are asked to take the Bible into ourselves, to let it sustain us, and to let it transform us, so that we can become what it proclaims.

Embrace and Ever Hold Fast: Our collect concludes with a final active phrase, "embrace and ever hold fast." This final phrase is not a command but a hope. The Bible is the story of God's great love for us, a story that is full of hope, a story that offers the gift and promise of everlasting life. God's hope is that we will embrace what has been offered. If we take the time to do our part, to follow these actions detailed by the collect, we will hear the story of God, who loves us, who embraces us as God's beloved children, and who holds fast to us, even when we wander and stray. In response, God calls us to reciprocate what God has already done for us: to embrace and ever hold fast the gift of God in Christ, the blessed hope of everlasting life.

For Reflection

✳ Have you ever sat down and read all or big portions of the Bible on your own? If so, what was that like? If you haven't, why not?

✳ Who is your favorite character from the Bible, and why is that person your favorite?

✳ In response to the biblical readings in worship, we proclaim "the Word of the Lord ... Thanks be to God." Because we understand the truth of scripture to be contained in the entirety of the Bible, we say this even when the readings are difficult or upsetting. How can we see difficult texts or texts that challenge us as God's Word?

✳ In our liturgy, we read the Bible from a lectern, using a book "of appropriate size and dignity" so that God's word is proclaimed from a fitting symbol. Many parishes have gospel processions, carrying the gospel book into the midst of the congregation with singing or torches. How do these actions affect our relationship with the Bible?

Chapter 15

Continually Given to Good Works
Salvation and Grace

Lord, we pray that your grace may always precede and
follow us, that we may continually be given to good works;
through Jesus Christ our Lord, who lives and reigns with
you and the Holy Spirit, one God, now and for ever. *Amen*.

—*The Book of Common Prayer*, pp. 234-235

Becoming a Christian, and more specifically an Episcopalian,
can make you feel like you need a dictionary. Our *Book of
Common Prayer* is full of beautiful but not often-used words
like inestimable and unfeignedly, oblation and penitent.
And churches have their own vocabulary—almost a distinct
language: We call the lobby a "narthex," the fancy outfits that
the clergy wear are "vestments," and the tabernacle where
we keep the blessed bread and wine is the "aumbry." In the
beginning, you'll probably have a lot of questions—and may
spend some time looking up words in a dictionary or online.

Some of the words we use in church are difficult, not because
they are unfamiliar but because their meaning is so rich

If you want to learn about some of the unfamiliar or strange words that we use in church, there are some great resources: Check out the *Episcopal Handbook, An Episcopal Dictionary of the Church*, or the *Oxford Dictionary of the Christian Church* to learn more. The Episcopal Church website (www.episcopalchurch.org) also has a very thorough glossary. Forward Movement offers some pamphlets that are perfect as a resource for you or to share with others. They include: "Episcopal Language"; "Welcome to the Episcopal Church"; and "Customs and Practices in the Episcopal Church." And you can always ask your priest!

and deep that they require exploration and discussion. Salvation and grace are two of these words. They are central to our vocabulary of our faith, and we say them often, yet they can take a lifetime to understand.

Being Saved

I grew up attending a Christian camp in the mountains of North Carolina every summer. It was a wonderful, beautiful place, where I got to do fun things like hiking and canoeing and archery. It was also a holy, inspiring place where I grew closer to God through daily worship, Bible study, and nightly devotions. On Sunday evenings, all of the campers and counselors would gather around the campfire to sing songs, and women from the oldest group of campers would give testimonies. Each summer I heard young women from all different places and backgrounds speak passionately and powerfully about the ways they had encountered God in Christ.

Over the years, I worked my way up from the youngest group of campers to the oldest, and finally it was my turn. I was expected to stand up in front of my fellow campers and give my testimony. And I had no idea what to say.

My friends and fellow campers had talked about their inspiring stories of being "saved." Some of them told stories of how they had been saved from helplessness or hopelessness. Others told of being saved from addiction or abuse. Some had tangible experiences of the risen Jesus or physically felt the Holy Spirit. Others had traveled with missionary parents to serve the least and the lost in far-flung countries of the world.

I was a middle-class white girl who had an uneventful childhood. I was a faithful Episcopalian more at home with ancient prayers than extemporaneous prophecy. I was the ultimate oldest child—I got good grades, followed all the rules, and never worried my parents. I had never had anything exciting or important happen to me. And as I tried to prepare my testimony, I had no idea what to say. What kind of story did I have to tell?

But as I prayed and read the Bible, I came to a realization: Jesus saved me from believing that I had to be or ever could be "good enough" to warrant salvation. Jesus saved me from believing I had to (or even could) earn God's love by always being perfect. As an overachieving child, my mantra in life had been to work hard, do better, be perfect. But the gospel of salvation is that there is nothing that I can do (or fail to do) that will cause God to love me any more or any less. I had spent most of my life trying to deserve God's love, believing, somewhere deep down, that I needed to be good and do good things for God to love me.

I meet lots of people who believe the same thing that I did: that they have to earn God's love by working harder, doing better, being perfect. And that belief is debilitating; trying to earn God's love is exhausting. It leads to lives full of endless striving, of always feeling "not enough." Being saved from this futile idea is no less (and no more) miraculous than the many other stories of salvation I have heard over the years. I was enslaved to the idea that I could earn God's love, and I desperately needed to be saved from a life of trying to be "good enough." Being freed from expectations of perfection allowed me to grow more deeply in my faith, to discover the love of God that knows no bounds, to begin to serve God, not out of obligation or fear but out of joy and gratitude. Realizing that I could never be good enough to earn God's love (and could never fail enough to lose it) set me free. The idea that Jesus saves us from trying to save ourselves is a central tenet of our faith. Another word for that is grace.

Grace

In *The Book of Common Prayer*, the Catechism defines grace as "God's favor toward us, unearned and undeserved; by grace God forgives our sins, enlightens our minds, stirs our hearts, and strengthens our wills" (858). This definition points us toward a couple of key ideas about grace.

The first is that grace is unearned and undeserved. This is a crucial point yet difficult to fully comprehend. We live in a culture that values pulling ourselves up by our bootstraps, and we're often told that "God helps those who help themselves." Yet neither of those ideas are found anywhere in the Bible and are, in fact, contrary to scripture and Christian teaching. People don't receive grace because they behave well or work hard or do the right things. God's grace isn't about us or about our actions at all—God's grace is about God's goodness, God's love, God's favor. Grace is about God, not about us. There is nothing good that we can do to earn God's love, and nothing bad that we can do to stop receiving God's love. Grace is the promise that God's love is a free gift to us, regardless of how badly we screw up or how often we fail to do the good that we intend.

Sit with that for a moment. Let it sink in. God loves you, no matter what you have done or failed to do. There is nothing that will make God love you any more or any less. That, in a nutshell, is grace. It is incredibly good news, for all of us, since none of us is perfect, yet all of us receive God's grace as a gift (Romans 3:23-24).

But here's the catch. The amazing, incredible gift of God's grace is for everyone, not only for you. You receive God's love, even when you don't deserve it. And so does your enemy, or the person you think is lazy, or the one whose opinion you disagree with. Grace is a free gift to everyone, not just those we like or agree with. Sometimes the hardest thing about grace is believing that God offers it to us, and other times the hardest thing about grace is realizing that God offers it to everyone else too!

Saved from Sin

The unearned, undeserved gift of God's grace is a good thing. If we're honest with ourselves, we know that we *don't* deserve the gift of God's love, and that, no matter how hard we might try, we could never do enough to earn it. The truth is, the world we live in is broken. And the people around us are broken. And we, ourselves, are broken.

We are broken because we don't do the things that we know we should do, and we do the things that we know we shouldn't. We act with selfishness, meanness, and judgment. We act out of prejudice or fear or anger. Sometimes it's not our action, but our inaction that is so troubling: we get too busy or too distracted or too tired, and we don't do the good, important, holy things that we know we *should* do. And sometimes, it's not our action or our inaction but our attitude that's the problem. We do the right things for the wrong reasons. Or we might act rightly, while still engaging in uncharitable thoughts. Another word for all of this brokenness, in ourselves and in the world, is sin.

Things Done and Left Undone

Our prayer book defines sin as "the seeking of our own will instead of the will of God, thus distorting our relationship with God, with other people, and with all creation" (848). Sometimes we sin through direct actions, such as hurting another person or wasting resources entrusted to us. Other times we sin by failing to act, such as our failure to stand with those who are oppressed. Even something as innocent as buying a new phone could involve sin, because the working conditions of those who made the phone may be intolerable and the raw materials to make that phone might come at the expense of environmental damage in countries we will never visit. It seems that our very participation in life—and in systems of commerce and oppression—can lead us to sin.

I grew up thinking that sinning was pretty much the same thing as not being nice to someone, but sin is much more pervasive than that and much harder to avoid. The reason to avoid sin is that it separates us from God and from other people. To reject sin is to choose union with God and our neighbor. But we cannot do it on our own. We need the free gift of God's grace to avoid sin and to be forgiven from those sins we inevitably commit.

Misunderstanding Grace

Since grace is a gift from God, we might be inclined to see it as license—tacit permission—to do whatever we want. If God loves us no matter what, then as long as we have prayed and asked Jesus' forgiveness, we should be able to do whatever we want and still "get in to heaven," right? Well, not exactly.

In the New Testament, we read in the Letter of James,

> What good is it, my brothers and sisters, if you say you have faith but do not have works? Can faith save you? If a brother or sister is naked and lacks daily food, and one of you says to them, "Go in peace; keep warm and eat your fill," and yet you do not supply their bodily needs, what is the good of that? So faith by itself, if it has no works, is dead. (James 2:14-17)

This is why the second part of the definition in the Catechism says, "by grace God forgives our sins, enlightens our minds, stirs our hearts, and strengthens our wills" (858). The gift of God's grace is active and powerful; grace works in our minds, our hearts, and our wills to enlighten, stir, and strengthen us. There is an expectation that the power of God's grace working in us will change us, enliven and inspire us, so that we can work on behalf of God's kingdom in the world.

Now, this isn't a tit-for-tat, where God has given us the gift of grace, and we have to spend the rest of our lives repaying that gift through our service or love or work. That wouldn't be a gift—that would be a loan. Grace is a gift, a free gift. We can't do anything to earn it, and we can't do anything to make God take it away. But we can (and should) live our lives in response to that love. The gift of God's grace is so astonishing that it urges us onward to do good things: not because we have to but because we want to, not out of duty but out of love. In fact, living lives of love and service in response to God's grace is how we were created to live.

As Paul writes, "For by grace you have been saved through faith, and this is not your own doing; it is the gift of God— not the result of works, so that no one may boast. For we are what he has made us, created in Christ Jesus for good works, which God prepared beforehand to be our way of life" (Ephesians 2:8-10). Paul's words are astonishing. The gift of God's grace allows us to become who we were created to be and to do what we were created to do.

In Genesis, God looked at humanity and said that humans were "very good" (1:31). We were created as good and created for good—living lives of generosity, love, kindness, and joy in relationship to God, humanity, and creation.

Saved for Something

One of the reasons I struggled so much with my testimony as a teenager was that I had a limited understanding of salvation. I thought of salvation as being saved from something: People are saved from addiction or abuse, or in my case, from self-reliance and self-sufficiency. And that is certainly true; Jesus saves us from sin and death and from all the other conditions and mindsets that enslave us.

But James and Paul and many other witnesses from the Bible and Christian tradition remind us that we are also saved *for* something. We are saved for abundant life, saved for service to God and God's people, saved for the building up of the kingdom of God on earth as it is in heaven. *Sozo,* the Greek word for salvation, contains a wealth of meaning, far beyond simply being saved from hurt or danger. *Sozo* means health and wholeness, wellness in the deepest sense of that word. Salvation in the Bible is about fullness of life.

When we limit salvation and grace to life in heaven, a life free from sin and death, we only get part of the picture. The salvation of Jesus Christ is about eternal life in heaven, but it's also about eternal life that begins now. In the service of Holy Eucharist in *The Book of Common Prayer,* the ministers distribute the bread and the wine while saying this sentence: "The Body (Blood) of our Lord Jesus Christ keep you in everlasting life." Have you ever noticed that verb "keep" before? It might seem like a small word, but it's a big theological statement. "Keep" reminds us that we have already begun experiencing everlasting life—right here and right now. When we are nourished with the Body and Blood of Christ in the eucharist, it is keeping us, sustaining us, in our eternal life, which is already underway.

From the moment that we receive God's grace, we are being saved for something, filled with God's grace that enlightens our minds, stirs our hearts, and strengthens our wills. Our salvation is lived out in this world, as well as in the world to come. The grace of God finds expression in the works that we do in God's name, not because we have to but because we want to, and because God, working in us, can do infinitely more than we can ask or imagine.

For Reflection

✳ In the Episcopal Church, we don't often hear sermons about sin and salvation; it's not language that we use comfortably. Why do you think this might be?

✳ In this chapter we hear about being saved *from* something and being saved *for* something. What have you been saved from, and what have you been saved for?

✳ There are two aspects of grace that can be hard to accept. One is to actually believe that God loves us, completely, no matter what. The other is that God loves everybody else too, completely, no matter what. How do you wrestle with these difficult aspects of grace?

✳ Tell a story of a time when you had a personal experience of God's grace.

Chapter 16

Accept and Fulfill Our Petitions

Prayer

Heavenly Father, you have promised to hear what we ask in the Name of your Son: Accept and fulfill our petitions, we pray, not as we ask in our ignorance, nor as we deserve in our sinfulness, but as you know and love us in your Son Jesus Christ our Lord. *Amen.*

—*The Book of Common Prayer*, p. 394

In a sense, this entire book is about prayer. We have walked through the liturgies, the scripted prayers, of the Episcopal Church. We have reflected on how we pray when we gather as a community for eucharist, baptism, and other special celebrations. And in Chapter 9, we explored in depth the Daily Office, the quintessential "Anglican" way to pray.

But so far, this discussion has been about our "prayers," the specific words and forms we use when we pray. In this chapter we will take a step back and talk more comprehensively about prayer (rather than prayers): what prayer is (and what it isn't), what prayer is "for," and different ways to pray, beyond our church's set liturgies.

According to the Catechism, "Prayer is responding to God, by thought and by deeds, with or without words" (856). That's an incredibly broad definition! Prayer includes both our thoughts and our actions; prayer happens both with and without words. Any response to God, whatever form it might take, is a kind of prayer. While it is wonderful to understand the umbrella of prayer as covering a great variety of territory, it can also be daunting to think of prayer so broadly. Luckily, the Catechism continues, describing seven particular kinds of prayer: adoration, praise, thanksgiving, penitence, oblation, intercession, and petition. By looking more closely at these particular kinds of prayer, we learn about what prayer is and the different ways that we are called to pray.

Types of Prayer

The Catechism begins the description of the principal kinds of prayer with two types that might be unfamiliar. **Adoration** is "the lifting up of the heart and mind to God, asking nothing but to enjoy God's presence" (857). This might be a surprising way to think about prayer, because adoration is less about a specific kind of action or a certain set of words and instead about an attitude, an orientation of our hearts and minds rooted in the enjoyment of God's very presence. This attitude of orientation is related to—but slightly different from—the next kind of prayer. **Praise**, the act of glorifying God because of God's goodness, is a fundamental part of who we are as humans. It is important to note that praise is not offering thanks to God for the things that God has done for us (that's thanksgiving, which we hear about next). Praise is simply expressing admiration and awe for who God *is*. "We praise God, not to obtain anything, but because God's Being draws praise from us" (857).

The third kind of prayer, closely related to the first two, is **thanksgiving**: giving thanks to God "for all the blessings of this life, for our redemption, and for whatever draws us closer to God" (857). Often, prayers of thanksgiving are more specific than those of adoration or praise; we move from adoring and praising God for God's very being to giving thanks to God for particular things, actions, or experiences in our lives and the lives of those around us.

These first three kinds of prayer described in the Catechism are prayers of joy. This is essential to our practice of prayer, rooting our relationship with God in an attitude of awe, enjoyment, and celebration. Of course, awe and joy are not all of the story. Because we live in a world that is broken by sin, and we ourselves are far from perfect, our prayers aren't exclusively words of celebration and joy. An essential part of prayer is being honest with God about our failures in prayers of **penitence**. "In penitence, we confess our sins and make restitution where possible, with the intention to amend our lives" (857). Prayers of penitence allow us to take an honest look at ourselves, at our lives and our shortcomings, so that we can acknowledge what we have done wrong and strive to do better in the future. In prayers of penitence, we submit ourselves to God, in the promise that God will forgive and renew us, so that we are not defined by the worst parts of ourselves. It is then, after honestly acknowledging our shortcomings, that we are ready to give ourselves over, fully, to God in prayers of **oblation**. "Oblation is an offering of ourselves, our lives and labors, in union with Christ, for the purposes of God" (857). Out of thanksgiving for all that God has done in and for us, we offer ourselves in service to God and God's purposes in the world.

The last two kinds of prayer described in the Catechism are probably the most familiar. In prayers of **intercession**, we bring "before God the needs of others" (857). Specifically, the forms for the prayers of the people in *The Book of Common Prayer* instruct us to make intercession for "the Universal Church, its members, and its mission; the Nation and all in authority; the welfare of the world; the concerns of the local community; those who suffer and those in any trouble; the departed" (383). This list reminds us of the breadth that our prayers for others can and should take. Intercession is not merely praying for our family and close friends who have asked for our prayers (though that is important); our intercessions should extend to the welfare of the community and, indeed, the whole world. We are commanded to pray particularly for those who suffer and are in trouble, our immediate friends and family, and those we may not know. In our prayers of intercession, we focus beyond ourselves to the whole human family, a reminder of Jesus' command to love our neighbors as ourselves.

Finally, our Catechism turns to prayers of **petition**. "In petition we present our own needs, that God's will may be done" (857). Bringing our needs before God is an important part of prayer; God deeply desires relationship with us, and being honest with God about our desires is a fundamental part of our relationship with God. We should not shy away from naming our needs before God in prayers of petition. And yet, as this definition reminds us, petition is presenting our needs *that God's will may be done.*

Too often we approach prayer as though God is some sort of vending machine, and if we simply "put in our money" (i.e. our prayers), we'll get our candy bar (i.e. whatever we're asking for). The Catechism reminds us that prayer is broader and deeper. We certainly pray to name our needs before God. But we also pray in order to rejoice in God's presence, to praise God's very being, to thank God for the blessings of our life, to ask forgiveness for the things we have done wrong, to offer ourselves more fully to God's service, and to make requests not only for ourselves but also on behalf of the whole world. And in our petitions, we do not pray in order to get what we think we want (for ourselves or others). We pray, just as Jesus himself did in the face of death, that God's will may be done.

One of my favorite ways of describing prayer is by saying that "prayer is a conversation that takes place in relationship." In fact, my relationship with God in prayer is a lot like my relationship with my spouse.

❖ Sometimes, my spouse and I spend time simply enjoying one another's presence. We don't have to say anything or do anything; we can simply sit in comfortable silence and *be* together. That's a bit like adoration.

❖ And sometimes I tell my spouse, through my words or in my actions, that I am deeply grateful, not for something specific he has done but simply for *who he is*: for his generosity and thoughtfulness. I am overwhelmed with gratitude that he is in my life. That's a little like praise.

❖ It's also important, for the health of our relationship, that I tell my spouse thank you on a regular basis. Sometimes I express gratitude for the big things that he does and sometimes for the little things that are easy to overlook; that's like thanksgiving.

❖ Often, I need to apologize to my spouse because I've done something wrong or forgotten to do something I was supposed to do. I try (though I often fail) to make those apologies real and not simply lip service; when I've really messed up, I work hard to make it right again. That's similar to penitence.

❖ When my spouse expresses frustration or is overwhelmed or needs something, I say, "How can I help?" Sometimes I step in and help without even being asked. I offer myself for support and assistance, however I can. That's kind of like oblation.

❖ And of course, my relationship with my spouse involves asking for things—for myself or for others. When I need help, I turn to my spouse for support and assistance. Sometimes that assistance is an action that helps "fix" a problem or achieve a goal. But often the support I seek is advice, reassurance, comfort, and strength in the midst of a struggle. Seeking help from my spouse, whatever form it might take, is akin to intercession and petition.

This is, on some level, what prayer is like—it's a conversation that takes place in relationship. It involves both talking and listening. It involves times of comfortable silence and enjoyment of one another's presence. It involves both words and actions. It involves both offering and receiving help. It involves both giving and taking (and sometimes just being together).

The truth is that my relationship with my spouse (or with any person) *needs* all these different kinds of interaction in order to be healthy. Our relationship would be badly damaged if I approached every interaction with an agenda. It wouldn't be a healthy relationship if I only talked to my spouse when I wanted or needed something from him, if I became angry if he didn't do exactly what I wanted all the time, if I never said thank you or apologized, or if I engaged in daily interactions with a tit-for-tat mentality.

The same is true with our relationship with God. Prayer isn't about one kind of interaction with God; it is about relating with God in the richness of adoration, praise, thanksgiving, petition, oblation, and intercession. Prayer is a conversation that takes place in relationship.

Why Do We Pray?

One of the questions I am most frequently asked as a priest is, "Does prayer *really* work?" Often, this question comes in response to a situation of deep pain: a person has prayed, fervently, for something that didn't happen—perhaps a job promotion that never came or a hope that was never realized or even physical healing for a loved one who died. These questions are painful and difficult; they are questions that believers throughout the ages have asked again and again: When we reach out to God in prayer, does it actually do anything? Does prayer matter?

How we answer that question depends on what we think prayer *is* and what we think prayer is *for*. If we believe that prayer is like a vending machine, where we put in our money and receive a product in exchange, then we become disillusioned when we don't get what we "paid for." If we think that prayer is an assignment at work—something we do in order to earn money or status or acclaim—then we become frustrated when we aren't rewarded for our hard work and good behavior. If we think of prayer as a voicemail that we leave for God and then wait for God to get back to us with an "answer" to our question, then we become angry when we never get a return phone call.

But thinking about prayer as a conversation that takes place in relationship fundamentally changes the way that we approach prayer, and it changes what "success" looks like. What if the goal of prayer is not simply to put in our money and get what we want but instead to engage in real, deep conversation with God? Then prayer works, not when you get what you want, but any time that you engage in conversation and you find relationship.

Prayer works because it is important, in any relationship, to be honest, to say what we really want and really hope for and really need, and the act of approaching God in prayer, of naming what we yearn for, in itself builds relationship. It works because, in the act of praying, we are changed—we realize that we are not alone, no matter how alone we feel. We find strength or comfort or at least release of the feelings that have built up inside of us. Sometimes, when I'm talking to my spouse, I just need to be "heard." I'll say, "I don't need you to fix this, I just need you to listen." At the end of our conversation, there might not be any change in the situation, in the outward reality of the world; nothing will be "fixed." And yet, the conversation has "worked" because I have been heard. Prayer is often very much like that.

That is not to say that prayer *only* changes us and our attitudes (though if and when that happens, it is a miracle as well!). The witness of scripture is clear that God sometimes miraculously intervenes to change circumstances—God protects the people when leading them out of Egypt (Exodus 14), feeds the Israelites with manna from heaven (Exodus 16), heals the sick and lame (Matthew 9:18-34), and sets prisoners free (Acts 16:25-34). The followers of Jesus continue to heal people in Christ's name (Acts 5:12-16). The prayers in our *Book of Common Prayer* reflect the reality that we believe God does intervene with mighty action in the world, and we can and should ask for God's presence and power among us.

But just as prayer takes a lot of forms, the outcome of prayer can take many shapes. Sometimes the thing that is changed is the result or the circumstance: the person we prayed for is healed or the deepest desire of our heart is fulfilled. Sometimes the thing that is changed is our attitude or approach; we are strengthened or comforted or better able to face the days ahead, or we are given insight so that we know what we are called to be or do, regardless of the circumstance. Sometimes the thing that is changed is someone else's heart or mind or actions, and that change impacts us. Sometimes the thing that is changed is our relationship with God; we find new ways of relating to God or a new dimension to our conversation and companionship.

Prayer is powerful, but it is also mysterious. We should approach any moral certainties about prayer with fear and trembling. We can do a great deal of damage to ourselves and one another if we pretend to know precisely *how* prayer works—any beliefs or assertions that "it must have been God's will" or "if only I'd prayed more or harder" move prayer out of the context of a conversation in relationship and into the context of an obligation or exchange—a deeply flawed context that damages our ability to relate to God. There are many ways to pray, there are many outcomes to prayer, and everyone's relationship with God in prayer is different. Much of prayer is beyond both our knowledge and control.

How Do We Pray?

Although we can never know exactly how prayer works, we can (and should) learn how to pray. Prayer, like any spiritual discipline, is a matter of practice. It won't always feel natural the first few times we do it. We might have to experiment with new ways of prayer in order to find the ones that help deepen our relationship with God.

In Chapter 9 we explored the Daily Office, one of the most essentially Anglican ways to pray. And toward the end of the chapter, we pointed you to dozens of different resources within *The Book of Common Prayer* for prayer. But of course, there are hundreds of other ways to pray beyond those found in our prayer book. You can pray by walking a labyrinth, by using rosary beads, or by creating icons or art. You can use different forms for prayer, from the Ignatian concept of Examen to Contemplative Prayer to *Lectio Divina*. You can pray kneeling or sitting or standing or moving. You can pray in sound or in silence. There is no one-size-fits-all form of prayer. Instead, there is a vast variety of different ways to pray, different methods for engaging in conversation with God.

But whatever method you use for prayer, the important thing is to engage in the relationship, making time and space to meet God in prayer. And there are some specific things that you can do in order to improve your relationship with God in prayer.

❖ Start small. If you have never prayed before, it can seem overwhelming at first. If you start out by saying that you are going to do the full Daily Office morning, noon, and night, then you might have set your sights too high (although if you do it—way to go!). The important thing about starting a life of prayer is to start somewhere. It could be grace at meals—every time—or daily morning prayer, or a weekly study session, or any number of things. Choose a prayer discipline that you want to try, and go for it. Commit to doing it daily for a period of time. Then, when you've gotten comfortable, spend more time in prayer, or add another component.

❖ Show up. If prayer is a conversation that takes place in relationship, then you have to show up so that the conversation can happen! The truth is, God is there— always waiting and hoping we will show up. Perhaps the most important thing we can do is schedule a time for prayer, and then show up—even when other things crowd the calendar, even if it is hard or uncomfortable.

Make a space in your calendar (every day) for God. And then follow through on that commitment.

❖ Keep trying. Relationships are hard work—ask anyone who has been married for a long time! Your relationship with God is no different. There will be some bumps in the road. You might try a prayer practice that you really hate or find that the way you have been praying for a long time may no longer work for you. Be ready to change your prayer practice and try new things. Ask for help from a priest or trusted friend if you need it.

One of the collects from *The Book of Common Prayer* says this:

> Almighty and everlasting God, you are always more ready to hear than we to pray, and to give more than we either desire or deserve: Pour upon us the abundance of your mercy, forgiving us those things of which our conscience is afraid, and giving us those good things for which we are not worthy to ask, except through the merits and mediation of Jesus Christ our Savior; who lives and reigns with you and the Holy Spirit, one God for ever and ever. *Amen.* (234)

God is always ready to hear us when we pray, longing to give us more than we desire or deserve. It is our turn to engage that conversation, to respond in adoration, praise, thanksgiving, penitence, oblation, and intercession to the God who is waiting and yearning to enter more deeply into relationship with each one of us.

For Reflection

- *The Book of Common Prayer* identifies seven different kinds of prayer: adoration, praise, thanksgiving, penitence, oblation, petition, and intercession. Name an example of each type of prayer.
- Which of the seven kinds of prayer is most difficult for you personally? Why?
- Which of the seven kinds of prayer is most comfortable for you personally? Why?
- In this chapter, we talk about prayer as a "conversation that takes place in relationship." Does that definition change how you think about prayer? How so or why not?

The Church

Chapter 17

That Wonderful and Sacred Mystery
The Church

O God of unchangeable power and eternal light: Look favorably on your whole Church, that wonderful and sacred mystery; by the effectual working of your providence, carry out in tranquility the plan of salvation; let the whole world see and know that things which were cast down are being raised up, and things which had grown old are being made new, and that all things are being brought to their perfection by him through whom all things were made, your Son Jesus Christ our Lord; who lives and reigns with you, in the unity of the Holy Spirit, one God, for ever and ever. *Amen.*

—*The Book of Common Prayer*, p. 280

Bob prayed at the church where I worked as a musician. Every week, after the service, Bob would stay in the church, alone with Jesus to pray. He had been doing this for years. Each week, we would chat: He would usually tell me a corny joke, and we would make small talk. But we also talked about prayer. He gave me my first rosary because he wanted me to know the gifts of God's presence that he enjoyed. I learned that he was going to retire from his factory job after decades of work. The next week, I began our conversation, "Bob! What did you do on your first day as a retired person, with loads of free time?" Without missing a beat, he said, "I went to a 7:30 a.m. Mass to give thanks to God for over forty years of work and good health. What else would I do?"

I've thought about Bob and our conversation many times over the years. Bob saw the church as central to his life of prayer—and to his whole life. It was second nature for him. I wonder how many years it took him to reach this point. Or maybe he was born with this charism—this holy gift. Either way, his life is a model for us all: The church should be central to our lives. When we have thanks to offer or pleas to cry out, we would do well to come to church.

It is tempting to think of church as a place to find ease, a place to be affirmed and comforted. But while these things may happen occasionally, that's not really what church is about. In simplest terms, church is the gathering of Jesus' followers. Speaking most broadly, people all over the world who claim to follow Jesus are gathered into one worldwide church. Locally, when we talk about "our church," we really mean the community of people with whom we gather to follow Jesus.

The church isn't an ordinary community. The scriptures promise that God abides in the church, in all its glory and ordinary life and problems. The church has great variety, because a great variety of people are its members. Saint Paul says it best:

> For just as the body is one and has many members, and all the members of the body, though many, are one body, so it is with Christ. For in the one Spirit we were all baptized into one body—Jews or Greeks, slaves or free—and we were all made to drink of one Spirit. Indeed, the body

does not consist of one member but of many. If the foot would say, "Because I am not a hand, I do not belong to the body," that would not make it any less a part of the body. And if the ear would say, "Because I am not an eye, I do not belong to the body," that would not make it any less a part of the body. If the whole body were an eye, where would the hearing be? If the whole body were hearing, where would the sense of smell be? But as it is, God arranged the members in the body, each one of them, as he chose. If all were a single member, where would the body be? As it is, there are many members, yet one body. The eye cannot say to the hand, "I have no need of you," nor again the head to the feet, "I have no need of you." On the contrary, the members of the body that seem to be weaker are indispensable, and those members of the body that we think less honorable we clothe with greater honor, and our less respectable members are treated with greater respect; whereas our more respectable members do not need this. But God has so arranged the body, giving the greater honor to the inferior member, that there may be no dissension within the body, but the members may have the same care for one another. If one member suffers, all suffer together with it; if one member is honored, all rejoice together with it. (1 Corinthians 12:12-26)

Differences that we might imagine (race, gender, political persuasion, sexual orientation, economic status) fall to the wayside in baptism, as we are grafted into Christ's body, the church. And yet that sacred body, the church, takes into itself each one of us in our diversity. We do not hide or deny who we were made to be as we join the church, but rather, we flourish as the people God has made us, and the church shines radiantly when its members gather in their unity and diversity. Another aspect of this body metaphor is that we understand that the church needs each of us in our diversity. We need people with many gifts and passions, and we each do our part to make the body healthy. Just as Saint Paul talks about a body needing its members, so too does the church need its many members. To have a church, for example, we need pastors, prophets, and teachers.

The body metaphor is one way to understand the church, but there are others. We also articulate our beliefs about the church in our creeds. For instance, in the Nicene Creed, we say that the church is one, holy, catholic, and apostolic. The answers are crisp and incisive in the Catechism (854):

"Q. Why is the Church described as one?

"A. The Church is one, because it is one Body, under one Head, our Lord Jesus Christ."

With so many denominations in the world, the idea of the church as one unified body can be hard to understand. But even though denominations have many differences, the vast majority of Christians recognize each other's baptisms and acknowledge other Christians as part of a universal church.

"Q. Why is the Church described as holy?

"A. The Church is holy, because the Holy Spirit dwells in it, consecrates its members, and guides them to do God's work."

When we say the church is holy, we do not say that the church is perfect. Far from it! Because the church is filled with humans, it will always be filled with human error. Still, we believe that God's presence abides in the church and that God's will is carried out through the church.

"Q. Why is the Church described as catholic?

"A. The Church is catholic, because it proclaims the whole Faith to all people, to the end of time."

Catholic means roughly the same thing as universal, so the catholic church is the universal church throughout the world. When people say "Roman Catholic," they are talking about a particular denomination, headquartered in Rome. But many other Christians use the term catholic to describe a church that is universal. We understand ourselves to be part of that universal church and bound by the theology and practice of that wider church.

"Q. Why is the Church described as apostolic?

"A. The Church is apostolic, because it continues in the teaching and fellowship of the apostles and is sent to carry out Christ's mission to all people."

To say that the church is apostolic means that it continues in the tradition of the apostles, that its faith and practices are rooted in those that Jesus' own followers taught and practiced. The word apostle comes from Greek, and it literally means one who is sent out. Thus to speak of an apostolic church is also to speak of a church that is continually reaching out into the world to proclaim good news of Christ and share God's love.

The Mission of the Church

In addition to explaining the definition of the church, the Catechism also articulates the church's mission: "The mission of the Church is to restore all people to unity with God and each other in Christ" (855). At first glance, this might sound a bit like the church's job is to be nice, because unity is nice. However, a quick scratch of the surface reveals a much more complex and challenging reality with our mission in the church.

For one thing, to be restored to unity, we must be reconciled. To be reconciled, we have to know who we are and why we are not already restored to unity. In reconciliation, as in recovery, the first step is admitting we have a problem. In order to be reconciled to one another and to restore the unity that God intends for us, we must first acknowledge the ways that we have fallen short of being the people that God has called us to be. Think about it like a friendship that is estranged. I cannot restore a broken friendship if I cannot see how the friendship was damaged and what role I played in the break. Moreover, unless I am willing to change my actions to prevent the same break again, the friendship is not restored through a simple apology. In other words, if I want to be restored to unity with God and with others, I have to be serious about it. There is nothing easy about this restoration. I need the church's help and the Spirit's guidance if I'm going to acknowledge who I am and what I've done and then live a new life in Christ.

Another phrase is also critical in our mission as the church: "All people." If the church's job is to restore all people to unity with God and each other in Christ, we need to do some evangelism, to tell people about the Good News of God in Christ and invite them to be grafted into Christ's body, the church. If we remain inside our church buildings, we cannot carry out our worldwide, universal mission of healing, wholeness, and restoration.

Anglican View of the Church

Christian agreement is far more widespread than disagreement. And so it is with the church. We Anglicans agree with most Christians that the church is ancient, universal, holy, and so forth. Still, there are some unique or special charisms to Anglican understandings of the church.

We look at Canterbury, England, as our spiritual motherland. Let us take a step back and look at our history. When the king of England fought with the pope over a number of issues in the sixteenth century, the church in England became independent of Rome. This was the result of a long-simmering division, one in which the English and Celtic churches had been at odds with others. Events such as the king's need for a divorce (and the pope's refusal to grant one) coupled with the foment of the Lutheran and Calvinist reformations ultimately caused King Henry VIII to sever ties with Rome. When those first independent Anglican Christians were articulating and justifying their faith, they understandably emphasized how the church is shaped by ancient, universal tradition as well as local practice and custom.

As English colonists spread around the world, so too did the Church of England and English culture and traditions. At the same time, Anglicans valued local culture as well. What this means today is that the liturgy is similar throughout the worldwide family of Anglican churches but also reflects local traditions integrated into the church's practice and worship. To be sure, the church has been corrupted with the sin of colonialism in much of its history, but when the church has been at its best, Anglicans have honored local tradition and universal faith.

So where does this leave us today? The Archbishop of Canterbury is viewed by Anglican bishops all over the world as the first among equals. While the Archbishop of Canterbury does not have authority like the Pope in the Roman Catholic church, the archbishop does have a persuasive spiritual authority by virtue of the office.

Our own Episcopal Church offers a liturgy that would feel familiar to Anglicans from nearly every part of the globe. There are certainly differences, but they are much smaller than our similarities. However, our heritage and our story have shaped our understanding of the church in important ways.

Why Go to Church?

Several years ago, I was asked to give a series of talks on why we should go to church. Fantastic! And then I started thinking. Beyond my own personal preferences, what *are* the best reasons to go to church? So I asked, on Facebook, if people could find scriptural warrant for Christians to gather in churches.

Some people cited Jesus' promise in Matthew, "For where two or three are gathered in my name, I am there among them" (18:20). While this passage affirms Christ's presence with his gathered followers, it is more about conflict resolution than corporate worship.

Others mentioned Pentecost, specifically the story about what life was like for the early Christians after they received the gift of the Holy Spirit.

> All who believed were together and had all things in common; they would sell their possessions and goods and distribute the proceeds to all, as any had need. Day by day, as they spent much time together in the temple, they broke bread at home and ate their food with glad and generous hearts, praising God and having the goodwill of all the people. And day by day the Lord added to their number those who were being saved. (Acts 2:44-47)

Certainly, this passage offers a compelling witness to the power of God at work in the Christian community, but it might be hard for modern Christians to connect to this dazzling, centuries-old experience.

I looked through Saint Paul's letters to find an answer to the question: Why church? Paul assumes that followers of Jesus will be gathered in churches. And he acknowledges that it won't always be easy. Churches will be filled with conflict, because they are filled with flawed humans. Each conflict is not a failure but rather an opportunity to practice the reconciling love of Christ with one another.

While Paul's letters offer wonderful advice to churches, the Letter to the Hebrews takes a different approach. Hebrews offers this exhortation:

> Let us hold fast to the confession of our hope without wavering, for he who has promised is faithful. And let us consider how to provoke one another to love and good deeds, not neglecting to meet together, as is the habit of some, but encouraging one another, and all the more as you see the Day approaching. (10:23-25)

We must not neglect to gather. There can be no solitary Christians. And why do we gather? To *provoke* one another to love and good deeds.

When I gave my series of talks on why we should go to church, I got some pushback on the word "provoke." It seems so … not very … nice. Yet even the original Greek has much the same meaning. Our task as Christians is to provoke one another—not to always be nice to one another. While it seems counterintuitive, this notion of the provocative church makes sense. We expect our close friends to tell us the truth, even when we're not sure we want to hear it. It follows then that we who are beloved in Christ are meant to be close to one another, to speak words of love and truth to one another at all times.

Sometimes our task is to be provocative. "You really need to reach out to your sibling and apologize for what you've done."

"You say you don't have time to pray, but don't you really mean that you don't *make* time to pray?" If we are "nice" to one another, we will never risk conflict or say something that might be received with difficulty, but that's not the Christian way. Jesus wasn't nice; he spoke the truth. That is our role as the church too.

When we gather as Christians, our task is to provoke one another to be better followers of Jesus, to be more Christ-like. The words of our liturgy provoke us. Good preaching and good teaching will do that too. And so too must we provoke one another. This is the fundamental point of gathering.

To put it more positively, we must inspire one another. Even Hebrews talks about encouraging one another. When I am feeling discouraged about my journey with Jesus, someone at the church may help me find hope again. Or maybe I will be the beacon for another. We can only encourage one another when we are in community.

What are the implications of these various understandings of church? The church is not like other secular, voluntary organizations. It has a sacred charter and is part of God's saving work for all people. The church is not one activity choice among many, something to do when it makes us feel good or is convenient. Rather, the church is the central way we encounter God and God's people, and its purpose is to encourage and provoke us to be more Christ-like. The church is a great gift to us and the world, and it is our task to share that gift with those around us.

For Reflection

* In the Catechism on page 854 of *The Book of Common Prayer*, the church is described as "one, holy, catholic and apostolic." Which of those three characteristics is most important to you and why?

* Why do you go to church?

* Did this chapter encourage you to think about going to church in a different way? How so or why not?

* How is the church different from other voluntary social organizations?

* Have you ever been to a church that is very different from your home church, either a different denomination or an Anglican church in another part of the world? What was similar and what was different?

Chapter 18

Defend
Your Church
Structure and Governance

Let your continual mercy, O Lord, cleanse and defend your
Church; and, because it cannot continue in safety without
your help, protect and govern it always by your goodness;
through Jesus Christ our Lord, who lives and reigns with
you and the Holy Spirit, one God, for ever and ever. *Amen.*

—*The Book of Common Prayer*, p. 232

The structure and governance of the Episcopal Church
balances two opposites in a beautiful dialogue. On the one
hand, our church is hierarchical. The word episcopal means
having to do with bishops, and so we have bishops with great
authority in some areas. There are plenty of churches in the
world whose governance is purely hierarchical. But ours also
has another side. Our church is democratic. At every level,
we insist that lay people and other clergy—not just bishops—
be involved in decision making. There are lots of churches
that are governed purely by local and regional meetings.
What makes Anglican Christianity different from many
other traditions is that we balance hierarchy and democracy.

In the last chapter, we talked about the church—the whole, global church—and why it is good for Christians to be part of a church community. In this chapter, we'll talk about how the Episcopal Church is structured and governed. The fancy, churchy word for this topic is polity. Polity comes from a Greek word that means form of government. Don't worry— this is way more interesting than it sounds!

Our insistence that lay people are included in the governance of our church at every level reflects our view that God has blessed people with the gifts of reason and skill and that it is important to give voice to those gifts. We value democracy and transparency, and we want our church to reflect truth in our own internal workings so that we can manifest it to the world with credibility.

The Episcopal Church is governed by a constitution and a set of rules called canons. Canons are, in essence, regulations the church adopts to govern itself. To change the constitution or canons of the Episcopal Church, the bishops and deputies at the church-wide, triennial General Convention must vote together to approve new text. If you are curious about the canons, you can download a copy at www.episcopalchurch.org.

Those who are called into positions of leadership—lay leaders, bishops, priests, and sometimes deacons—are given authority and power over other people to discharge their duties within the limits of church regulation. Our church's rules describe how particular temporal things (church buildings, money, corporations) are to be under the authority of elected groups or, sometimes, individual clergy. When authority is given, it is never unlimited or unquestioned authority but is carefully spelled out in our canons. It is also notable that ordained people promise that they will obey those in authority over them. This is another example of how our church bears marks of a hierarchical church but with transparency and accountability at all levels. Together, hierarchy and democratic governance function as a kind of check and balance system for each other.

We will now look at polity at three levels: congregation, diocese, and church-wide. Like most of the rest of this book, we're simplifying complicated subjects here, so please check out some of the additional resources listed in the appendix.

Congregations

Congregations are usually led by a priest and a group of elected lay leaders. These lay leaders function both as the board of directors of the church as a nonprofit institution and as spiritual leaders who, with the clergy leader, lead the vision for the mission of the church. Typically, the leaders are organized into what is called a vestry. However, if the church is under the supervision of a bishop, they may be called a bishop's committee or mission council.

The clergy person who leads the church serves as the chair of the group of lay leaders and may vote on matters that require a vote. However, the lay leaders are able to vote their conscience. This contrasts with some denominations in which the clergy have sole control over financial and other matters. Generally these vestry and leadership meetings are open, so if you are curious what's going on in your church, find out when the leaders meet and attend the gathering. The group will review financial reports, discuss important matters that concern the church's material or spiritual well-being, and often share time together in Bible study or Christian formation.

Nearly all congregations have an annual meeting, to which all voting members are invited. Most churches permit all communicants in good standing to vote, and this is defined in the Episcopal Church canons as those "who for the previous year have been faithful in corporate worship, unless for good cause prevented, and have been faithful in working, praying, and giving for the spread of the Kingdom of God" (Canon I.17.3). This means that membership in the church is different from a voluntary society: Members are expected, as a normal practice, to work, pray, and give to support God's work. And the standard for worship attendance is pretty high, suggesting that one should be in church every week, "unless for good cause prevented." Details on these definitions will vary, but the point here is that on the one hand, the church is quite open, saying that lots of people have voting interest in the congregation's affairs. On the other hand, there is a standard of discipleship at work; one cannot simply pay dues and be considered a member in good standing.

The priest who leads a church is often called a rector. Rectors have tenure, like a professor. When a church needs a new rector, the vestry usually delegates a search committee with the task of recruiting and identifying suitable candidates; one or more candidates are presented to the vestry, and the vestry elects the person who they believe is called by God to be their next rector. This decision is then ratified by a bishop.

In some cases, the priest who leads the congregation is called a vicar, which means that the congregation is under the care of a bishop who has delegated leadership to a vicar, appointed by the bishop. Vicars generally serve at the pleasure of the bishop. A priest-in-charge is generally given a time-limited agreement, perhaps for a year or two or three, to lead the congregation. Priests-in-charge are sent by the bishop, but the vestry has the right to approve or reject the choice. All of this may vary widely based on diocesan regulation, state law, or local custom.

At the annual meeting, voting members usually elect members to the vestry or bishop's committee and representatives to diocesan gatherings, approve financial reports and perhaps budgets, and review ministries and events of the church's life.

Episcopal congregations have a good deal of autonomy in some ways. Each congregation makes its own financial decisions and governs many of its affairs. But the Episcopal Church is not a congregational church, meaning that our primary organizational unit is not the local church. Instead, we are fundamentally organized by diocese. Each congregation contributes some of its budget to support ministry in the diocese, such as campus ministries, camps and conference centers, urban ministries, diocesan program staff, and the work of the bishop. Congregations have some autonomy, but the bishop also exercises authority over the church, and many aspects of life together—especially worship—are governed by *The Book of Common Prayer*, as we saw in earlier chapters.

Dioceses

When I was a parish priest, people new to the Episcopal Church would sometimes ask about our diocese. What is it? What is its function? I would provide all the textbook answers, but I would usually suggest that if they really want to learn about the diocese, they should attend the annual diocesan convention. There, you see clergy and lay leaders from every corner of the diocese gathered for worship, fellowship, and legislative deliberation. All of this is led by the bishop, and this is the closest we can get to seeing what an abstract idea ("the diocese") looks like in real life.

Each diocese is led by a bishop, who serves until retirement or resignation. When there is a vacancy for bishop, the diocese receives nominations and a committee forms a slate of nominees. The diocesan convention, consisting of elected lay members and clergy, elects its next bishop from the slate. An important principle of this process is that lay people and clergy together elect their bishop.

From the earliest times, the church was organized around bishops. At first, each city would have its own bishop, and that bishop would be assisted in worship by many deacons or presbyters. Thus the bishop was at the center of the sacramental and liturgical life of the diocese. Baptisms, confirmations, and ordinations, among other sacraments, were to be performed by the bishop. When the bishop could not be present, worship was delegated to presbyters to act on the bishop's behalf. Clergy were meant to have a pastoral relationship with their bishop. So our pattern in the beginning was that practically and sacramentally, diocesan life flowed out from the bishop.

Today we have added layers of complexity, and our dioceses are too geographically large for bishops to be as embedded in the practical and sacramental life of the diocese as they once were. Still, it continues to be true that presbyters are acting in the bishop's stead and that all sacramental life in a diocese flows from the bishop.

Our bishops are advised by a group of lay leaders and clergy called a Standing Committee. These people advise the bishop on leadership of the diocese and must consent to certain actions, such as clergy discipline or selling property.

Bishops govern with the consent of clergy and lay people. And bishops safeguard the doctrine of our church, and could, for example, remove a priest who preached false teaching. But bishops are not dictators, and the rights and prerogatives of congregations and clergy are protected, especially by our tradition of transparency and democracy. A bishop is not a pope; bishops cannot force lay people to believe or say certain things in order to be eligible for sacraments.

Of course, the diocese is more than just a bishop and Standing Committee. Most dioceses also have a group of elected and appointed leaders called a council or board as well as other committees of lay leaders and clergy that typically oversee the programmatic life of a diocese. And then there is the annual diocesan convention, in which clergy and elected lay leaders come together for worship, for formation, and to make decisions.

Church-wide

The Episcopal Church is led by a presiding bishop, whose title also includes descriptive add-ons, chief pastor and primate. Chief pastor refers to the Presiding Bishop's work as the pastor to all other bishops and to the whole church, especially as it involves speaking to and on behalf of the church on social or moral issues. Primate is a funny word that means "senior-most bishop" in a country or church. The Presiding Bishop of the Episcopal Church leads a staff of people, many of whom work in the headquarters office in New York City. This group provides program resources for the whole church, as well as administers the resources of the church.

The General Convention of the Episcopal Church meets once every three years, and it is the chief authority within our church. This triennial gathering is part legislative assembly, part revival, part marketplace, and part family reunion. Though our church is large, as leaders gather regularly, old friendships are renewed and new friendships are forged. Meanwhile, over in the exhibit hall, vendors from advocacy groups, sellers of church goods, bookshops, schools, and church organizations sell their wares and tell their stories.

General Convention is a public gathering. Anyone can come and wander through the exhibit hall or attend daily worship. The center of General Convention is the legislative process, and each item goes through a hearing process. Anyone can come and listen to testimony or sign up to speak about the issue being discussed. The legislative gatherings are open to guests. You might have to register onsite, but you are most welcome to come and see what the Episcopal Church looks like in all its global diversity —glory and warts.

In recent years, much of the convention has been live streamed on the web for people who want to follow along but who cannot attend in person. Learn more about recent and upcoming General Conventions at www. generalconvention.org.

Every day, thousands of people gather to raise their voices in song and praise, as General Convention attendees celebrate massive worship services together.

Officially, General Convention is a bicameral legislative body, consisting of a House of Bishops and a House of Deputies. The presiding bishop is the head of the House of Bishops, and the House of Deputies is led by a president, who may be a lay person, a priest, or a deacon. During the convention, legislation must be agreed upon by both houses for ratification. There are eight deputies—four lay people and four priests or deacons— from each diocese. With just over 100 dioceses, the legislative body is quite large, with 800-plus deputies. With few exceptions, every bishop is eligible to take part in the House of Bishops, so there are usually around 200 bishops.

The General Convention votes on matters of liturgy and worship, social policy, budgeting, and church governance.

Free and open debate is a hallmark of the General Convention, and anyone can attend the convention and watch the houses debate matters or even speak at legislative hearings.

When the convention is not in session, the church is governed by an Executive Council consisting of about forty elected and *ex officio* members, including lay people, bishops, priests, and deacons. The Executive Council, which also functions as the board of directors of the corporate body for the Episcopal Church, meets several times each year.

As you can see, at every level of the Episcopal Church, democratic participation and transparency are core values, along with participation by lay people, bishops, priests, and deacons. And yet the same structures call and empower leaders who exercise authority specific to their context and role.

While most of us will spend the majority of our time in local congregations, it is worth noting the vast church that lies beyond our community. This wider church connects us to other Christians in our own state or region and to Anglicans around the world.

In all that we say about our church, we do not claim perfection but rather seek to admit and correct error when we find it. One of our prayers covers this very subject.

> Gracious Father, we pray for thy holy Catholic Church. Fill it with all truth, in all truth with all peace. Where it is corrupt, purify it; where it is in error, direct it; where in any thing it is amiss, reform it. Where it is right, strengthen it; where it is in want, provide for it; where it is divided, reunite it; for the sake of Jesus Christ thy Son our Savior. *Amen.* (816)

Just as Anglicans see the human life as a pilgrimage of sanctification, in which we are constantly growing into the full stature of Christ, we see the church as an imperfect institution that is always growing toward being a perfect icon of God's kingdom on earth.

For Reflection

✳ In our church governance, we balance two opposing values: hierarchy and democracy. What are some of the gifts of this balance? What are some of the challenges?

✳ As a lay person, you can take your place in the governance of the church at a local, diocesan, and church-wide level. How is this important to you? In what ways can you imagine living into this calling?

✳ What might our church be like without lay involvement?

✳ How have you, at your church, experienced the ministry of your bishop?

✳ As an Episcopalian, you are a member of three levels of polity: your congregation, your diocese, and the larger Episcopal Church. What are some ways that you could make connections on each of these levels? How might each level impact your faith?

Chapter 19

A Great Cloud of Witnesses

The Communion of Saints

Almighty God, you have surrounded us with a great cloud of witnesses: Grant that we, encouraged by the good example of your servants, may persevere in running the race that is set before us, until at last we may with them attain to your eternal joy; through Jesus Christ, the pioneer and perfecter of our faith, who lives and reigns with you and the Holy Spirit, one God, for ever and ever. *Amen.*

—*The Book of Common Prayer*, p. 250

Being a Christian is a powerful thing, in part because it means we are never alone. God is with us always: God who became incarnate for the explicit purpose of being fully with us as Emmanuel, and God the Holy Spirit who dwells in us and empowers us to do God's work in the world. We also have, as we explored in Chapter 17, the presence of the church, a community of believers surrounding us who challenge and support us through all the times and seasons of our lives. Further, as Christians, we are a part of the communion of saints, a great cloud of witnesses who have lived lives that proclaim the Jesus that they know and love.

There is often confusion about what it means to be a saint. Saint comes from the Greek word ἅγιος (*hagios*), derived from the verb ἁγιάζω (*hagiazo*). These words literally mean to set apart, to sanctify, or to make holy. Thus saints are those who are set apart, sanctified, or being made holy.

On November 1, or the Sunday after, the church celebrates All Saints' Day as a principal feast. This is a day to celebrate all the heroes of the faith, the saints we have remembered across time and culture. Think of all the saints: Saint Paul, Saint Mary, Saint John, and so forth, and that's who we celebrate on All Saints' Day. Then the next day, we commemorate what is often called All Souls Day, though its formal name is the Commemoration of All Faithful Departed. On this day, we remember all the Christians dear to us who have gone on to their glory. So on November 1, we celebrate Saint Andrew and Saint Martha, but on November 2, we remember Uncle Andy and Granny Martha. To help differentiate, this chapter uses Saints with a capital S to refer to those the church honors on All Saints' Day.

In a very real sense, this means baptized Christians are saints. Followers of Jesus Christ are set apart from the world. We believe that we are sanctified by God, and we are made holy by the power of the Holy Spirit through Jesus Christ. In the Bible, the word saints often refers to believers; Paul writes in his letter to the Romans, "To all God's beloved in Rome, who are called to be saints: Grace to you and peace from God our Father and the Lord Jesus Christ" (Romans 1:7). And to the Corinthians, Paul writes, "To the church of God that is in Corinth, to those who are sanctified in Christ Jesus, called to be saints, together with all those who in every place call on the name of our Lord Jesus Christ, both their Lord and ours" (1 Corinthians 1:2). In both these passages, saints means all the believers in Jesus. And yet, the church through the ages has recognized certain people as Saints (with a capital S). One of the earliest actions of the church was to remember specific saints and martyrs; the first generations of Christians gathered to pray and give thanks for those who proclaimed their faith, even in the face of death. Early Christians saw those Saints both as examples to emulate and as companions in life. The early martyrs and other examples of extraordinary faithfulness continue to be remembered through the ages, and over the years, more Saints have been added to their number.

The Episcopal Church follows this ancient tradition of recalling and remembering the Saints. The men and women whom the church officially recognizes as Saints are found in The Calendar of the Church year, on pages 19-30 of *The Book of Common Prayer*. The church does not *make* Saints; the church merely *recognizes* people whom God has made Saints. The Saints listed in *The Book of Common Prayer* are those that the Episcopal Church has, as a body, agreed to recognize and honor. The list of Saints is full of rich variety: young and old, lay and ordained, recent and ancient, from every race and ethnicity and nationality. The supplemental book, *Lesser Feasts and Fasts*, contains a biography and collect for each Saint, as well as readings from the Bible related to the Saint. These collects and readings can be used in personal prayer or at public services of worship in a church. By learning about these Saints, observing their feast days, and praying with and for them, we can be inspired and encouraged in our own lives of faith.

A feast day is the day designated to observe a certain saint; it is called a feast because it is a day of great celebration! Most saints are observed, not on their birthdays, but instead on the date of their death. So, for example, the Episcopal Church recognizes Martin Luther King Jr. not on the federal holiday in January (near his birthday) but instead on April 4, the date of his death. This is a reminder that we celebrate Martin Luther King Jr. not as a civic leader, but as a Saint whose life and words fearlessly proclaimed the witness of Jesus Christ. We observe Saints on the date of their death as a reminder that, for Christians, death is not an end but a new beginning of eternal life with God.

The list of Saints in the Episcopal Church is rich and varied, full of extraordinary and sometimes surprising people. In addition to modern saints like Martin Luther King Jr.,

As of this writing, the Episcopal Church's official sanctoral calendar (the list of the saints recognized by the Episcopal Church) is found in *Lesser Feasts and Fasts 2022. The Book of Common Prayer* includes this list in The Calendar of the Church Year. Changes or additions to the sanctoral calendar are made by the General Convention, because it is important that the wider church agrees upon the person's extraordinary example of Christian faithfulness.

The Book of Common Prayer also gives guidelines for individual communities to observe other saints who are important to their context, using the Common of Saints, found on pages 246-250. So, for example, your community could observe a deacon who offered extraordinary service or a lay person from your community whose life and witness proclaimed Jesus Christ to those around her. By using the prayers and carefully selecting readings from the options in *Lesser Feasts and Fasts,* local saints can be raised up and observed wherever they are found.

our calendar includes ancient examples of faithfulness like Perpetua and her Companions: a group of young women who are among some of the earliest martyrs in the Church. Although Perpetua was wealthy and the mother of a newborn child, she was unwilling to deny her faith in order to save her life. In the face of questioning she proclaimed "I am a Christian" and was sentenced to death along with her companions. Our sanctoral (Saint) calendar includes authors like C.S. Lewis, who wrote meaty theology and imaginative fantasy to bring both young and old into deeper relationship with God in Christ. There are monastics (monks and nuns) like Saint Francis of Assisi and Saint Teresa of Avila, who lived out their faith in lives deeply committed to both prayer and the service of the poor. And there are musicians like J.S. Bach, who wrote music to the glory of God and used that music to draw others more deeply into the praise and worship of God.

> If you want to learn more about the stories of some of the saints in The Episcopal Church, check out *Celebrating the Saints*, a one-year curriculum from Forward Movement, or explore Lent Madness (www.lentmadness.org), an annual Lenten devotional on the lives of the saints.

As we look through the list of Saints observed by the Episcopal Church, we find an incredibly important and oft-overlooked resource in our life of faith. The lives, writings, actions, and experiences of the Saints reveal to us what is possible through God's indwelling Spirit. Their witness shows us how the story of Jesus doesn't end with the empty tomb or even with the generation of apostles and disciples who immediately followed Jesus. The lives of the Saints continue the Christian story, stretching from the time of Jesus and to this very day.

But Saints are not simply figures embedded in the past that we read about in history books; they are meant as companions who, through time and space, journey with us and spur us on to love and good deeds. Whenever we say the Apostles' Creed, we affirm the communion of Saints. Communion means "together with," testifying to the mystery that the Saints are present with us, even now, reminding us that we are not alone and showing us that the difficulties and questions that we encounter are not new but have been wrestled with and struggled over by many who have gone before us.

And that's an important thing to remember about Saints: Saints are not immune to questioning or struggle. Saints are not perfect people; they have foibles and flaws just like the rest of us. In fact, among the saints you'll find Peter, who denied Jesus not once, but three times. Saint Augustine was infamous for living a profligate life in his early years. Almost all of the Saints encounter moments of deep doubt; many of them also struggled with pride, anger, or prejudice.

Saints struggle and sin, just as we do. Yet they allow God's light to shine through their imperfect selves. They allow even their imperfections to be used to serve God in the world, to glorify God. Saints are not people who are already fully holy, but people who have submitted themselves to be *made holy* by God. Their imperfections remind us that we too can serve God in amazing and radical ways, as imperfect as we are.

Saints are also not superheroes; they don't have any extra, special powers. They weren't bitten by radioactive spiders, and they don't come from an alien planet. The amazing things they do aren't because of any magical power they have themselves but because of God's power working through them, God's life living in them. Their humanity reminds us that we don't need superpowers in order to witness to God's power and promise; we can do that as fully human as we are.

And yet, a Saint is not just a "good person." Our culture gives us lots of lists of great human beings and influential people. Saints are not another of those lists. Saints are special, not because of the good that they did but because of the way that they proclaimed, not only with their lips but also in their lives, the God who is made known in Jesus Christ. They are notable, not for themselves, but for the power of God working in them. Saints are people whose good deeds or extraordinary actions point, clearly and powerfully, to Jesus. In other words, Saints are not known for being status keepers or revolutionaries (though some were); they are not revered because of a special skill or excellence in a certain realm of experience. Saints are known for being excellent disciples— students and followers of Jesus.

As witnesses to Jesus, the Saints have a great deal to teach us, both about the historic faith and about the way that faith impacts our daily lives. When we study the lives of the Saints, when we read their writings, and when we pray with and for them by observing the feasts of Saints included in the calendar of the church year, they teach us. They teach us theology as they encounter ideas about God and discover what is within the bounds of what we call Christianity and what lies beyond. They teach us church history, as they show us what it looks like to live out the Christian life and faith in different ages and places. They teach us spiritual disciplines, as they struggle with how to encounter God in their daily lives and how to live faithfully in and among the culture. They teach us how to live, and perhaps just as important, how to die, as they face trials and dangers without fear, neither denying nor defying death, but trusting in the One who created them and loves them always.

One of the collects "Of a Saint" in *The Book of Common Prayer* speaks to the mystical union we have with all the saints:

> Almighty God, by your Holy Spirit you have made us one with your saints in heaven and on earth: Grant that in our earthly pilgrimage we may always be supported by this fellowship of love and prayer, and know ourselves to be surrounded by their witness to your power and mercy. We ask this for the sake of Jesus Christ, in whom all our intercessions are acceptable through the Spirit, and who lives and reigns for ever and ever. *Amen.* (250)

Here we are reminded that we are one with all the Saints, deeply connected to them as part of the Body of Christ. This is a unity that transcends the differences of space and time; although they have died, the Saints both support and surround us as we walk through the journey of our lives.

Episcopalians do not pray to the Saints in place of praying to God or Jesus, as though we need a Saint to talk to God in our place. Instead, we pray *in companionship with the Saints*. We might ask the Saints (or a specific Saint) to pray for or with us, just as we would ask a friend to pray for or with us. In this way, the Saints join us as part of our community of faith, supporting us with their prayers.

The idea that we are surrounded by Saints who have died can sound kind of strange, or even scary, not unlike a famous quote from the movie *The Sixth Sense:* "I see dead people." Yet, the communion of Saints is not meant to be scary but sacred (and hopefully comforting). As Christians, we believe that baptism is forever, indelible, and ties us to God and to one another in a way that defies time and space. Just as we are tied to our earthly family through blood and birth, so we are tied to our Christian family through baptism and new birth. As the Catechism tells us:

"Q.   What is the communion of saints?

"A.   The communion of saints is the whole family of God, the living and the dead, those whom we love and those whom we hurt, bound together in Christ by sacrament, prayer, and praise (862)."

The communion of Saints is the whole family of God, our family. And our lives as faithful people are richer because of their presence and witness. The Saints remind us:

❖ **We are not alone.** We have companions in our journey of faith to comfort, support, and challenge us. We have people who are on our side in the struggle to follow Jesus.

❖ **We are surrounded and upheld by prayer.** In our eucharistic prayer each week, we join our prayers together with the Blessed Virgin Mary and all the saints. The great cloud of witnesses prays with and for us, not only on Sundays but throughout our lives.

❖ **Our faith is not in vain.** When we struggle and wonder if there's hope for our world or a possibility for us to do the right thing, others who have gone before us inspire and show us how to follow Jesus in our own time. The Saints through the ages have brought light into some of the darkest places and periods of history. They remind us that we, too, are the light of the world, and our faith can and does make a difference.

For Reflection

✳ Is there a Saint who has been important to you in your life of faith? Who was that person, and why are they important?

✳ Have you ever asked a Saint to pray for you? Why or why not?

✳ Saints are typically celebrated on the dates of their death rather than their birthdays. What might this say to us about the life of faith and about how we approach death?

✳ The Saints include people who have committed nearly every sin, and yet God has worked through them to be bearers of Christ's love in the world. Do you find it empowering or discouraging to think about Saints as flawed humans? Why?

Chapter 20

The Work You Give Us to Do

Vocation

Almighty God our heavenly Father, you declare your glory and show forth your handiwork in the heavens and in the earth: Deliver us in our various occupations from the service of self alone, that we may do the work you give us to do in truth and beauty and for the common good: for the sake of him who came among us as one who serves, your Son Jesus Christ our Lord, who lives and reigns with you and the Holy Spirit, one God, for ever and ever. *Amen.*

—*The Book of Common Prayer*, p. 261

Vocation is not a word we hear much in our world. We are much more interested in occupation. We ask children: "What do you want to do when you grow up?" We ask teens headed off to college: "What do you want to study?" We ask young adults nearing college graduation: "What do you want to do with your degree?" And once individuals join a profession, we stop asking about their dreams and aspirations; we assume they have found what they want to do and are simply doing it.

We are preoccupied with occupation, and we fail to ask people of all ages: "Who are you? Who do you hope to be? Who is God calling you to be?" These are questions, not of occupation, but of vocation.

The word vocation comes from the Latin word *vocare*, which means to call, and is also related to the word for voice. This etymology gives us insight into what we mean by vocation: It is your calling—who God calls you to be and what God calls you to do. And vocation is your life's way of speaking; it is your individual voice that only you can offer to the world.

Growing up in the South, I often heard people talk about when someone "got the call," as in "he was working in his daddy's law firm until he got the call and went to seminary to be a pastor." This presumed that vocation was reserved for ministers, those who work in the church. And we often still use the word in that way. But our Catechism calls us to think much more broadly about vocation. In the Episcopal Church, all Christians are ministers! In fact, *The Book of Common Prayer* features a beautiful collect, "For all Christians in their vocation":

> Almighty and everlasting God, by whose Spirit the whole body of your faithful people is governed and sanctified: Receive our supplications and prayers, which we offer before you for all members of your holy Church, that in their vocation and ministry they may truly and devoutly serve you: through our Lord and Savior Jesus Christ, who lives and reigns with you, in the unity of the Holy Spirit, one God, now and for ever. *Amen.* (258)

Vocation isn't only for priests or bishops or monks—it's for all Christians. Each of us is called by God to serve God in ministry.

Figuring Out Our Vocation

So what does that mean, exactly? How do we figure out what God is calling us to be and to do? If vocation is about more than just serving God in the church, how do we serve God in the world and in our daily lives?

When I began wrestling with my own vocation, trying to understand what it means to be called and to understand what exactly God was calling me to, a quotation by the noted theologian Frederick Buechner helped in my discernment. To this day, these words from his book, *Wishful Thinking: A Seeker's ABC*, are the most powerful and most deeply true thing I have heard to explain calling: "The place that God calls you to is the place where your deep gladness and the world's deep hunger meet."

This definition strikes an important balance. On the one hand, your vocation is a place of deep gladness. You are called by and through the things that you love, the things that bring you joy, the things that uniquely define you. God created each of us with unique gifts, skills, passions, and talents. God's call is for us to be more truly ourselves, not for us to try to be someone else. This is where God stands in direct conflict with culture. Television, Facebook, newspapers, and sports teams all promote certain people as role models. We see these stars, politicians, or athletes, and we want to be like them. It is fine for us to admire other people and their skills. We can, of course, be inspired and encouraged by the examples of others; the communion of Saints is a powerful reminder of that!

But wanting to *be* them or even be *like* them to the exclusion of being ourselves isn't what God has in mind for us. A story in the Jewish *midrash*, or commentary on the Hebrew scriptures, tells about a man named Rabbi Zusya. Reflecting on his own life, particularly in relationship to the Jewish patriarchs and prophets of the Old Testament, he reportedly said: "In the coming world, they will not ask me: Why were you not Moses? They will ask me: Why were you not Zusya?" I think that is the question that God asks each of us. I am never going to write like C.S. Lewis or paint like Rembrandt, much as I might wish to do so. But the question of my vocation is not why I wasn't more like some famous writer or artist, more accomplished or articulate, artistic or literary. The question God asks me, not just at the end of my life, but every day, is: "Why were you not yourself?" Embrace who you are rather than wishing you could be someone else.

Finding your vocation means living into who God created *you* to be. You need to ask yourself important questions to discover and explore your deep gladness: What are you doing when you feel most alive? What actions or activities bring you deep joy? When do you feel most fully yourself? These are questions of vocation, of calling.

It would be easy to think, based on this description, that vocation is an every-man-for-himself sort of thing; you figure out what you like best and you do it, regardless of anyone or anything else. But that is where the second part of Buechner's understanding of vocation comes into play: "The place that God calls you to is the place where your deep gladness *and the world's deep hunger meet.*"

God isn't just calling you to be yourself in some new-age sense of the phrase, where you live totally on your own, independent, focused solely on your deep gladness. Such a life is neither fruitful nor ultimately fulfilling. Your passion, the thing that brings you joy, is only half of the calling. The other half is to find where those passions fit into the hunger—the needs—of the world. We hear this intention clearly in the collect from *The Book of Common Prayer*:

Almighty God our heavenly Father, you declare your glory and show forth your handiwork in the heavens and in the earth: Deliver us in our various occupations from the service of self alone, that we may do the work you give us to do in truth and beauty and for the common good: for the sake of him who came among us as one who serves, your Son Jesus Christ our Lord, who lives and reigns with you and the Holy Spirit, one God, for ever and ever. *Amen.* (261)

We are not called to serve ourselves alone but instead to do our work "in truth and beauty and for the common good." We must search for the place where the things that bring us joy answer a need in the world and serve others. At the same time, we are not called to serve the world at the expense of ourselves. Our vocations can and should be difficult and sometimes costly, if we are following the example of Jesus, but they should not be joyless. If we are serving the world, but we are not finding truth, beauty, and joy in that work, then we have not yet found our true calling.

Thus vocation is what happens at the intersection of our gladness and the world's need; it is the thing that we do both because we find fulfillment within ourselves and because we are filling a gap in the fabric of the world. The wonder of God is that God made us to feel deep gladness and made the world with places of deep hunger so that, if we are listening to our lives, we slide into our unique niches in the world. We are most fully alive not when we are focused on the things that bring us individual joy but when we can find deep gladness in meeting the hunger of the world.

This work of vocation can take surprising forms. Once, I was meeting with a newcomer at my church, a woman named Caitlin. She shared that she wanted to serve God in the church, but she wasn't really sure how. She had been approached to help with Sunday School, but she didn't really enjoy teaching. She had observed the ministry of the lectors and chalice bearers, but she had a paralyzing fear of speaking or serving in public. She had carefully read the notices asking for various church volunteers, but none of them seemed to be the right fit. I asked Caitlin, "What are some things that you love to do? Or where do you feel close to God?" With an embarrassed laugh, she said, "Well, I really love to iron. When I'm feeling overwhelmed or confused, I get out the ironing board and iron my shirts or even my sheets. It's a time when I can focus and concentrate and reflect on life and maybe even talk to God. But that's not really a church ministry."

I couldn't help but smile at God's sense of humor. What Caitlin didn't know is that, the night before, I had been at a very tense altar guild meeting. The members of the altar guild were faithful, dedicated people who loved tending the sanctuary, keeping the sanctuary lamp blazing and bright, laying out vestments, and quietly preparing the church for worship. But, to a person, they all hated cleaning and ironing the linens. It had become a battle, where members were angry and resentful with one another about who had to launder the linens that week. Into that void stepped a person who found deep joy and connected with God in the act of ironing. When I told Caitlin about the dilemma, her face lit up. She heard that the place of her deep gladness was the very place of the church's deep need. She had found her vocation within the church.

As Christians, we are called to take part in the life of the church and to share our time and talent alongside our treasure. Like Caitlin, it might take a while to find the right fit, to find *our* vocation within the work of the church. The good news is that there are a variety of different vocations within the church, so there is something for everyone!

❖ Liturgical ministries offer ways for people to participate in leading and facilitating the worship of the church.

Acolytes carry the torch and cross, light candles, and lead processions. Altar guilds help with the care of the sanctuary and set up for church services, tending to the holy vessels of the church. Eucharistic ministers help administer communion. Lectors read the lessons. Ushers assist in directing people. These and many other liturgical ministries allow people to find their vocation within the worship of the church.

❖ Education ministries offer ways for people to participate in teaching and forming disciples. Most congregations have Sunday school teachers, youth leaders, Bible study and book group facilitators, all of whom work to help people love God with their minds as well as their hearts.

❖ Outreach ministries are ways that the church focuses outward rather than inward and serves the needs of the community. Many churches have feeding ministries, tutoring programs, community partnerships, and other ways to seek and serve Christ in all persons.

And there are hundreds of other ways to put your gifts, skills, and passions to work for the common good. Those who get excited about spreadsheets and balance books can volunteer as treasurer or help with the stewardship drive. People with a passion for art or music can serve the art and music ministries of the church. Those who find deep joy in tilling the earth might offer to help tend the grounds or start a community garden. If you are seeking your vocation in the ministry of the church, don't hesitate to talk to your priest or church leadership. You might be surprised that the thing that brings you deep gladness is exactly what the church most needs!

Yet it's important to resist the idea that vocation is only about ministry within or for the church. The reality is that we spend much more of our time outside the church than we do within it. Our collects are clear: our vocations are found in our "various occupations," in the work that we do on a daily basis and the lives that we live in relationship with our families and with the world. Our sense of vocation should extend to our secular occupations. We need to find the place where our deep gladness and the world's deep hunger meet in our daily lives.

This can be a difficult thing, and it is often a long endeavor. Some people are lucky and find their vocation early in life; others might go through multiple careers in search of their calling. Sometimes it can be hard to balance the differing demands: How can we stay faithful to our deep gladness and also support our families financially?

One of the first things that we have to do is shift our understanding of vocation. We must realize that any *occupation* can be a vocation. Vocation is not limited to the church, nor is it confined to the "helping professions," people like doctors and teachers and counselors. These are wonderful professions where some people find their vocation. But vocation is not one-size-fits-all. There are as many ways to serve God as there are people in the world, and any profession can be a vocation when it involves our deep gladness and meets the world's deep hunger.

Several years ago, I was looking for a place to get some car repairs. A friend recommended a local shop run by a man named Gary. I loved going there—and not just because Gary did great work at a fair price. Being around him was a delight. Gary loved figuring out what was wrong with cars, fixing them, and helping car owners understand what was going on. Sometimes he would call me into the garage to pop the hood open and show me what was wrong. He practically glowed with enthusiasm. He was also really good at solving difficult problems. I think of Gary whenever I think of vocation. Of all the people I've ever known—bishops, priests, doctors, teachers, lawyers—this man lived out his vocation in the most authentic way I've experienced. He found deep joy in what he was doing, and he used his skills to meet a need in the world. Truly, God called this man into auto-repair ministry!

The truth is, we don't have just one vocation in life. We have many. We have our vocations to be in relationship—to be spouses and parents and friends and neighbors. We have our vocations in our daily life and work—in professional callings where we exercise our gifts and meet society's needs. We have our vocations as members of the church—to be faithful in worship, service, and giving for the spread of the kingdom of God.

In all the occupations of our lives, both within and beyond the church walls, we have to do the hard work of discernment in order to discover our vocations. Discernment is the process of thoughtfully evaluating decisions and situations to determine God's desire for our lives. Discernment requires asking tough questions, spending time listening to the witness of our own lives and the wise words of trusted advisors, and carefully evaluating the choices we face. In the work of discernment, we must always remember that saying yes to something means saying no to other things. When we say yes to a promotion, we might be saying no to more family time or starting over in a new field. Or by saying yes to a job change, we might be saying no to more money or time at church. But when we do this hard work—of saying yes and saying no, of discerning what things to hold on to and what things to let go of, of figuring out who we are called to be and what we are called to do—then we begin to find our vocation, to find the place where our deep gladness and the world's deep hunger meet.

Process of Discernment

Whether you're trying to decide what kind of career to pursue, whether to get married or have children, or what ministry you are called to be a part of in your church, discerning your vocation can be a confusing thing. There is no magic-eight-ball solution, no single, foolproof process for making the correct decision. But there are a number of basic steps we can take in order to listen to what God is calling us to do and who God is calling us to be.

1. **Pray.** This first step in discernment is both obvious and easy to overlook. But if we are trying to figure out what we are "supposed" to be doing, it is important to start in conversation with the God who made us, loves us, and calls us each by name! You might use some of the collects for vocation in *The Book of Common Prayer* or you might use your own, extemporaneous prayers. Whatever you choose, make sure to bring your questions and decisions to God. And don't forget that prayer is a two-way conversation. Take time to stop talking and start listening to God as well. Listen for how God's voice might speak to you—in the silence of your heart, in the pull of your affections, in the voices and words of those you love. If you are wrestling with discernment in your life, commit to praying about it daily for a period of time. See if that dedicated time of prayer adds some greater clarity.

2. **Reflect.** The second step of discernment is intentional reflection, looking back over the course of your life and getting in touch with your current feelings, desires, and thoughts. Explore questions such as: *Where is my deep gladness? Where do I see the world's deep hunger? What am I doing when I feel most myself? What do my times of deep spiritual joy look like—what am I doing and who am I with? What would I be saying yes to with this decision? What will I be saying no to with this decision? Who do I imagine I will be in five years if I pursue this new opportunity? Who do I imagine I will be in five years if I say no to this decision?*

These questions are just a starting point; others will be specific to your own discernment. Some people are able to simply reflect on these questions in their mind; others find it helpful to journal or make lists in order to bring clarity of thought.

3. **Discuss.** Our lives do not exist in a vacuum, and God often speaks to us through other people. Though any discernment should *begin* with you and God, it is important to involve other people in the act of discernment. You might talk with a spouse, a trusted friend or family member, or your priest or spiritual director. Be careful to frame the conversation not as a request for *advice* but instead as an opportunity for discernment. Begin by asking them to simply listen, giving you time to voice your own reflections aloud. Ask them about the things that they see in you that you might be unable (or unwilling) to see. This time of discussion is not about having someone else make a decision for you; instead, try to seek out people who will help inform and support you as you move forward in your own decision.

4. **Pray.** Return, once again, to prayer (in fact, praying all along the way is a good idea!). You might have new things to offer up to God in prayer, or you might hear what God is saying to you in a new way.

For Reflection

✳ This chapter is based on the idea that God calls everyone to particular work or purpose. Sometimes we have limited the idea of calling to only those ordained. Is this broader way of thinking about calling helpful to you? Why or why not?

✳ Can you see a difference between doing the things that might be immediately gratifying to you and doing the things that God calls you to do? When might these be the same and when might they be different?

✳ Who are the people you know who are most clearly or abundantly living out their vocation? How can you tell they are doing what God called them to do?

✳ Do you believe that you are doing what God has called you to do with your life? If so, what is that like? If not, why not?

A Trinitarian Life

Chapter 21

Grateful Enjoyment of Your Abundant Creation

God the Father and Creation Care

> We give you thanks, most gracious God, for the beauty of earth and sky and sea; for the richness of mountains, plains, and rivers; for the songs of birds and the loveliness of flowers. We praise you for these good gifts, and pray that we may safeguard them for our posterity. Grant that we may continue to grow in our grateful enjoyment of your abundant creation, to the honor and glory of your Name, now and for ever. *Amen.*
>
> —*The Book of Common Prayer*, p. 840

One Sunday—and one Sunday only—each year, the church celebrates a doctrine. On the Sunday after the Day of Pentecost, we focus on the Doctrine of the Holy Trinity. We sing hymns and hear preaching about God as Father, Son, and Holy Spirit: the Holy Trinity. If you wanted to pick a good Sunday to hear a heretical sermon, you'd do well to pick this Sunday. You see, it's pretty common for preachers to make the mistake of trying to simplify the Holy Trinity. And in our efforts to downsize the ineffable into something we can grasp, we almost always mess it up.

We are much better off leaving the Holy Trinity as a divine mystery, something that we enter into with joy and a bit of uncertainty. Without trying to boil the whole thing down to a bumper sticker, there are a few things we can say about the Holy Trinity. At its core, the Holy Trinity reveals that our God is a God of relationship. Father, Son, and Holy Spirit are in a beautiful, careful, and timeless dance. The Holy Trinity reveals to us that God is unity, diversity, and majesty. The Holy Trinity keeps us from making the mistake of reducing God to something comprehensible, to a God that our brains can hold.

For much of its history, the church has preferred to speak of God the Father, God the Son, and God the Holy Spirit. In recent decades, feminist theologians have rightly pointed out that this places limits on our understanding of God. If we only ever speak of God as Father, we run the risk of beginning to think that God is literally male. Theologians agree that God is not a male or a female but rather transcends human gender, and a growing tradition seeks to enrich our speech about God, including addressing God as Mother. This is not completely new: Julian of Norwich (c. 1342 to c. 1416) spoke of God as Mother. This perspective can help us expand our understanding of God.

Some people today prefer to avoid all pronouns for God, using instead functional descriptions for God as Creator, Redeemer, and Sanctifier. This de-personalizes God in a way that does not resonate with the scriptures, and it also limits our understanding of God to particular functions for the persons of God. The scriptures say that God the Son, for example, is involved in our creation, redemption, and sanctification, so we wouldn't want to limit Jesus to redeemer only.

If all this seems confusing, it is. The Holy Trinity is not meant to be easy to grasp, and if we put it in a box we can hold, we confine God to the limits of our minds. We do well to savor what is best about the traditional language for God, even as we look for fresh ways to speak of God.

With this chapter, we begin a three-part exploration of the Christian life. These are, admittedly, artificial constructions, but they can still be a helpful guide to exploring the Trinity and our life in faith. This chapter will look at the connections between God as Creator and our enjoyment of and care for God's creation. Next, we will look at God in Christ—the Incarnate Son—and implications for our understanding of humanity and our treatment of others. Finally, we turn to God as Spirit, thinking about how our relationship with the Holy Spirit might inform our discernment and exercise of spiritual gifts.

God as Creator

To start, we begin at the beginning. Our understanding of creation is grounded in the idea that God is the creator. We profess in our creeds that God the Father has created all that is, and we affirm that the eternal Christ was present and active in the creation also. Indeed, the church also teaches that the Holy Spirit hovered at the moment of creation. The entire Trinity lovingly brought the universe into being and life into the world.

If you open a Bible and start reading, you will immediately encounter the story of God creating the universe (begin reading at Genesis 1:1, page one of any Bible!). In the story, we read again and again that God saw creation as good. God saw the light, the land and sea, the plants, the stars, and the animals. And they were all good. When God created people, they were created, male and female, in God's very image and likeness. And God saw that they were very good.

When God created people, God said to them that they should multiply. God also gave them dominion over the animals. Some Christians have read this to mean that people have unbridled power to use or to destroy animals for their pleasure alone, but this reading does not stand up to scrutiny. For one thing, this whole story takes place before the Fall— the moment when sin crept into human existence. At this point in the story, people have not sinned against God or God's creation. No selfish acts would be possible. Also, it's important to read the word dominion in a biblical context. While it's true that dominion means to rule over, it is also true that the Bible almost always sets out an ideal for rulers who are just and compassionate. God elevates mercy as the ideal, not absolute power.

To tell the story of the biblical view of creation is, in a way, to tell the entire story of the Bible. God gives people the earth, along with its fruits and animals, to use and care for. Later in the story, God obliterates almost every person and animal because of their flagrant and endemic sin. In the various laws, God constrains the use of the land, especially in ways that ensure the poor are cared for. Fields are to be left fallow every seven years so the land can rest, but the poor are to be given access to the gleanings—the leftovers—of these fields.

Psalm 19 begins, "The heavens declare the glory of God." In Psalm 8, verses 4-5, the writer praises God, saying, "When I consider your heavens, the work of your fingers, the moon and the stars you have set in their courses; what is man that you should be mindful of him, the son of man that you should seek him out?" Psalm 148 is a raucous hymn of praise in which the whole created order joins in the hymn.

> Hallelujah!
> Praise the Lord from the heavens;
>   praise him in the heights.
> Praise him, all you angels of his;
>   praise him, all his host.
> Praise him, sun and moon;

praise him, all you shining stars.
Praise him, heaven of heavens,
   and you waters above the heavens.
Let them praise the Name of the Lord;
For he commanded and they were created.
And he made them stand fast for ever and ever;
   he gave them a law which shall not pass away.
Praise the Lord from the earth,
   you sea-monsters and all deeps;
   Fire and hail, snow and fog,
   tempestuous wind doing his will;
Mountains and all hills,
   fruit trees and all cedars;
Wild beasts and all cattle,
   creeping things and winged birds;
Kings of the earth and all peoples,
   princes and all rulers of the world;
Young men and maidens,
   old and young together.
Let them praise the Name of the Lord,
   for his Name only is exalted;
   his splendor is over earth and heaven.
He has raised up strength for his people,
   and praise for all his loyal servants,
   the children of Israel, a people who are near to him.
Hallelujah!

Notice how beasts, kings, sea monsters, maidens, trees, snow, fog, young men, and shining stars all join together in praise. The fabric of creation binds all together.

Jesus used agrarian language regularly. He spoke of faith the size of a mustard seed, knowing that his hearers would understand this to be a tiny amount of faith, like a tiny seed. He spoke of scattering seed on rocky soil, thorny ground, or fertile ground, knowing that his listeners would understand something about how seeds take root and grow. Indeed, for us to understand Jesus and his teachings, we have to know something about the land and the plants and animals that live around us. Likewise, the importance Jesus places on land teaches us something of God's priorities: The creation matters.

Of course, it's not just the scriptures that shape our understanding of creation and our relationship to it. *The Book of Common Prayer* is infused with teaching about creation. Since we gather most often as a community to partake in Holy Eucharist, let's look at the eucharistic prayers.

Rite I, Prayer II, begins with a reminder about creation, "All glory be to thee, O Lord our God, for that thou didst create heaven and earth, and didst make us in thine own image" (341). Creation is so important that its invocation begins the prayer. Similarly, in Rite II, Prayer B begins, "We give thanks to you, O God, for the goodness and love which you have made known to us in creation" (368).

Prayer C offers more robust teaching about creation. The prayer begins:

> God of all power, Ruler of the Universe, you are worthy
> of glory and praise.
> *Glory to you for ever and ever.*

> At your command all things came to be: the vast expanse of
> interstellar space, galaxies, suns, the planets in their courses,
> and this fragile earth, our island home.
> *By your will they were created and have their being.*

> From the primal elements you brought forth the human
> race, and blessed us with memory, reason, and skill. You
> made us the rulers of creation. But we turned against you,
> and betrayed your trust; and we turned against one another.
> *Have mercy, Lord, for we are sinners in your sight.* (370)

Here we see the important idea that God entrusted us to rule creation, and we squandered this gift, turning against God, against creation, and against one another. Prayer D picks up this same theme: "We acclaim you, holy Lord, glorious in power. Your mighty works reveal your wisdom and love. You formed us in your own image, giving the whole world into our care, so that, in obedience to you, our Creator, we might rule and serve all your creatures. When our disobedience took us far from you, you did not abandon us to the power of death" (373).

The Book of Common Prayer offers many lovely prayers about nature and creation.

For the Right Use of God's Gifts

Almighty God, whose loving hand hath given us all that we possess: Grant us grace that we may honor thee with our substance, and, remembering the account which we must one day give, may be faithful stewards of thy bounty, through Jesus Christ our Lord. *Amen.* (827)

For the Conservation of Natural Resources

Almighty God, in giving us dominion over things on earth, you made us fellow workers in your creation: Give us wisdom and reverence so to use the resources of nature, that no one may suffer from our abuse of them, and that generations yet to come may continue to praise you for your bounty; through Jesus Christ our Lord. *Amen.* (827)

For the Harvest of Lands and Waters

O gracious Father, who openest thine hand and fillest all things living with plenteousness: Bless the lands and waters, and multiply the harvests of the world; let thy Spirit go forth, that it may renew the face of the earth; show thy loving-kindness, that our land may give her increase; and save us from selfish use of what thou givest, that men and women everywhere may give thee thanks; through Christ our Lord. *Amen.* (828)

If we are to live faithfully according to the vision set out in scripture and echoed in our liturgy, we must see God at work in creation; we must honor the gift of creation, and we must use this gift to the good of others.

Our culture pushes us toward two dangerous sins that are relevant here. First, our culture prizes individualism and the idea that each of us is responsible for ourselves alone—others can solve their own problems. Taking individualism to an extreme, we can begin to believe that we are our own saviors, that we don't need anyone else, much less God. The other dangerous sin of our time is consumption. Our culture promotes a take-what-you-want notion, that we should have what we want when we want it and our horizon need extend only to our own pleasure.

When we think about creation as a gift, these great sins are challenged. Each of us is indicted for our complicity in climate change and global forces of destruction. Just as it is true that no one can live the fullness of a Christian life apart from Christian community, it is also true that when we sin, our sins go beyond our own individual lives. Choices that we make impact the climate elsewhere. Using more electricity than we need might mean that a coal-fired plant somewhere is belching dangerous gas into the atmosphere. Buying new electronics more often than we need them results in the double destruction of the earth to mine elements for computer chips and the dumping of toxic chemicals as our machines are discarded. All of this takes place out of our sight, but we are still responsible.

The commandment to love our neighbors should be sufficient to keep us from poisoning them by our lifestyle. However, like most ethical matters, there is great complexity in our actions and their consequences.

Every Christian would do well to take stock of what we consume. Do we consume more than we need? Are the things we discard handled in a responsible way? Can we use alternative materials (for example, compostable plastics) instead of materials that will last for centuries after we die? And what about our church buildings? Can we ensure that they are heated and cooled efficiently? Can we make sure that we are not recklessly putting plastic bottles or cups into landfills, when durable alternatives might exist? Think about how the care of creation plays out in your life and in the life of your church community.

The important consideration is to treat creation as a gift—a gift that should be enjoyed equally by all people for countless generations to come. As with all gifts, we begin with gratitude, thanking God for creation. Then, as with all gifts, we seek to use them well. And if we cannot use a gift from creation (food, for example), then we try to find someone else who can enjoy that gift, perhaps by sharing leftovers with someone else. Care for God's creation impacts our whole lives and everything we buy, use, or discard—and is every bit as important as how we treat other people.

For Reflection

✴ The Bible says that God has made us rulers of creation. Yet we also recognize that creation is a gift from God that we are asked to care for—to be stewards of—so that those who come after us can enjoy as well. How do you understand the differences between ownership (dominion) and stewardship?

✴ Does it change the way you think about your actions if you see care of creation as a spiritual practice instead of environmentalism, which is purely goal-oriented? How so or why not?

✴ Read Psalm 148. How does it change your attitude toward the world around you when you think of creation itself praising God?

✴ What are some specific actions you can take to be a better steward of God's creation? What are some things your church community can do?

Chapter 22

Wonderfully Restored

God the Son and Incarnation

O God, who wonderfully created, and yet more wonderfully restored, the dignity of human nature: Grant that we may share the divine life of him who humbled himself to share our humanity, your Son Jesus Christ; who lives and reigns with you, in the unity of the Holy Spirit, one God, for ever and ever. *Amen.*

—*The Book of Common Prayer*, p. 252

Sometimes Christians think of Jesus as little more than a historical figure, albeit one with special powers. But to see Jesus only as one who entered into our history for a time is to glimpse only a tiny part of God the Son, Jesus Christ. This is why it's important for us to think about the theology of incarnation.

When we talk about Jesus' incarnation, we are referring to the radical idea that the eternal God took on human flesh of a particular person at a particular moment in history. As we discussed in Chapter 13, the "carn" part of incarnation comes from the same root as *carne*, which means meat. When we talk about Jesus' incarnation, we are literally talking about the enfleshment of God. In Jesus Christ, God took on flesh, the same flesh as us.

Unlike ordinary human beings though, Jesus Christ did not begin his existence with birth but rather at the beginning of time. The Gospel of John opens with a lovely poem about the majesty and splendor of Christ. "In the beginning was the Word, and the Word was with God, and the Word was God" (John 1:1). John waxes eloquently about Jesus' role in creation, in bringing beautiful, radiant life into being.

> He was in the beginning with God. All things came into being through him, and without him not one thing came into being. What has come into being in him was life and the life was the light of all people. The light shines in the darkness, and the darkness did not overcome it. (John 1:2-5)

Even before Jesus' love was revealed to us in Bethlehem, he was God. But in the incarnation, God did something extraordinary. As *The Message* version of the Bible explains, "The Word became flesh and blood, and moved into the neighborhood" (John 1:14). God dwelled among us, as one of us.

By affirming Jesus' incarnation, the enfleshment of God, we are affirming Jesus Christ as fully divine (the Word present at the beginning) and fully human (a helpless baby born in a remote village of ancient Palestine). God voluntarily took on human frailty, knowing our weaknesses, our joys, our sorrows, and our temptations. God even knew the sting of death. This puts to rest any idea that our God is remote, distant from us.

In the life of Jesus Christ, everything we need to know about God is revealed. As Saint Paul wrote to the Colossians, Jesus "is the image of the invisible God, the firstborn of all creation" (Colossians 1:15). Philippians contains a lovely hymn about the power of this humility:

> Let the same mind be in you that was in Christ Jesus,
> who, though he was in the form of God,
>> did not regard equality with God
>> as something to be exploited,
> but emptied himself,
>> taking the form of a slave,
>> being born in human likeness.
> And being found in human form,
>> he humbled himself
>> and became obedient to the point of death—
>> even death on a cross. (Philippians 2:5-8)

In other words, since God loves us so much that God is willing to share all our sorrows and pain, so we too should strive to love others in the same sacrificial way. For God, it's all about humility and self-offering, not about power and might.

While Jesus had access to unlimited power as God, he did not coerce anyone to follow him. Jesus' teaching and life were about invitation. Jesus invited people to give up everything to follow him. Jesus invited his followers to love everyone, especially those on the margins—the people whom conventional wisdom called unlovable. But Jesus also challenged everyone he met to experience an abundant, transformed life. God loves everyone, but God also wants people to repent—to turn from the direction they're going— to change and to live lives shaped by the incarnation.

So what does this incarnational theology look like when it's lived out in the church? About 1,600 years ago, John Chrysostom was Archbishop of Constantinople. He was known as a brilliant preacher who did not hesitate to preach the gospel. He famously said, "If you do not find Christ in the beggar at the church door, neither will you find him in the chalice." This is a consequence of the incarnation.

You see, if we cannot see Christ, behold Christ, in the poor and marginalized, we will not behold him in our liturgy or sacraments. One of our baptismal promises commits us to "seek and serve Christ in all persons." We do that because all of us, and our neighbors, are bearers of God's image and beneficiaries of God's graciousness in taking on our human nature.

It's not just that we see Jesus in the sacraments and this helps us to see him in the world. The reverse is true, too. When we can see Jesus in the world, we can see him in the sacraments.

Bishop Frank Weston, the late bishop of Zanzibar, put it eloquently:

> If you are Christians then your Jesus is one and the same: Jesus on the Throne of his glory, Jesus in the Blessed Sacrament, Jesus received into your hearts in Communion, Jesus with you mystically as you pray, and Jesus enthroned in the hearts and bodies of his brothers and sisters up and down this country. And it is folly—it is madness—to suppose that you can worship Jesus in the Sacraments and Jesus on the Throne of glory, when you are sweating him in the souls and bodies of his children. It cannot be done. (*Concluding Address*, Anglo-Catholic Congress, 1923)

An incarnational life demands much of us. We must look for Jesus in the poor *and* in sacraments. We are called, at every turn, to see ourselves and those around us as people whose very being has been sanctified by God's enfleshment, by God taking on our human nature.

One aspect of the incarnation is that God shows up. When we offer our presence to loved ones, to strangers, to anyone who needs us, we are taking seriously our incarnational work. Not only does God show up, but also the incarnation teaches us about where to look for God. The incarnation of God occurred in a place and time of vulnerability. Jesus was born a helpless baby, like all other babies. He was born to traveling parents under what must have been regarded as suspicious circumstances. He was born in a remote village in an occupied backwater nation in the Roman Empire. It would be hard, if not impossible, to find power or might in the story. And yet this is how God chose to enter our world, our history. It is a powerful reminder that we should especially look for God among the vulnerable, the weary, the traveler, the unexpected. God can come near in the person who may seem to be of dubious circumstances.

Another aspect of the incarnation is that it's messy. Most of our experiences of God are quite tidy. Our Episcopal church services are well ordered. We starch and iron things. We read in a particular way. We often shun disorder and messiness in our worship. So it wouldn't be too hard for us to think that God was similarly ordered as well. But the incarnation shows us that God gets real and messy. Jesus was born in a completely ordinary way. Of course, birth is a very beautiful event. But it's also messy under any circumstances, especially in a dirty stable next to sheep and cows! And we have every reason to think that Jesus was as messy and chaotic as any child growing up. If someone suggests that the church shouldn't do something because it's unseemly or messy, we might do well to recall the reality that God didn't enter the world in a neat and tidy way.

Incarnation insists that God in Jesus Christ is both fully divine and fully human. Church teaching holds that Jesus' life was like ours in every way, except that he did not sin. We understand sin to be separation from God, and so Jesus Christ, who was God Incarnate, could not be separated from himself. And yet, Jesus Christ was fully human, too. That means, in his humanity, he experienced pain, joy, betrayal, friendship, sorrow, learning, sadness, growth, love, temptation, and even death. Of course, after his death, God raised him to new life, but prior to death, his experience of life was very much the same as ours. God did not hold back or stay away. When Jesus wept at the grave of Lazarus, they were real tears of grief. When he celebrated at a wedding or spent time with friends or talked with strangers, he was engaging with real emotions and experiences, just like us. And so our emotions and all of life are sanctified by Jesus. God blesses us in the experience of entering our world and our lives. We do not need to be ashamed when we experience pain, joy, betrayal, friendship, sorrow, sadness, growth, love, or temptation. Death no longer has dominion over us, because we know that God's love is stronger than death. The incarnation frees us to savor this earthly life and all that it brings.

The Bible teaches us that God is loving and God is full of surprises to our conventional thinking and ways of seeing. So we should expect surprises. And above all else, we should see in the incarnation that God's love for us is so great that God is willing to dwell in our neighborhood, even among all our frailties and faults. Thanks be to God.

For Reflection

✳ How do you experience Christ's presence in the sacraments? How do you experience Christ's presence in the people you encounter? How are those two things related?

✳ Read the Nicene Creed from "We believe in one Lord, Jesus Christ" through "he came down from heaven" (*The Book of Common Prayer*, 358). How does this focus on Jesus' existence before his birth expand your understanding of him and his work?

✳ Incarnation is messy business. The incarnate Jesus cried and bled and got dusty and tired, just like all of us. How does this challenge you to get your hands dirty in ministry?

✳ Our culture tends to treat the poor and marginalized as people to avoid and diminish, and yet the teaching of the church says just the opposite. How does the church's understanding shape your life as a Christian and a citizen?

Chapter 23

Strengthened for Your Service

God the Holy Spirit and Spiritual Gifts

Almighty and most merciful God, grant that by the indwelling of your Holy Spirit we may be enlightened and strengthened for your service; through Jesus Christ our Lord, who lives and reigns with you, in the unity of the Holy Spirit, one God, now and for ever. *Amen.*

—*The Book of Common Prayer*, p. 251

After Jesus died, his disciples felt lost. Jesus, the Word made flesh, had brought God close to them once again. The disciples, who had walked and talked and eaten and served with Jesus, had experienced God's presence in a new and powerful way. Without the person of Jesus, they were bereft and adrift. They were afraid, hiding in locked rooms (John 20:19). And they returned to "life as usual," going back to the fishing nets they had abandoned when they first followed Jesus (John 21).

Then, the amazing happened. The resurrected Jesus appeared to them. They were filled with astonishment and surprise.

We can only imagine how overjoyed they must have been, believing, perhaps, that Jesus had returned to stay with them forever. But that was not, of course, the case. Jesus appeared to the disciples in resurrected form, but he had not come to stay forever. He would soon ascend to heaven, to sit at the right hand of the Father. It must have been a roller coaster of emotions for the disciples, to have Jesus, then lose him to death, receive him back, resurrected, and then see him leave them again at the ascension.

Yet Jesus made the disciples—and all of us—a promise. Jesus told his disciples that when he returned to the Father, he would not leave them comfortless (John 14:18). In fact, Jesus promised to send the Holy Spirit, God's presence, to be with them—and us—always. In Acts, we hear what happens when God fulfilled that promise, sending the Holy Spirit into the midst of the disciples and to the church through the ages.

> When the day of Pentecost had come, they were all together in one place. And suddenly from heaven there came a sound like the rush of a violent wind, and it filled the entire house where they were sitting. Divided tongues, as of fire, appeared among them, and a tongue rested on each of them. All of them were filled with the Holy Spirit and began to speak in other languages, as the Spirit gave them ability. Now there were devout Jews from every nation under heaven living in Jerusalem. And at this sound the crowd gathered and was bewildered, because each one heard them speaking in the native language of each. Amazed and astonished, they asked, "Are not all these who are speaking Galileans? And how is it that we hear, each of us, in our own native language? Parthians, Medes, Elamites, and residents of Mesopotamia, Judea and Cappadocia, Pontus and Asia, Phrygia and Pamphylia, Egypt and the parts of Libya belonging to Cyrene, and visitors from Rome, both Jews and proselytes,

Cretans and Arabs—in our own languages we hear them speaking about God's deeds of power." All were amazed and perplexed, saying to one another, "What does this mean?" But others sneered and said, "They are filled with new wine." But Peter, standing with the eleven, raised his voice and addressed them, "Men of Judea and all who live in Jerusalem, let this be known to you, and listen to what I say. Indeed, these are not drunk, as you suppose, for it is only nine o'clock in the morning." (Acts 2:1-15)

God joined the disciples—but in a surprising way. The Holy Spirit did not appear, as Jesus did, in human flesh as a baby lying in a manger or a person who walked and talked and taught. Instead, God's presence in the person of the Holy Spirit was "like the rush of a violent wind" and appeared as "divided tongues, as of fire." And rather than the presence of a person, the Holy Spirit came as a power *within* people— the disciples were "filled with the Holy Spirit" and "the Holy Spirit gave them ability." There is no question that, in the person of the Holy Spirit, God is powerfully present in the midst of humanity but in a new and different way than God was present in the person of Jesus Christ.

This is not to say that the Holy Spirit is new to the scene. As a church, we proclaim that the Holy Spirit was present from the beginning of creation, moving as the breath of God over the waters in Genesis 1:2. The Holy Spirit spoke through the prophets of the Hebrew Bible, proclaiming God's love and salvation before the coming of Christ. The Holy Spirit descended on Jesus at his baptism, proclaiming him the beloved Son of God. But at Pentecost, as described in Acts 2, the disciples and the church experience the presence of the Holy Spirit in a new way, and they are empowered by the Spirit to do new and amazing things.

Episcopalians are often wary of the Holy Spirit. We mention the Holy Spirit in our prayers, but we don't spend a lot of time talking about the Holy Spirit. This might be because the Holy Spirit isn't typically depicted as a person. We can imagine Jesus as a person and even sometimes God the Father as a person. But the Holy Spirit is most often depicted as a dove, as fire, or as wind—abstract images that are not explicitly personal. This makes the Holy Spirit harder to wrap our brains around and less accessible than the other persons of God.

Perhaps we also shy away from the Holy Spirit because we are a little bit (or a lot) afraid. The Holy Spirit is unpredictable, dangerous, and demanding. When the Holy Spirit showed up at Pentecost, it was like a rushing wind and a mighty fire—powerful, uncontrollable things. The Holy Spirit caused people to speak and say things they normally wouldn't say (in other languages), and the Spirit allowed people to understand things they normally wouldn't be able to understand. The whole experience was so bizarre that onlookers believed the disciples were drunk! For those in the Episcopal Church, who often value order and propriety, this idea of an indecorous Holy Spirit can seem upsetting and undesirable.

But, if we keep reading in Acts, we see that the presence of the Holy Spirit, while unconventional and unusual, was also powerful and amazing. Empowered by the Holy Spirit, Peter preached to those gathered, and 3,000 people asked to be baptized (Acts 2:41). (Wouldn't those be impressive numbers on a church's report!) The followers of Jesus began to act in incredible, inspiring ways:

> They devoted themselves to the apostles' teaching and fellowship, to the breaking of bread and the prayers. Awe came upon everyone, because many wonders and signs were being done by the apostles. All who believed were

together and had all things in common; they would sell their possessions and goods and distribute the proceeds to all, as any had need. Day by day, as they spent much time together in the temple, they broke bread at home and ate their food with glad and generous hearts, praising God and having the goodwill of all the people. And day by day the Lord added to their number those who were being saved. (Acts 2:42-47)

Through the power of the Holy Spirit, people devoted themselves to prayer and fellowship, gave sacrificially to those in need, had generous hearts, and praised God. Yes, the Holy Spirit is dangerous and demanding, because the Holy Spirit inspires conversion and change, and change is always hard and scary! And yet, the results of a life lived through the inspiration of the Holy Spirit are awe-inspiring: People worship God fully, serve others sacrificially, share what they have generously, and proclaim the good news of Jesus Christ abundantly.

When we look at the Holy Spirit's presence in the Bible and in the early church, we see that the Holy Spirit shows up most powerfully *in community*. The Holy Spirit appeared at Pentecost when the followers of Jesus were "all together in one place" (Acts 2:1). And the Holy Spirit's action in the early church caused people to create and sustain community: "all who believed were together and had all things in common..." (Acts 2:44).

The Holy Spirit is personal, empowering each of us with spiritual gifts, but the Spirit's presence and power are not primarily individual. Our spiritual gifts are given to us for the community and often come in relationship with the Christian community. It is when we are together, as the Body of Christ, that we most fully experience the power of the Spirit, with each one of us taking our place as a part of the whole.

In fact, scripture tell us that we can see, visibly and powerfully, when people's lives are filled with the Holy Spirit. Galatians 5:22-23 lists fruits of the Holy Spirit—visible, describable traits that you find in people in whom the Holy Spirit dwells: "the fruit of the Spirit is love, joy, peace, patience, kindness, generosity, faithfulness, gentleness, and self-control." Disciples of Jesus, who receive the Holy Spirit that God promised, should stand out from the crowd. Through the presence of the Holy Spirit, we are empowered to live lives that show forth to the world these fruits, this love and joy and generosity.

This can sound like an impossible task—how can we possibly do all those things?! But our faith teaches us that we do not do these things *of our own power*, but that God's Spirit, working in us, empowers us to live in these ways. The fruits of the Spirit are not some impossible standard that we strive to achieve. The fruits of the Spirit are the visible signs of a life that is lived through the power of God.

To say it another way, a life empowered by the Holy Spirit is a gift, not a goal. The disciples didn't work hard to earn the Holy Spirit—it descended upon them as a gift from God. Through the power of the Holy Spirit, the disciples were able to do things that they did not imagine possible without God's power—preaching prophetically, sharing generously, praying constantly, and serving joyfully. So too, we are told, God sends the Holy Spirit to each of us, empowering us with spiritual gifts.

You might be surprised to learn that, as a disciple of Jesus, you are *already* filled with the Holy Spirit and you have been given powerful spiritual gifts! The Bible lists some particular gifts of the spirit in Romans 12:6-8, 1 Corinthians 12:4-11, 1 Corinthians 12:27-31, and Ephesians 4:11-12. The lists vary but include gifts of prophecy, ministry, teaching, exhortation, generosity, leadership, cheerfulness, knowledge, faith, discernment, tongues, interpretation, servanthood, wisdom, healing, apostleship, evangelism, and shepherding.

It is impossible to go into detail about all of these gifts or to interpret and define exactly how they might be expressed. How is the gift of wisdom different from the gift of knowledge? What exactly does apostleship entail? But there are some important things to note about spiritual gifts:

> "Tongues" is one of the gifts listed in the Bible, and it often gets a lot of attention. This is because of the description of Pentecost and because of Pentecostal churches, which place a lot of emphasis on this particular gift. It is important to note that "tongues" is just one gift listed among many and in no way is deemed more important (or more universal) than other gifts of the Spirit.

❖ Everyone gets them! Spiritual gifts are not something reserved for church leaders or awarded to certain special people. "To each is given the manifestation of the Spirit for the common good" (1 Corinthians 12:7). That means that *everyone*—including you—has spiritual gifts. In fact, you might have a few spiritual gifts, because some naturally work together.

❖ There are a variety of gifts, and none are better than others.

> For as in one body we have many members, and not all the members have the same function, so we, who are many, are one body in Christ, and individually we are members one of another. We have gifts that differ according to the grace given to us: prophecy, in proportion to faith; ministry, in ministering; the teacher, in teaching; the exhorter, in exhortation; the giver, in generosity; the leader, in diligence; the compassionate, in cheerfulness (Romans 12:4-8).

❖ All of the different spiritual gifts are necessary in the building up of the kingdom, and in fact these gifts work together to share God's love with the world. Your gift is important … and so is everyone else's! Be willing to recognize that others have gifts that you don't. That's why we need one another.

❖ Your spiritual gifts are a free gift from God. Those gifts are yours—to use or not. Gifts of the Holy Spirit are not things you have to work for and try to earn; they are attributes that you already have and have to decide to explore and use. Learning about your spiritual gifts is similar to reading a manual for a present you've received; it's a way to figure out how the thing that you already have works! By learning about our gifts, we can cultivate and strengthen them. Sometimes just being aware that something is your gift can help you focus on offering and exercising it.

❖ The gifts of the Holy Spirit are given "for the common good" (1 Corinthians 12:7). It is your *duty* to share the gifts that you've been given with the rest of us. You shouldn't engage in false humility, saying that you don't have any gifts. And you can't be selfish, hoarding your gifts for yourself or your immediate family. Your gifts are meant to be shared, and by exercising your gifts for the common good, you take your place in the Body of Christ.

❖ No person has every spiritual gift! The number of gifts might vary—some will have a single gift, while others might have several. What is important is for us to treasure whatever gift or gifts God has sent our way.

❖ It is important to find ways to use our gifts and not to try to exercise gifts we may not have been given. For example, if I don't have the gift of teaching, I won't be

Discerning Spiritual Gifts

Now that you've learned that everyone receives spiritual gifts, how do you figure out your spiritual gifts? The Bible doesn't include a handy spiritual gifts inventory or social media quiz, leaving us instead to do the work of discernment as individuals and as a community. If you'd like a book or resource to guide your reflection, ask your priest for suggestions; she can help you find one that approaches spiritual gifts from an Episcopal perspective.

You can also do your own discernment:

1. Read the passages in the Bible that talk about spiritual gifts, especially 1 Corinthians 12, Romans 12, and Ephesians 4. As you read these passages, notice whether any of the gifts jump out at you. Do you find certain gifts more intriguing or appealing? Which ones sound most like you? Which ones are most challenging for you?

2. Spend some time reflecting carefully on your life thus far. What are some of your moments of greatest spiritual fulfillment, and what were you doing in those moments? When have you felt most fully integrated into the Body of Christ and what were you doing in those times? When have you felt most helpful to your brothers and sisters in Christ? When have you felt most disconnected from the Body of Christ?

3. Ask others—trusted friends or advisors—what they think your spiritual gifts are. Sometimes others see us more clearly than we see ourselves!

4. Try a few gifts and see what you discover. Maybe you've never had a chance to exercise leadership, or you've never tried healing prayer. Give yourself an opportunity to explore new spiritual gifts; you might discover a spiritual gift you never knew about.

Many times, this work of discovering our spiritual gifts is related to our work of discerning vocation. When we are lucky, our spiritual gifts support us in our various vocations. Knowing our spiritual gifts can also help us live more fully into our life's vocations, building on our strengths while growing deeper in our discipleship as Christians.

a very good Sunday School teacher. When we look for people who carry out ministries in our churches, we should be looking for spiritual gifts, not just for willing volunteers.

God promises to be with us always. God came into the world in the person of Jesus Christ, living and breathing and loving and dying as one of us. And God continues to come into the world and into our lives as the Holy Spirit, inspiring and empowering us to do God's work in the world. God's Holy Spirit is both an amazing gift and an incredible responsibility. Just like the earliest disciples, we too are "filled with the Holy Spirit," and "the Holy Spirit [gives us] ability" to be prophets and teachers, to be wise and cheerful, to be leaders and evangelists and much more.

For Reflection

✳ We are accustomed to praying to God the Father or God the Son. Do you often invoke the Holy Spirit in your prayers? Why or why not?

✳ What do you find most comforting about the presence and power of the Holy Spirit? What do you find most challenging?

✳ Some might say, "The Holy Spirit was here," when we are pleased with an outcome or situation. How can we tell our own emotions or feelings apart from the presence of God's Spirit? When might they be the same or different?

✳ Do you recognize any of your spiritual gifts in today's chapter? Are there any that you wish you had?

What's Next

Chapter 24

According to Your Will
Finding Spiritual Practices

Grant to us, Lord, we pray, the spirit to think and do always those things that are right, that we, who cannot exist without you, may by you be enabled to live according to your will; through Jesus Christ our Lord, who lives and reigns with you and the Holy Spirit, one God, for ever and ever. *Amen.*

—*The Book of Common Prayer*, p. 232

Most of us would like to have a fuller, deeper life of faith. But often we're just not sure where to start or what to do. One important way for a Christian to grow in faith is to take on spiritual practices, especially daily spiritual practices. These could include prayers, actions, meditation, and movement. There are nearly as many different spiritual practices as there are people. Beyond the dizzying array of choices, it's also pretty common to get discouraged or to give up. But doing so won't help us reach our desire for a deeper life of faith.

Perhaps a metaphor will help. I like to think of developing spiritual practices as a bit like exercise. We all agree, I think, that exercise is good for us. Some is better than none. More is usually better. Exercise helps make our bodies healthy. Spiritual practices are similar. Some is better than none. More is usually better. They help make our spiritual lives healthy.

If you are a couch potato, walking around the living room might be the first step in the right direction. If you walk around your house, then walking around the block is improvement. A brisk walk is better still. You don't have to go straight from couch potato to marathon runner. There are lots of steps between. And there are different types of exercises: Some people are great joggers. Others prefer biking or kayaking or yoga. The point is to get ourselves moving and to stretch ourselves a bit.

Whatever our exercise regimen, at some point we usually get stuck. Maybe I bike to and from work, which used to be taxing, but now I'm used to it, and my body doesn't work very hard. Or maybe I've chosen a kind of exercise that uses the same muscles over and over again. At some point, we have to change our habits. We have to bike more or faster. Or we have to add or change our regimen to get different muscles working.

So it is with spiritual practices. Perhaps you've been showing up at church occasionally for years. Even though you might be (and I mean this lovingly) a Christian couch potato, you decide to go on a metaphorical walk around the living room. Maybe you sit in on a class at church. Maybe you start saying a familiar table grace at meal time. Maybe you take home the service leaflet and have a quick look at the scripture readings after church. Anything is a step in the right direction.

At some point, after dabbling a bit here and there, it's time to think about a next step. Prayer? Study? Movement? Where to begin?

Several years ago, I worked for an employer with a very generous benefit: They would pay for me to join a gym—and a nice one at that. I wasn't very athletic as a child, and I'm not exactly a gym rat. What sold me on the gym is that the membership came with a few sessions with a trainer. At my first visit, the trainer asked, "Are you looking for tone, endurance, or strength?" Blank stare. "Okay, let's start at the beginning. What are you hoping for?" I said I had no idea, but I thought maybe it would be good for me to lift some weights and so forth.

The trainer took me over to one of the weight rooms, and he showed me how to use various machines, how much weight to set up, and how many times to repeat. He gave me a good order of progression from one machine to the next. When I got to the rowing machine, he became ecstatically encouraging. "Look at that! You're a natural! You could do this competitively!" I'm not sure I believed him, but it was nice to hear. The point is that he took my desire to be healthier and helped me focus. He gave me some specific suggestions and a roadmap. Over the next few weeks, I checked in occasionally, and he helped me revise the plan.

If you're trying to choose and then take on spiritual practices, it helps to have a trainer. This could be anyone who has more experience than you do. One option is a spiritual director—someone who is trained to help people attend to their spiritual lives. They help people see God at work in their lives and in the world around them, and they often encourage particular spiritual practices at certain times. But a priest or wise friend can also point you in the right direction. And of course, you can also Google or buy books or read blogs.

It does help to have a trainer or a coach of some sort. Several years ago, someone I respect spoke eloquently about the goodness of centering prayer, a practice of prayer that is rooted in long periods of interior silence. I tried it for quite a while. I kept thinking I wasn't doing it right or that I must be missing something. It didn't work for me. And then I had a conversation with a wise person who freed me from feeling like a lousy Christian by telling me that not every spiritual practice works for every person. Maybe centering prayer just isn't a good fit for me! I was so relieved. I moved on to praying with a rosary and found a spiritual practice that I could keep. I love the tactile sense of the beads, and it helps keep me focused. If I'd had a mentor, I could have avoided some angst.

If you don't have a daily spiritual practice or if you think it might be time for a change, I encourage you to consider a new practice. If you don't have a guide, it's perfectly fine to try stuff out on your own. If you get stuck, try something else or get help. Unlike exercise, it is unlikely you'll hurt yourself with a spiritual practice done incorrectly!

As we said earlier, there are nearly as many spiritual practices as people, and there's no way to discuss all of them. But some common practices and principles might help you get started. For other ideas and more information, check the resource list at the end of the book, speak with a priest, do some Googling, or talk with a wise friend. Remember, if you try one and it doesn't seem right, give the practice a bit of time, and then try another. Think about which practice or practices you want to take on and how much time you can devote to them. Set achievable goals first; you can always increase later.

Prayer

Daily prayer is important for every Christian. The good news is there are lots of different kinds of daily prayer. Here are some kinds of prayer, from easy to more complicated.

Author Anne LaMott, in her book *Traveling Mercies*, writes about how she began a habit of daily prayer with two simple prayers. In the morning, she prayed to God, "Help me, help me, help me!" *Help me get through the day, God.* Then at night, just before sleep, she prayed, "Thank you, thank you, thank you." *Thank you, God, for all the blessings of this day.* These prayers take only a few seconds, yet if they are prayed fervently, they can change our lives.

Table graces are an easy way to develop habits of prayer. *The Book of Common Prayer* has a few short, easy-to-memorize mealtime prayers on page 835. Or your family might have a favorite prayer. This is a good time to remember how God blesses us and to remember those who have less than we do. Just say a quick prayer—memorize one or make one up on the spot—each time you eat. You can say it silently or out loud, alone or with your dining companions.

It's perfectly fine to just talk to God. Many people begin or end their day by talking to God, sharing their concerns, hopes, thanksgivings, and praises. You can do this by yourself or with others.

The Book of Common Prayer offers Daily Devotions for Individuals and Families (pages 137-140). These prayers for morning, noon, evening, and night include a bit of a psalm, a short scripture reading, some time for free prayer, the Lord's Prayer, and a collect for that time of day. It just takes a couple of minutes, and they work well for people by themselves or for families of all kinds.

The Daily Office is the richest form of daily prayer. Rooted in ancient tradition, the Anglican version of these prayers focuses especially on morning and evening prayer, though there are also short forms for noon and night time. These prayers include multiple scripture readings, psalms, collects, responses, and other prayers. Each day, the readings and prayers change based on the liturgical season, whether or not there is a saint to commemorate, or other reasons. If you're getting started, the easiest way is to use an app or website such as the *Forward Day by Day* app or Daily Prayer website (prayer.forwardmovement.org). If you are more tactile and like books, you can use *The Book of Common Prayer*, a Bible, and *Lesser Feasts & Fasts* (for all the saints' information). Using these together takes some effort, but it can be very satisfying. Some churches offer morning or evening prayer daily, and it is especially nice to say these prayers with other people. (See Chapter 9 for more details about the Daily Office.)

Praying with beads works well for some people. You can get a traditional rosary at a Roman Catholic or Anglican religious store or online, and the prayers are readily available. Using a rosary, you say certain prayers with certain beads as you work your fingers around the circle of beads. Sets of prayers are available to commemorate sorrowful or joyful "mysteries" and to meditate on various themes as you repeat the Hail Mary and other prayers. Anglican prayer beads have a different number of beads than the Roman Catholic rosary, and the prayers are all scripturally based, often without extra themes layered on or an emphasis on Mary. People who like tactile prayers will appreciate this form of prayer. To find the prayers, ask where you bought the rosary or just Google "praying the rosary" or "praying with Anglican prayer beads."

In our visual age, **praying with icons** is another good option. There is an ancient Christian tradition of depicting Jesus and the saints in iconography using certain traditional techniques. These images diminish the icon painter's individual creativity and focus our gaze on the depicted figure and beyond. Icons are sometimes described as windows into heaven. So, for example, I can gaze at an icon of Mary, the mother of Jesus, and see in her strength and generosity a model for Christian living. Or I might be reminded in seeing a portrayal of Saint Michael the Archangel that heavenly powers are on my side when I contend against evil forces.

Many people like to walk a **labyrinth**. It may appear as a maze, but labyrinths are actually one-way, winding paths that take you on a circuitous journey to the center of the circle, where some time is spent in quiet prayer before winding one's way back out. People usually offer one set of prayer concerns on the way in and a different set on the way out. Many churches have permanent labyrinths (indoor or outdoor) and even some parks have them now. This form of prayer is good for people who like to stay moving and to pray with their whole bodies.

Centering prayer or **contemplative prayer** are two ways of praying in silence, where the focus is on listening for God's still, small voice. Techniques for these kinds of prayer may involve repeating a phrase to focus the mind, or just the opposite, attempting to clear the mind of thoughts. People interested in centering or contemplative prayer should seek an experienced practitioner for guidance and support.

Yoga can be a good spiritual practice, and it's also good for the body. It's possible in many communities to find Christian yoga where the leader will encourage prayer or meditation on scripture verses or Christian themes during the yoga session.

Scripture

Beyond prayer, scripture engagement is an excellent spiritual practice. You can try reading your way through the Bible. Make sure you get a Bible you love. There are modern language versions and thee-and-thou ones; hot pink leather or paperback; fancy scholarly notes or simple readers' editions. You can get the Bible on an app, in a book, or as an audiobook.

It's pretty common for would-be readers to give up after the first few chapters. Many people struggle with trying to read the Bible like a regular book—because, as we've discussed, it's more like a library of sixty-six books with different styles of writing and purpose. Some genres are easier to read than others. See Chapter 14 for more information about the Bible.

A number of tools are available to help you engage with scripture. *The Path: A Journey Through the Bible* offers the grand, sweeping narrative of the Bible in an accessible, novel-like format. Some people like *The Bible Challenge*, created by Episcopal priest Marek Zabriskie. In this way of reading the Bible, you read three chapters from the Old Testament, a psalm, and one chapter from the New Testament every day (except Sundays) for a year. At the end of the year, you've read the entire Old Testament, the Psalter twice, and the New Testament all the way through, plus a bit of the beginning twice. Visit www.thebiblechallenge.org to learn more.

You might like to try *lectio divina*, which invites us into the scriptures through four steps: read; meditate; pray; contemplate.

Giving and Money

One of the greatest spiritual challenges of our time is consumerism. We are constantly pressured to want new things and more things. Things, things, things! Americans have loads of credit card debt and almost no savings. Our charitable giving is not especially impressive. Are we stuck that way? Is there a different way?

If we can learn to look at how we spend our money, we can learn to spend our money differently. Jesus says, "Where your treasure is, there your heart will be also" (Matthew 6:21). Where we spend our money is where our heart goes. If we spend our money on clothing, that's what is important. If we want our concern for the poor and needy to be the focus of our hearts, then we need to send some money that way. This spiritual practice is about evaluating our income and our spending and deciding if we want or need to make a change.

A common financial principle is to give some money, save some money, spend some money. We give some money for God's work. We save some money for our future needs. We spend what is left on things that we need and things that we want (and we know the difference between those two!).

> The church teaches that we should give ten percent of what we receive back to God, for God's work. Ten percent sounds like a lot, until you flip it around. Suppose someone walked up to you and said, "I will give you a million dollars, but I need you to give $100,000 back." You do the math and realize you just received $900,000, free and clear. "Yes, please, I'll take the million!" That's a bit how it is with all our stuff. Everything we have is a gift from God. So God says to us, you can have this and this and this, and I want ten percent as an offering.

Keep Practicing

In addition to the practices we've discussed, there are many others. Some spiritual practices include obviously "churchy" activities like prayer or worship, while others might be less obviously spiritual—growing food, caring for the sick, or caring for one's body. In this chapter, we have looked at a few ideas to get you started. Try one or two. See how it goes.

Again, talk with a wise friend or a priest or a spiritual director. And remember, you're not doing these spiritual practices to earn God's love or get on God's good side. God already loves you more than you can imagine, no matter what you have done or will do. These spiritual practices help us see God at work in our own lives and in the world around us. Spiritual practices help us practice gratitude for our blessings and share that gratitude with others. Spiritual practices help us to keep our perspective, so that we always remember we are first and foremost followers of Jesus Christ.

And one more important note: these are called practices for a reason. We are always practicing. And when we mess up or fall short, it's another chance to try again. Thanks be to God.

For Reflection

✻ What spiritual practices have been important in your life of faith thus far?

✻ Are there any spiritual practices that you would like to try but haven't? Why not? What would you need in order to try them?

✻ Spiritual practices take time. Do you make time in your life for spiritual practices? How so? If not, why not?

✻ Generosity is a spiritual practice. How has your experience of being generous changed your life? Have you ever tried tithing as a spiritual practice? If so, what was it like? If not, why not?

Chapter 25

Our Witness
to Him
Knowing Our Story

Everliving God, whose will it is that all should come to
you through your Son Jesus Christ: Inspire our witness to
him, that all may know the power of his forgiveness and
the hope of his resurrection; who lives and reigns with you
and the Holy Spirit, one God, now and for ever. *Amen.*

—*The Book of Common Prayer*, pp. 816-817

All of us who are Christians enjoy our faith because someone,
somewhere, shared the story of faith with another. About
2,000 years ago, Jesus himself proclaimed a new way to his
followers. His followers shared their faith with others, and
on and on for generations, across cultures, centuries, and
nations. If we want others to know the joy of our faith, we
need to share that joy with others.

The practice of sharing our faith is evangelism. The word
comes from the Greek *evangelion* and means to bring
good news. Some people think we shouldn't use the word
evangelism or even practice it, because a few Christians have

employed coercive tactics, threatening or bullying people into conversion. But evangelism doesn't and shouldn't mean that, and it is time that we reclaim the word and live out its meaning of bringing good news.

Jesus urged the people around him to practice evangelism. In Luke, Jesus healed a man and then told him, "Return to your home, and declare how much God has done for you." The gospel continues, "So he went away, proclaiming throughout the city how much Jesus had done for him" (Luke 8:39). This is a good model for us; sharing the good news can be as simple as telling others what God has done for us. In the beginning of the Book of Acts, we read about Jesus' mandate to the church. Jesus said to his disciples, "But you will receive power when the Holy Spirit has come upon you; and you will be my witnesses in Jerusalem, in all Judea and Samaria, and to the ends of the earth" (Acts 1:8). The earliest followers were to witness not just in familiar Jerusalem but throughout their land and indeed the whole world. So we too are to witness to God's power in our lives, not just in our familiar places but throughout the land and indeed the world.

Evangelism is sharing the good news, no more and no less. But that raises an important question. What is the good news? When we talk about the Good News of God in Jesus Christ, we might talk about our redemption, about being freed from death, our liberation from sin, or any number of other aspects of Jesus' life and ministry. Another way to talk about good news is to share what Jesus is doing in our own lives. Either way, if we're going to practice evangelism, to tell others the good news, then we have to know it ourselves: We have to know our story.

Let's start with the grand, cosmic story of God in Jesus Christ and then we'll talk about the local, personal story of God at work in our own lives.

One great way to learn or to remember the grand story of God's love for us in Jesus is to read scripture. As we discussed in the last chapter, there are many different ways to read scripture and encounter the story of God's boundless love for us and for creation.

Each Sunday we hear a summary of the grand story of God's love for us in our celebration of Holy Communion. There are six different eucharistic prayers in our prayer book, and each one retells the story a bit differently. Here it is from Prayer B, which starts on page 368 of *The Book of Common Prayer*:

> We give thanks to you, O God, for the goodness and love which you have made known to us in creation; in the calling of Israel to be your people; in your Word spoken through the prophets; and above all in the Word made flesh, Jesus, your Son. For in these last days you sent him to be incarnate from the Virgin Mary, to be the Savior and Redeemer of the world. In him, you have delivered us from evil, and made us worthy to stand before you. In him, you have brought us out of error into truth, out of sin into righteousness, out of death into life.

Then we re-tell the words Jesus spoke when he blessed the bread and wine and shared them with his disciples. We talk about the Spirit's work in us and in the gifts we offer, and then the story cuts to the end of time:

> In the fullness of time, put all things in subjection under your Christ, and bring us to that heavenly country where, with all your saints, we may enter the everlasting heritage of your sons and daughters; through Jesus Christ our Lord, the firstborn of all creation, the head of the Church, and the author of our salvation.

We remember that God has loved us from creation, through the prophets, through the love and sacrifice of Jesus, and will love us until the consummation of history, when Jesus Christ rules over all creation.

I think it's helpful for Christians to be able to tell this grand story in their own words. This helps us own the story, that is, to take it on as our own. This is how I might tell the story:

> Even before creation, God loved us more than we can imagine. God the Holy Trinity brought all things into being, creating a perfectly good world. Then God created us humans in God's own image. God trusted us and gave us our freedom, but we squandered that gift. We turned away from God, choosing selfishness over God. God sent prophets and messengers into our world, again and again reminding us who we are and calling us to turn back to God. Sometimes we would listen for a while, and we would know the blessings of living as God hopes we will live. But every time, we turned against the prophets and against God.

> Finally, God entered our world as Jesus Christ, to show for us Perfect Love. In Jesus, we could see everything we need to know about God. We could see a God whose values are vulnerability, humility, and generosity. We could see a God who reaches out to those who some might say are unlovable to offer them costly, beautiful love. We could see a God who stood with the powerless and who challenged the authorities to be righteous, just, and merciful. We could see a God who loved everyone, but who loved them in a way that constantly challenged them to repent, to turn back to God and to God's love.

> The powers of this world feared perfect love (just as they do today), and so the authorities did their best to extinguish that love. They arrested Jesus, tortured him, and finally killed him. God loves us so much that the almighty God who made heaven and earth was willing to

endure a cruel death. The authorities might have thought they had defeated God's love, but they could not have been more wrong.

On the third day, God raised Jesus from the dead. Though he had been stone-cold dead, Jesus was brought to new life. He appeared to many people, literally showing them the power of God's love, which is so strong that not even death could defeat it. In time, Jesus returned to dwell with God the Father in heaven but not before blessing his followers to carry on his work and sending the Holy Spirit to abide with them and give them strength for their work.

And this is where we are in the story. We too are Jesus' followers. He has given us everything we need to carry on his work of proclaiming the kingdom of righteousness, justice, and mercy. Jesus has shown us what God's love looks like, and he has sent the Holy Spirit to help us.

Spoiler alert! We know how the story turns out. In the end, Jesus comes as Lord and judge. He will offer consolation and blessing to those who have suffered greatly in this life. He will render justice to those who have failed to honor God's image in others. And in the end, God's generous, amazing, brilliant love will fill the universe with its life and light.

Our marching orders are given by Jesus: Love God with our whole being and love our neighbors as ourselves. Or, to put it another way, Jesus says we are to love everyone as he has loved us. That is nearly impossible for us ordinary humans to do, but we have the power of the Holy Spirit to help us.

Isn't this amazing news? God has loved us from the beginning of all time. God has sent messenger after messenger to teach us. God has shown us exactly what perfect love looks like.

We know God's love cannot be defeated by anyone, no matter what. The Holy Spirit has our back. And in the end, God's people live, literally, happily ever after. Astounding. That's something worth sharing!

The way I tell the story of faith might seem too abstract for some. Maybe your story is instead found in talking about God's love at work in your life or in the people around you. You don't have to be a theology expert or a Bible scholar to talk about God's love as you see it!

I think of friends whose lives seemed hopeless due to addiction, and then God's mighty power helped them regain their lives. I think of relationships that seemed completely broken until God's gentle love bound up their wounds and led to restoration. I think of people who reject power and worldly goods in favor of humility and generosity.

In my own life, I can remember times when I wasn't paying attention, and the Holy Spirit prompted me to notice things about people around me so that I could respond to their needs. I think of how God called me away from a pretty happy career making a pretty good salary into the ordained ministry, a vocation that is tremendously challenging but that offers me more joy than I could have dreamed. Quite often in worship, it is as if the thin veil between heaven and earth has been lifted, and God's glory becomes radiantly present for me.

It's great news, isn't it, that God can work in our lives? That's definitely worth sharing.

I encourage you to learn and to steep yourself in the grand narrative of God's great love for you and for creation. Here are a few suggestions for doing that work:

❖ Read the scriptures. Try studying particular passages deeply as well as reading the whole Bible to get a sense of the big story. If it seems like too much to read the whole Bible, then try *The Path, The Story*, or another digested version of the Bible.

❖ Get a *Book of Common Prayer* for your home and read the eucharistic prayers. See chapters 4-5 in this book for guidance about these prayers, which retell the story of salvation.

❖ In your *Book of Common Prayer*, look up the readings for the Easter Vigil (starting on page 285). They offer a wonderful survey of the story of God's salvation of us and creation.

❖ Think about times when you have felt God's presence in your life. Record them in a journal, and re-read your entries several times.

❖ Begin each day giving thanks to God. A friend thanks God for 100 things during his morning walk with his dog. This is a terrific way to shape our minds toward gratitude for all that God has done for us.

❖ Talk with spiritual friends about how important your life of faith is—and why. Listen carefully to the other person's story, and be vulnerable and generous when you share your story.

Now that you know your story, it is time to tell others, to share the good news so that all might know God's love.

For Reflection

＊ Who was the first person to share the Good News of God in Jesus Christ with you? How did they do this? What was it like for you?

＊ How does the story of God in your life connect to the larger story of God's saving work from the beginning of time in creation?

＊ Many of us learned some of the stories of salvation when we were small children, but that might have been a long time ago. Which parts of the story of God do you wish you knew better? What steps can you take to learn more about them?

＊ The chapter ends with some ways that we might steep ourselves in God's story. Which ways have worked for you? Which might you try?

Chapter 26

Proclaim to All People

Telling Our Story

Give us grace, O Lord, to answer readily the call of our Savior Jesus Christ and proclaim to all people the Good News of his salvation, that we and the whole world may perceive the glory of his marvelous works; who lives and reigns with you and the Holy Spirit, one God, for ever and ever. *Amen.*

—*The Book of Common Prayer*, p. 215

We have talked about the amazing story of God's love for us, especially as we see God's love revealed in Jesus Christ. God is working in each of us, doing amazing things, and this gives us our own story of God's love. Now that we have a sense of what the Good News of God in Christ is for us and for the world, it's time to start sharing it. Of course, that is easier said than done.

When we find a new restaurant, we often tell people how great it is. We tell people about bargains or beautiful parks or movies we enjoyed. We find it easy to share good news about things that are trivial, but we find it difficult to share the all-important Good News of God in Christ.

Yet sharing the good news, telling our story of God's love, is so important that it is one of our baptismal promises. We promise to "proclaim by word and example the Good News of God in Christ." It is not enough that we should live an inspiring life that visibly manifests the good news but also that we should talk about it and share the hope that is within us. As with all of the seemingly impossible baptismal promises, we will never manage to fulfill them on our own. That is why it's worth remembering that we say we will do this with God's help. Remember that part in the last chapter about the Holy Spirit having our back? This is what we're talking about!

We don't tell the story of God's love in our lives merely to fill our pews or prop up struggling churches. We share the good news because we promised we would. And because God asks us to. In Matthew 28, Jesus gives some of his last instructions to the disciples, telling them to go and make disciples of all nations and to teach them to obey his commandments. Perhaps the best reason to share our faith is that through the process, we become so filled with the joy of God's love in our hearts that we can't help but keep sharing it! We practice evangelism because we want to share our joy, to share God's love.

It is not our task to convert people, and it certainly isn't our job to coerce people away from another faith or convince them that we are right and they are wrong. Our only work is proclaiming the Good News of God in Christ; what happens after that is up to the Holy Spirit.

Now, Episcopalians are not very good at this. I've seen statistics that say we share our faith once every few decades.

We need to change this. We must change this. People are eager to hear a word of hope. They are hungry for God's grace and love. And yet we still don't share our faith. Why? Perhaps we are afraid, fearful of doing it wrong or causing offense.

Several years ago, I worked with a Muslim man. One day, as I was sitting in his office munching on some candy from his desk, I suddenly remembered that it was Ramadan, the Muslim month of fasting. Here I was, sitting in his office, merrily eating sweets, while he watched, unable to drink even a glass of water, let alone eat food, during the day. I profusely apologized, and he told me, "No need to apologize. We fast to remind ourselves of our need for God, and so if I get hungry, that is helpful. And if I hadn't wanted anyone to eat the candy, I would have put away the dish." What a generous response. That began a series of conversations about our mutual faiths. He gave me a copy of his scriptures and told me about his life as a Muslim in America. Neither of us tried to convert the other, but our friendship was strengthened by this time of deep, real conversation about our faiths.

When I think about that experience or recall other times I have spoken with someone about my faith or theirs, I recognize that each of those conversations has been a blessing. If I was talking with a stranger, I've been grateful for a brief moment of serious connection. With friends, our relationship has grown and deepened. Maybe we should stop worrying about offending people and simply share our faith. Perhaps these are opportunities to build deep connections. And if we mess up and say the wrong thing, we can always apologize.

Sharing our faith doesn't need to be hard. Here are a few ideas for ways to tell the story of God's love. Discover ways to practice evangelism that work best for you. And practice helps: The more we do it, the easier it gets.

Invite someone to your church. This is one of the easiest ways to practice evangelism. You don't have to say much more, though if you can talk about why you attend church, it can help. Pick any Sunday to bring along a friend, but it's easier to invite guests for some special occasions in the life of a church. Here are a few examples of invitations that you could use:

❖ I love the carols we sing at our Christmas Eve service. It's the high point of the whole season. Would you like to join me?

❖ We are blessing animals this weekend at my church. I bet your dog would love to come and receive a blessing. I always love the joy of seeing all the animals and worshiping with God's creatures.

❖ We're having special music at my church this Sunday. I know you love music, so maybe you'd enjoy hearing it with me.

❖ Welcome to the neighborhood! If you are looking for a spiritual home, I hope you'll check out the church I attend. I'd love to give you a ride.

Offer to pray with someone. If people you know—neighbors, friends, co-workers—are struggling with something in their lives, offer to pray for them. Nearly everyone will receive this offer as a precious gift. And saying these prayers will be a blessing to you. You don't have to say much. "I'm sorry to hear this. Can I pray for you?" You can pray right then and there (be brave!), or you can say you'll pray later. Just make sure you follow through! If you decide to pray with someone on the spot, you can certainly use a prayer from *The Book of Common Prayer*, but you can always use your own words. There are no wrong or right ways to talk to God, and whoever you share this gift with will be grateful. Your prayer can be brief and to the point. "Almighty God, be with Mary as she struggles with cancer. Amen." "Dear Jesus, you know our pain and sorrow, help Juan as he grieves the loss of his friend. Amen."

Practice your Christian faith and say why. There's a folk song with the refrain, "They'll know we are Christians by our love." Do our lives show forth our faith? Chances are your life is a beacon of Christ's love sometimes—and other times, not so much. That's normal, and no one gets it right all the time. But when we get it right, we manage to follow Jesus in extraordinary ways in our ordinary lives. There are lots of ways to show that we are Christians. For example, in a time of division, instead of piling on against those with whom we disagree, offer words of compassion. Then tell someone that you act this way because your faith demands compassion. You can reject a racist or sexist comment and explain that you believe everyone is made in God's image, and we shouldn't denigrate anyone, ever, for any reason.

Serve the poor, and say why. Tell someone why you work at the homeless shelter or the soup kitchen or the Habitat House. Explain that, in Matthew 25, Jesus promised that when we serve the poor and others, we meet and serve Jesus himself. You could even invite others to join you in service. Talk about the joy of serving others and of looking for Christ in those around you. Talk about how good it feels to be generous with others. Talk about how gratitude wells up in your own life as you encounter the poor and those at the margins.

When you have a spiritual high, share it! Sometimes we think we shouldn't talk about our spiritual highs because it's bragging. But nothing could be further from the truth. Jesus told us not to hide the lamp of faith under a basket but rather to place it where it can shine for others. We talk about how our families make us happy, so why not the most important thing in our lives? Perhaps you could say, "Lately I've had such a feeling of peace and comfort. I'm so grateful for my faith." Or maybe, "There's so much fear and violence in the world, I'm so grateful for God's love in my life, which gives me hope and empowers me to work for a better world."

Remind people that God loves them. Maybe you have a friend who is discouraged, struggling with a relationship or perhaps looking for purpose. The person might feel that he or she has done something horrible and cannot be forgiven. Any time someone is struggling, it can be helpful to be reminded of God's great love—that there is hope for a better future, and that whatever we have done, God still loves us. You don't have to preach a sermon; just offer simple reassurance.

Like most things in life, evangelism gets easier with practice. And if the words don't come out right one day, apologize and try again. Next time will be better. Jesus has promised that the Holy Spirit abides with us, and that is never more true than when we are sharing our faith, a faith that offers untold gifts to those around us.

For Reflection

✳ Why is it important for us to share the Good News of God in Christ?

✳ Have you ever shared the Good News of God in Christ with someone else? How did you do it? What was it like?

✳ What are some of the barriers to sharing the good news? How can we overcome those barriers?

✳ Briefly tell the story of how God has been involved in your life. Were you able to do this? What was it like to do this?

Afterword

Congratulations! You have made it through an overview of the beliefs and practices of the Episcopal Church. If you are new to the Episcopal Church, we hope this helps you feel at home quickly. If you are a long-time member, we hope you are encouraged to renew your journey as a disciple of Jesus.

In a book of this size, covering this much ground, we had to leave out important topics and provide only the most cursory glance at other vital aspects of our faith. If you are curious to learn more, please explore some of the materials we've listed in the Resources section in the back of the book. You'll also do well to talk with your priest or an Episcopal friend as you seek a broader and deeper exploration of the Anglican way of following Jesus.

Though you are at the end of a book, we Christians are always at the beginning of a journey. Each day, we must die to our old selves and discover how God is offering us an abundant life in Christ's new creation. On our journey, we find that a deeper appreciation of Christian practices leads to an enriched faith, and that an enriched faith leads to deeper Christian practices.

We began this book with a scripture verse, and it is now our wish and our blessing for you. *Walk in love, as Christ loved us and gave himself for us, an offering and sacrifice to God.*

Resources

General Books

- *Faithful Questions: Exploring the Way with Jesus* by Scott Gunn and Melody Wilson Shobe (Forward Movement, 2015)
- *Praying Shapes Believing: A Theological Commentary on the Book of Common Prayer* by Leonel Mitchell (Morehouse Publishing, 1991)
- *Inwardly Digest* by Derek Olsen (Forward Movement, 2016)
- *Why Sacraments?* by Andrew Davison (Cascade Books, 2013)
- *The Liturgy Explained* by James Farwell (Morehouse Publishing, 2013)
- *Liturgical Sense: The Logic of Rite* by Louis Weil (Seabury Books, 2013)
- *The Episcopal Handbook* (Morehouse Publishing, 2015)

Baptism

- *Preparing for Baptism in the Episcopal Church* by Anne Kitch (Church Publishing, 2015)
- *Being Christian* by Rowan Williams (Eerdmans, 2015)
- *Why Sacraments?* by Andrew Davison (Cascade Books, 2013)

Eucharist

- *Being Christian* by Rowan Williams (Eerdmans, 2015)
- *The Meal that Jesus Gave Us* by N.T. Wright (Westminster John Knox Press, 2015)

- *For the Life of the World* by Alexander Schmemann (St. Vladimir's Seminary Press, 1973)
- *Why Sacraments?* by Andrew Davison (Cascade Books, 2013)
- *Gifts of God for the People of God* by Furman L. Buchanan (Forward Movement, 2019)

Confirmation and Marriage

- *The Marriage Journey: Preparations and Provisions for Life Together* by Delbert Glover and Linda Grenz (Church Publishing, 2003)
- *The Art of Being Together* by Francis Wade (Forward Movement, 2005)

Healing and Confession

- *Joy in Confession: Recovering Sacramental Reconciliation* by Hillary D. Raining (Forward Movement, 2017)
- *Reconciliation: Preparing for Confession in the Episcopal Church* by Martin Smith (Cowley Publications, 1985)
- *The Sacrament of Anointing the Sick* by Lizette Larson-Miller (Liturgical Press, 2005)

Ordination

- *Many Servants: An Introduction to Deacons* by Ormonde Plater (Cowley, 2004)
- *On Being a Priest Today* by Rosalind Brown and Christopher Cocksworth (Cowley, 2002)

Daily Office

- *A User's Guide to the Book of Common Prayer: Morning and Evening Prayer* by Christopher Webber (Morehouse, 2006)
- *Hour by Hour* by Edward Gleason, ed. (Forward Movement, 2003)
- *Inwardly Digest* by Derek Olsen (Forward Movement, 2016)
- *Daily Prayer in the Early Church: A Study of the Origin and Early Development of the Divine Office* (Wipf and Stock Publishers, 2008)

Church Year

- *Celebrating Liturgical Time* by J. Neil Alexander (Church Publishing, 2014)
- *Waiting for the Coming: The Liturgical Meaning of Advent, Christmas, Epiphany* by J. Neil Alexander (Pastoral Press, 1994)

- *The Origin of Feasts, Fasts, and Seasons in Early Christianity* by Paul Bradshaw and Maxwell Johnson (Pueblo Books, 2011)

Holy Week and Easter

- *The Scriptures, the Cross, and the Power of God* by Tom Wright (Westminster John Knox Press, 2006)
- *Offering the Gospel to Children* by Gretchen Wolff Pritchard (Cowley Publications, 1992)
- *Seven Last Words: An Invitation to a Deeper Friendship with Jesus* by James Martin (HarperOne, 2016)
- *Cross-Shattered Christ: Meditations on the Seven Last Words* by Stanley Hauerwas (Brazos Press, 2011)
- *The Last Week* by Marcus Borg and John Dominic Crossan (HarperOne, 2007)
- *Easter Triumph, Easter Joy: Meditations for the Fifty Days of Eastertide* by Scott Gunn (Forward Movement, 2022)

Burial

- *Accompany Them with Singing—The Christian Funeral* by Thomas Long (Westminster John Knox Press, 2013)
- *Faithful Living, Faithful Dying: Anglican Reflections on End of Life Care* by Jan C. Heller (editor) (Morehouse Publishing, 2000)

Creeds

- *The Creed: What Christians Believe and Why it Matters* by Luke Timothy Johnson (Image, 2004)
- *"I Believe": Exploring the Apostles' Creed* by Alister McGrath (IVP Books, 1998)
- *The Apostles' Creed for Today* by Justo Gonzales (Westminster John Knox Press, 2007)
- *Loving the Questions: An Exploration of the Nicene Creed* by Marianne Micks (Seabury Books, 2004)

The Bible

- *The Path: A Journey Through the Bible* (Forward Movement, 2016)
- *Opening the Bible* by Roger Ferlo (Cowley Publications, 1997)
- *The Good Book: Discovering the Bible's Place in Our Lives* by Peter Gomes (HarperOne, 2002)

- *The Bible Challenge: Read the Bible in a Year* edited by Marek Zabriskie (Forward Movement, 2012)
- *The Heart of Christianity* by Marcus Borg (HarperOne, 2004)

Grace

- *What's So Amazing About Grace?* by Philip Yancey (Zondervan, 2002)
- *Saving Salvation: The Amazing Evolution of Grace* by Stephen Smith (Morehouse Publishing, 2005)
- *The Ragamuffin Gospel* by Brennan Manning (Multnomah, 2005)
- *Amazing Grace: A Vocabulary of Faith* by Kathleen Norris (Riverhead Books, 1999)

Prayer

- *The Practice of Prayer* by Margaret Guenther (Cowley Publications, 1998)
- *Prayer: Finding the Heart's True Home* by Richard Foster (Zondervan, 2002)

The Church

- *Searching for Sunday: Loving, Leaving, and Finding the Church* by Rachel Held Evans (Thomas Nelson, 2015)
- *Church: Why Bother?* by Philip Yancey (Zondervan, 2015)

Episcopal Church (Polity)

- *The Episcopal Handbook, Revised Edition* (Morehouse, 2015)
- *The Episcopal Story: Birth and Rebirth* by Tom Ferguson (Morehouse Publishing, 2015)
- *Anglicanism: A Very Short Introduction* by Mark Chapman (Oxford University Press, 2006)
- *What We Shall Become: The Future and Structure of the Episcopal Church* ed. Winnie Varghese (Church Publishing, 2013)

Communion of Saints

- *Lesser Feasts and Fasts 2022* (Church Publishing, 2022)
- *Celebrating the Saints* curriculum (Forward Movement, 2015)
- *Brightest and Best: A Companion to the Lesser Feasts and Fasts* by Sam Portaro (Cowley Publications, 1998)

- *The Oxford Dictionary of Saints* by David Farmer (Oxford University Press, 2011)
- *My Life with the Saints* by James Martin (Loyola Press, 2007)
- *Luminaries: Twenty Lives That Illuminate the Christian Way* by Rowan Williams (SPCK Publishing, 2019)

Vocation

- *Listening Hearts: Discerning Call in Community* by Suzanne Farnham (Morehouse Publishing, 2011)
- *Crossing the Jordan: Meditations on Vocation* by Sam Portaro (Cloister Books, 1999)
- *Let Your Life Speak: Listening for the Voice of Vocation* by Parker Palmer (Jossey-Bass, 1999)
- *Callings: Twenty Centuries of Christian Wisdom on Vocation* by William Placher (Eerdmans, 2005)

Creation Care

- *Scripture, Culture, and Agriculture: An Agrarian Reading of the Bible* by Ellen Davis (Cambridge University Press, 2008)
- *Serve God, Save the Planet* by Matthew Sleet (Zondervan, 2007)
- *Soil and Sacrament: A Spiritual of Food and Faith* by Fred Bahnson (Simon & Schuster, 2013)
- *From Nature to Creation: A Christian Vision for Understanding and Loving our World* by Norman Wirzba (Baker, 2015)
- *The Creation Care Bible Challenge* edited by Marek Zabriskie (Forward Movement, 2022)

Incarnation

- *Jesus the Savior: The Meaning of Jesus Christ for Christian Faith* by William Placher (Westminster John Knox Press, 2001)
- *Jesus: A Very Short Introduction* by Richard Bauckham (Oxford University Press, 2011)
- *Knowing Jesus in Your Life* by Carol Anderson (Morehouse Publishing, 1993)
- *The Secret Message of Jesus* by Brian McLaren (Thomas Nelson, 2007)

Spiritual Gifts

- *The Holy Spirit* by Stanley Hauerwas and William Willimon (Abingdon Press, 2015)
- *Discerning Your Spiritual Gifts* by Lloyd Edwards (Cowley, 1988)
- *After You Believe: Why Christian Character Matters* by N.T. Wright (HarperOne, 2012)
- The ELCA has a helpful online quiz that can help in discernment of your spiritual gifts: https://www.elca.org/Our-Work/Congregations-and-Synods/Faith-Practices/Spiritual-Renewal/Assessment-Tools

Spiritual Practices

- *Practicing our Faith* by Dorothy Bass (Jossey-Bass, 2010)
- *Mudhouse Sabbath: An Invitation to a Life of Spiritual Discipline* by Lauren Winner (Paraclete Press, 2015)
- *An Altar in the World: A Geography of Faith* by Barbara Brown Taylor (HarperOne, 2010)
- *Celebration of Discipline: The Path to Spiritual Growth* by Richard Foster (HarperSanFrancisco, 1998)
- *Liturgy of the Ordinary: Sacred Practices in Everyday Life* by Tish Harrison Warren (InterVaristy Press, 2016)
- *The Way of Love: A Practical Guide to Following Jesus* by Scott Gunn (Forward Movement, 2020)

Knowing our Story

- *Transforming Evangelism* by David Gortner (Church Publishing, 2008)
- *Evangelism for "Normal" People* by John Bowen (Augsburg Fortress, 2002)

Telling our Story

- *Transforming Evangelism* by David Gortner (Church Publishing, 2008)
- *Evangelism for "Normal" People* by John Bowen (Augsburg Fortress, 2002)
- *How to Revive Evangelism: 7 Vital Shifts in How We Share Our Faith* by Craig Springer (Zondervan, 2021)
- *Acts to Action: The New Testament's Guide to Evangelism and Mission* by Susan Brown Snook and Adam Trambley (Forward Movement, 2018)

Acknowledgments

No author writes a book alone, and that is certainly true for us. Your two authors have worked together, but there are other people to thank. Certainly our families have tolerated lots of time away as we researched and wrote. We are grateful to early readers of the manuscript, especially several colleagues from the Acts 8 Movement: Brendan O'Sullivan-Hale, Derek Olsen, Steve Pankey, David Simmons, and Adam Trambley. Manoj Zacharia also gave us valuable feedback. Jason Sierra was kind to go back and forth with several iterations of a lovely cover design. Alexis Fortuna Caoili made the interior design beautiful. Len Freeman patiently edited the book early on. We are especially grateful to Richelle Thompson, who cajoled us to meet deadlines (or catch up quickly when we fell behind), who masterfully edited the manuscript, and who made all the pieces of a complicated project come together. Above all, we give thanks to God, who is the source of all good gifts and the origin of the love that we both have for the church and its ministries.

About the Authors

Scott Gunn is executive director of Forward Movement, a ministry of the Episcopal Church that inspires disciples and empowers evangelists. Scott travels widely as a speaker, retreat leader, and preacher. Before his work at Forward Movement, he was a parish priest in Rhode Island. He has worked in technology at nonprofits, a media company, and a university. His hobbies include photography and travel. You can read his blog at www.sevenwholedays.org.

Melody Wilson Shobe is an Episcopal priest who has served churches in Rhode Island and Texas. A passionate lover of the Bible, she hears God speaking in a new way every time she reads this extraordinary story. A graduate of Tufts University and the Virginia Theological Seminary, Melody serves as the associate for children and families at Good Shepherd Episcopal Church in Dallas, Texas. Melody, her husband, and their two daughters live in Dallas, where she spends her spare time reading stories, building forts, conquering playgrounds, baking cookies, and exploring nature.

Scott Gunn and Melody Shobe have also co-written *Faithful Questions: Exploring the Way with Jesus* (Forward Movement, 2015), an introduction to the Christian faith for seekers and explorers.

About Forward Movement

Forward Movement inspires disciples and empowers evangelists. While we produce great resources like this book, Forward Movement is not a publishing company.

We are a discipleship ministry. Publishing books, daily reflections, studies for small groups, and online resources are important ways we live out this ministry. People around the world read daily devotions through *Forward Day by Day,* which is also available in Spanish (*Adelante Día a Día*) and Braille, online, as a podcast, and as an app for your smartphone. We actively seek partners across the church and look for ways to provide resources that inspire and challenge. A ministry of the Episcopal Church since 1935, Forward Movement is a nonprofit organization funded by sales of resources and gifts from generous donors.

To learn more about Forward Movement and our work, visit us at forwardmovement.org or venadelante.org. We are delighted to be doing this work and invite your prayers and support.